Elizabeth Gaskell and the English Provincial Novel

First published in 1975, this book places Elizabeth Gaskell amongst the major novelists of the nineteenth-century. It considers how she has sometimes been overlooked, or admired for very few of her works, or for reasons that are not in fact central to her art. W. A. Craik looks at Gaskell's full-length novels with three main purposes: to analyse her development as a novelist, her achievements, and the nature of her very original work; to see what she owes to earlier novelists, what she learns from them, and how far she is an innovator; and to put her in relation to those other novelists who write on similar themes with comparable aims. This book establishes Elizabeth Gaskell's excellence in comparison with her peers by demonstrating how far she extended the possibilities of the novel, both in materials and techniques.

Elizabeth Gaskell and the English Provincial Novel

W. A. Craik

Routledge
Taylor & Francis Group

First published in 1975
by Methuen & Co Ltd

This edition first published in 2013 by Routledge
2 Park Square, Milton Park, Abingdon, Oxon, OX14 4RN

Simultaneously published in the USA and Canada
by Routledge
711 Third Avenue, New York, NY 10017

Routledge is an imprint of the Taylor & Francis Group, an informa business

© 1975 W. A. Craik

Publisher's Note
The publisher has gone to great lengths to ensure the quality of this reprint but points out that some imperfections in the original copies may be apparent.

Disclaimer
The publisher has made every effort to trace copyright holders and welcomes correspondence from those they have been unable to contact.

A Library of Congress record exists under ISBN: 75309747

ISBN 13: 978-0-415-83466-7 (hbk)
ISBN 13: 978-0-203-48378-7 (ebk)
ISBN 13: 978-0-415-83491-9 (pbk)

W. A. CRAIK

Elizabeth Gaskell
and the
English Provincial Novel

METHUEN & CO LTD
LONDON

First published in 1975
by Methuen & Co Ltd
11 *New Fetter Lane London* EC4P 4EE
© 1975 *W. A. Craik*
Printed in Great Britain by
Butler & Tanner Ltd, Frome and London

ISBN 0 416 82630 X (hardbound)
ISBN 0 416 82640 7 (paperback)

Distributed in the USA by
HARPER & ROW PUBLISHERS, INC.
BARNES & NOBLE IMPORT DIVISION

for M. R. Heaslip

Contents

Preface

Elizabeth Gaskell, the Brontës – Charlotte, Emily and Anne – Anthony Trollope, George Eliot and Thomas Hardy form a group apart from the other great novelists of the nineteenth century, for they all write of a world which is – in no dismissive sense – provincial. They also form a progression, since their combined writing period extends from *Jane Eyre* and *Agnes Grey* in 1847, to Hardy's last novel *Jude the Obscure* in 1895. All these seven novelists see the world from a viewpoint which is not metropolitan. London, which, with the culture and standards which it implies, has been the accepted if unconscious social and moral point of reference for the English novel, is felt in their work, when it appears or is referred to, as a world or social order outside and apart from that which the writer and his novel inhabits. Independent of the traditional values and social order of London, the Brontës' Yorkshire, Elizabeth Gaskell's northern England, Trollope's Barset, George Eliot's Midlands, and Hardy's Wessex, all enable them to interpret anew the world they live in, to see life steadily and see it whole each in his way, as nearly as the human mind may; to write of the individual in relation to his fellow-men, in a changing, developing society, with new and changing ideas, not merely about social problems of the day, but about the human spirit, and the universe it inhabits.

The provincial novelists are thus in many ways separated from Thackeray and Dickens, for whom London – though their novels may at times depart from it – is the centre of the social world which, though they can criticize and disparage it, is felt as a norm against

A*

which character, ethics and society may be measured. They are distinct also from another group whom they more closely resemble, the novelists of social reform, like Disraeli and Kingsley who, though they write with knowledge of what goes on in industrial cities, and in the declining countryside, do so to reform, with a metropolitan, even cosmopolitan audience in mind, to whom injustice and wrong must be made clear; and do so also from knowledge, which, though first-hand, is consciously 'learned up' as well, from reports and research. The provincial novelists have in common that they write of life as they know it from living or sharing in it themselves, in novels that, though they may often explore injustice and wrong, are not primarily vehicles for a particular message, but interpretations and explorations of the universal human predicament.

They have in common also basic beliefs and attitudes towards their art, which make them avoid romance and cling to what they regard as 'real', or 'truthful'.

The Brontës, George Eliot and Hardy have all had the attention bestowed upon them that they richly deserve. Elizabeth Gaskell has not. Though she is admired, it is for a few of her works, and for reasons not central to her art. The general reader knows *Cranford*, the student of literature reads *Mary Barton* and *North and South* as novels of social concern, while *Wives and Daughters*, probably by general critical consensus felt to be her greatest novel, is seen as the rich nineteenth-century descendant of the art of Jane Austen.

Elizabeth Gaskell wrote five full-length novels: *Mary Barton* (1848), *Ruth* (1853), *North and South* (1855), *Sylvia's Lovers* (1863), and *Wives and Daughters*, left not quite finished at her death in 1866. It is on these five that I wish to concentrate in the following pages, with three main purposes. The primary one is to examine her development as a novelist, her achievement, and the nature of her art; the second is to see her development from previous novelists, what she learns from them, and how far she is an innovator; the third is to put her in relation to those other novelists who write on similar subjects and themes, and with comparable aims, in order to establish her own excellence in relation to her contemporaries, how they enrich each other, and how far she herself extends the possibilities of the novel, both in materials and techniques, for those who follow her.

To do so I have been compelled to subordinate and omit much that it would have been pleasant to include. Elizabeth Gaskell was not only a prolific short-story writer of distinction, but also wrote one of the finest biographies in English of another writer, *The Life of Charlotte Brontë*. I regret being unable to deal with this and two or three of her best works, such as the long-short stories *Lois the Witch* – a unique handling of the New England Salem witch-hunts – and the poignant *Cousin Phillis*, and also her most popular work, *Cranford*. Not being full-length novels, none of these comes within my brief, even *Cranford*, since it was never conceived as such, growing out of a single tale for Dickens's periodical *Household Words*, into a series of delicately-linked episodes which, even entire, do not reach the length of a novel, nor achieve even the structural coherence of Dickens's own similarly conceived *Pickwick Papers*.

I have deliberately omitted, also, any comparison in *Mary Barton* and *North and South* with historical, political and social evidence for how far the situation she deals with corresponds with 'fact'. Elizabeth Gaskell herself clearly lays down her own purposes in the preface to *Mary Barton* in the original edition of 1848:

> to give some utterance to the agony which, from time to time, convulses the dumb people; the agony of suffering without the sympathy of the happy, or of erroneously believing that such is the case.

I admire and am indebted to many who have already written on Elizabeth Gaskell. She has been fortunate in that, though her reputation has been modest, it has been rightly based, since she is a writer easy to underestimate, but not to misapprehend. I acknowledge particular indebtedness to the work of Edgar Wright in *Mrs Gaskell: the Basis for Reassessment* (Oxford, 1965), and Arthur Pollard in *Mrs Gaskell: Novelist and Biographer* (Manchester, 1965) and to his invaluable edition, jointly with J. A. V. Chapple, of the *Letters of Mrs Gaskell* (Manchester, 1966). References to these and other secondary sources have been kept to a minimum in the interests of concentrating on the novels. The bibliography itself is a measure of my indebtedness to other scholars.

In quoting from the novels I have used the text of the Knutsford Edition, edited by A. W. Ward (Smith, Elder & Co., 1906) – still the nearest thing to a complete edition of the works – identifying quotations by chapter reference.

For the use of their facilities I am indebted to the library staffs of the University of Aberdeen, the British Museum, Manchester

Public Libraries, and the Portico Library, Manchester; for typing the manuscript, to Miss Lily Hay and Mrs Constance Keith. For invaluable help in discussing and arranging my ideas I am grateful to my colleagues and students in the English Department at Aberdeen University and to my friends Dr William Ruddick of the University of Manchester and Dr Angus Easson of Royal Holloway College, London. Finally, I acknowledge my debt to Miss Marjorie Heaslip, to whom this book is dedicated, as the first person to guide me in reading and appreciating the English novel.

I

Mary Barton

Mary Barton in 1848 is new ground for the English novel. It has new materials, presents new ways of seeing and handling both its own materials, the world in which any writer finds himself, and the human nature which it is an essential part of most writers' task to reveal. Elizabeth Gaskell, by beginning her writing career in other forms than the novel, and by not seeing herself at first as a professional novelist – or even a professional writer – makes as nearly as can be a fresh beginning to the novel as a form. Like the primitive in other arts, she virtually unconsciously creates an unobtrusive, wholly invigorating and wholly beneficial revolution. That she is not aware she is an innovator is a great advantage both to herself and to the later novelists who in their own ways derive from and extend beyond her. She leaves herself always free to grow and to extend her powers; each of her novels is different in subject from the previous one, wider in range and more assured in its achievement. She never develops a mere formula for success, so, consequently, her influence is never that of a formula or doctrine. She points ways, and reveals means, so that novelists as widely different as Anthony Trollope, George Eliot and Thomas Hardy have the way to their own different kinds of greatness charted for them by the writer who began seven years before Trollope (*The Warden*, 1855), ten years before George Eliot (*Scenes of Clerical Life*, 1858), and twenty-three years before Hardy (*Desperate Remedies*, 1871). All these writers, like Elizabeth Gaskell herself, begin somewhat tentatively and develop rapidly. All, having discovered and established what it is in them to create, reveal her aid in their most mature, greatest, and most original novels. This is not to say they deliberately imitate her, or that they consciously model themselves on her; hers is the most vital and fruitful sort of help to those who come after her, in that the new areas and skills she herself develops offer further areas, and exploitable and extensible techniques, to those who, coming after her, explore the areas further, and develop and extend the techniques, not only for the purposes she herself has, but for other, sometimes more profound, ends of their own. Elizabeth Gaskell not only touches greatness herself; she enables others to reach their own kinds of greatness.

Elizabeth Gaskell is obviously well placed to write 'A Tale of Manchester Life' as she subtitles *Mary Barton*. She had been, when she wrote it, for fourteen years absorbed within that life in her role as the active wife of a Unitarian minister. Her childhood and up-bringing were close to it, only a few miles away at Knutsford in Cheshire. She saw and experienced and was part of what she writes.

But situation cannot account for success. One needs only to re-collect the innumerable other similar but unsubstantial 'tales' turned out in the course of the age – all too often by women – which faded and left not a rack behind. First-hand experience is *per se* very useful to a writer. So, also, is detachment. Elizabeth Gaskell has both. *Mary Barton*, her first novel, stands apart from her others in being, professedly, a novel of social reform, exploring injustice, abuse and inequity. Like Disraeli's and Kingsley's novels, it deals with industrial and poor provincial workers and their plights; like theirs, it is factually accurate in its account; like theirs, its author cares passionately about the conditions she reveals. As a novelist of social reform, Elizabeth Gaskell has the advantage over them of per-sonal experience and personal contact, of having not only observed, but known, visited, and helped men like John Barton and the other mill-workers, or households like that of the Wilsons; as well as having visited and known socially mill-owners and industrialists like the *nouveau riche* Carsons. Elizabeth Gaskell has also the asset of being provided by circumstance with the right degree of dissociation. Her Knutsford background – the place she knew and loved and balanced against her feelings of commitment to and distaste for Manchester – gives her the detachment that even her own characters could achieve from their imprisoning circumstances, as they do in the opening of *Mary Barton*, where the Barton and Wilson families, parents and children together, can have a brief and idyllic walk in the modest south Lancashire countryside. Just as that idyll proportions and intensifies the troubles their town life inflicts upon them, so Elizabeth Gaskell's own detaching awareness enables her to do justice to their miseries, never underestimating them, but never exaggerating with excessive pathos or melodramatizing past belief, as did, on occasion, the city-based Disraeli before her or the invincible Londoner Dickens after her. At intervals in her story – even at times of greatest misery, the urban cloud lifts for a while. Mary, desperately pursuing the sailor Will Wilson, whose evidence is to save Jem from being hanged for murder, goes by train from Manchester to Liverpool, and sees from her back seat 'the cloud of smoke which hovers over Manchester' and looks with unseeing eyes at 'the cloud-shadows which give beauty to Chat-Moss, the picturesque old houses of Newton'; and then, being rowed down the Mersey in pursuit of Will Wilson's ship, she sees Liverpool too become something distant and detached, from the 'glassy and motionless [river], reflecting tint by tint of the Indian-ink sky above' (XXVI).

These advantages of personal situation are perhaps even less important than her approach as a writer. Her first steps in writing were not novels. She began[1] with a poem in the manner of Crabbe called 'Sketches Among the Poor',[2] written jointly with her husband; next came a little descriptive essay, an account of a visit to Clopton Hall in Warwickshire;[3] then 'Libbie Marsh's Three Eras'[4] (a short tale of a lonely young sewing woman's brief friendship with a crippled boy, and her final coming together with the boy's mother when he dies), published in *Howitt's Journal* along with another short tale 'The Sexton's Hero', which in the following year brought out her 'Christmas Storms and Sunshine'.

Mary Barton however is both more than the customary novel of social reform, and different from it. Though its overt aim may be didactic, its fundamental ones are neither didactic nor reformatory; its author is not a clergyman or political figure who elects to use the

[1] Though one could mention that her writing might be considered to begin with 'My Diary: The Early Years of my Daughter Marianne', begun in 1835 (privately printed, Clement Shorter, 1923), it would be even less fair to take this as her first literary composition than it would be to consider her letters in the same light. It was an entirely private piece of writing, not even intended for friends' eyes, still less the public's.

[2] *Blackwood's Magazine*, XLI (January 1837), pp. 48–51.

[3] Introduced by W. Howitt into his *Visits to Remarkable Places* (1840), pp. 130–46.

[4] 'Libbie Marsh's Three Eras: A Lancashire Tale', *Howitt's Journal*, I (1847).

novel to further his beliefs. She is a novelist first, an artist whose aims are wider than those of the reformer. She is concerned with one of the ultimate subjects of all literature – the predicament of men within their mortal span of life. So her novel has not 'dated' as social reformers' novels do, losing all but their historical interest when the conditions they deal with no longer survive. She is paradoxically less cynical, artistically speaking, than the novelist with a purpose, who exploits the medium as a means to non-artistic ends. She is, naturally, not a mere documenter of facts. Her religion is at the heart of her and of all she writes, and her social concern for those of whom she writes is a practical manifestation of that religion. In this way she is a novelist with a moral purpose in the same sense that Jane Austen is, and in this way is perhaps the last voice speaking from that position of securely-held belief that ends somewhere in the mid-nineteenth century. The fact is perhaps not so evident in *Mary Barton* as in *Ruth*, *North and South* or *Sylvia's Lovers*, whose themes and characters question orthodox belief, but its truth is proved by the absence of doubt, contrasted with later writers. George Eliot in *Adam Bede* (1859), writing of an age and society in which Christian belief is secure, is neither secure herself, nor depends on that security in her readers. She is detached not only from the extreme Wesleyanism of Dinah, but from the orthodox inert Christianity of the clergyman Mr Irvine. Trollope, who would seem committed to handling creed by choosing to write of clerics, avoids in his Barchester novels all but the most rudimentary morality, and has virtually no dealings with Christian belief.

When Elizabeth Gaskell does have a specific social aim in writing, as here and in *Ruth* (and somewhat in *North and South*), it is rather to inform than to reform. She acts on the faith that if facts are known, then improvement may follow, and so feels no obligation to exaggerate, or dramatize or heighten. One can often feel indeed that Elizabeth Gaskell needs the social aim only to justify writing at all; that it arises as much from personal diffidence as from social zeal. Her turning away from vexed social questions in her later novels reinforces the feeling.

Elizabeth Gaskell is apart from novelists of her time, as well as social reformers. She is a 'primitive', working out her own art and craft of the novel for herself, enlarging and perfecting it in the course of her career, very much independently of novelists before her, and those around her. Naturally, therefore, she blunders, she sometimes lacks assurance, she sometimes over-emphasizes. These faults of a beginner are most visible in *Mary Barton*, as is another fault of a very interesting kind. Elizabeth Gaskell shows she is aware that she is learning her craft, by the way that in some parts of this novel she depends on and uses the traditional material of the novel, such as the love story of a young heroine, the subject of seduction, sensational and improbable happenings, and a test of heroism for her central characters. *Mary Barton* suffers from being an amalgam of what can be seen as two distinct novels, one of them a quite original tragic novel, the other a much more conventional one which, though in many ways congenial and suited to her, is yet a sign of her depending on what she knows will be acceptable to a novel-reading public. The tragic novel concerns John Barton, driven by his sense of justice, his loyalties to his fellow mill-workers and to his Trade Union, into the extreme act of murdering his employer's son; through it Elizabeth Gaskell explores his social problem of the struggles between masters and men. It has its end in the superb reconciliation between the broken and dying Barton, and the father of the murdered man. The theme is great enough for a novel and gives enough scope on its own, as the wiser Elizabeth Gaskell of *Sylvia's Lovers* – her great and achieved tragic novel – would have known. Her second story is that of John's daughter Mary, the much more orthodox heroine, who hesitates between her real love, the workman Jem Wilson, and the dazzling wealthy lover Harry Carson; who, rejecting the one, on the murder of the other suffers the terrible dilemma of having to save Jem from being hanged, without revealing her father's guilt. This exciting plot, with the capacity for a (qualified) happy ending, is both more conventional and more sensational. Providing a study of the moral and spiritual growth of a young girl, it suits its author, and it provides some of the novel's finest scenes. Yet undoubtedly the two stories are too much for a single work, and account for many of its incidental failures in emphasis and proportion. Yet *Mary Barton* is an exciting whole, for its originality of subject matter, of character, and of methods, and impressive for the unobtrusive assurance of its writer, not least when she appears quite unaware that what she is doing is wholly new.

In discussing this novel, like *Ruth*, and unlike her other three full-length works – *North and South*, *Sylvia's Lovers* and *Wives and Daughters* – one must examine, account for, and assess the signs of unsureness, as well as the originality, initiative and success. One must look backwards to the novel as it existed as a tradition and a model before her, as well as forwards to the novelists after her, who developed in their own ways and for their own purposes the new ground she opened up for them and herself, and the new means she created of handling it.

Manchester is not only the setting for *Mary Barton*, it is its world. Elizabeth Gaskell herself, all her characters, the experiences that shape them and rule their lives, the present world from which they view life, religion, eternity, are within it. It is the life and time from which they view the rest of the universe, and from which we, the readers, view it during our reading. This is its great strength and its main originality. Earlier novels had often taken regional settings; Maria Edgeworth wrote of Ireland, Disraeli and Kingsley had deliberately chosen their areas of the English provinces; but with all these there is the authorial remoteness that comes from writing with the feeling of a metropolitan audience, and from a standpoint that accepts metropolitan standards as a norm, from which those of the novel are departures and regional aberrations.[5] Almost all of Elizabeth Gaskell's innovations as a provincial novelist rise from her unconscious acceptance of the world she chooses as a valid norm in itself, from which to understand and interpret the great issues of human life. She ignores social and geographical detachment, recognizing and revealing, not the 'otherness' of Manchester compared with London, but of London and elsewhere compared with Manchester; and feeling the present time of 'ten or a dozen years ago' (1838) of the opening of *Mary Barton*, from which all other times – even the 1848 of its publication – are past or future. She is not, naturally, devoid of artistic or moral detachment, but her judgements rise from and get their worth from her ability to participate, at the same time as she assesses. This stance in relation to her setting and subject is the most obvious gift she bestows on the nineteenth-century novelist – bestowed in the way of most such gifts, so that the beneficiaries are unaware of receiving it. George Eliot, writing her first fiction, *Scenes of Clerical Life*, ten years later, is in no sense an imitator of Elizabeth Gaskell; nor is Trollope in his first Barchester novel *The*

---

[5] Scott is a different case, since he wrote of Scotland for the Scots, aware more of a universal than an English set of values. A fairer parallel with Maria Edgeworth, on the Scottish scene, would be Galt, who writes his provincial topics from a standpoint which like the others' is aware of a norm from which his characters are aberrations.

Warden in 1854; Thomas Hardy creating Wessex still later, is even less so; but all three have the way to their own separate, and original, areas of greatness made smooth by her opening of the road. Charlotte Brontë, bringing out *Shirley* only a year later, was aware of the similarity between her own subject and her friend's, but the two novels are separated by their different aims: Charlotte's, despite its Yorkshire West Riding cotton-mill milieu, is, like all her novels, more a progress of the soul of its main character than a view of the world, quite apart from being also a study of the Napoleonic period.

Elizabeth Gaskell's assumptions about the novel are clear from the beginning, her main one being that its material must be the actual present world of everyday observation. Hence, though in later novels she may move in time (*Sylvia's Lovers* is historical) or disguise place (Milton instead of Manchester, or Cranford or Hollingford instead of Knutsford), no conventionalizing to fit a literary mode takes place. Hence, naturally, she presents herself enormous problems. Her method must be one rather of comprehensiveness than selection, of total understanding rather than detachment, allowing judgements to emerge by a multitude of juxtapositions and comparisons, rather than by heightenings, or sharp changes of tone and mood.

Therefore, she is closest among her great precursors to Scott at his best, who can in *Old Mortality* present with equal fairness the fanatical Balfour of Burley and the aristocratic cavalier Marquis of Claverhouse; and range socially, in *Heart of Midlothian*, from the humble Deans family to the illustrious Duke of Argyll. Elizabeth Gaskell's range in *Mary Barton* is less great, because Manchester offers less spread: the factory-owning Carsons are her highest; Alice Wilson, living by dispensing herb-medicines from her one-room damp cellar, and the prostitute Esther, who lives nowhere at all, are her lowest. But Elizabeth Gaskell's richness and fullness of creation is accordingly much greater. Resembling Scott, however, does not mean literary influence by Scott. It is as hard to detect any definite literary borrowing or learning from him as it is from any other previous novelist. The very signs of insecurity in this first novels are signs of her courage, and reveal her lack of dependence on those before and around her.

The relation between author and reader is one of any novelist's most powerful assets, and most personal traits, as well as perhaps one of his

greatest problems. It is a great source of Elizabeth Gaskell's power
and distinction, and causes her apparently few uneasinesses. She once
wrote that the idea of a reader caused her uneasiness and distress, yet
she shows few signs of having, even in her first full-length work, to
grapple with the problem. At her best, she is assured, candid, unassuming, engaging to her reader in assuming their complete equality
and communion of intellect and beliefs, and in having no reserves
from him. She never hectors a public, as Dickens sometimes does; has
no suspicions, such as Thackeray has, as to the reader's good nature or
goodwill; nor any detaching irony such as George Eliot can show.
At first reading, in her opening, her tone is so transparent as to seem,
deceptively, almost naïve, as when she speaks thus of Green Heys
Fields, outside Manchester:

> Here in their seasons may be seen the country business of hay-
> making, ploughing, etc., which are such pleasant mysteries for
> townspeople to watch: and here the artisan, deafened with the
> noise of tongues and engines, may come to listen awhile to the
> delicious sounds of rural life; the lowing of cattle, the milk-
> maid's call, the clatter and cackle of poultry in the old farmyards.
> You cannot wonder, then, that those fields are popular places of
> resort at every holiday time; and you would not wonder, if you
> could see, or I properly describe, the charm of one particular
> stile, that it should be, on such occasions, a crowded halting-
> place. (1)

She goes on to describe it delightfully. Such a tone immediately
establishes trust in the speaker, faith in her accuracy, and willingness
to go where she leads. She can then lead to strange, new, even repellent places, scenes, events, opinions and conclusions. She can describe
the Davenports' cellar, for instance, without arousing disbelief.

> Never was the old Edinburgh cry of *Gardez l'eau!* more
> necessary than in this street. As they passed, women from their
> doors tossed household slops of every description into the gutter;
> they ran into the next pool, which overflowed and stagnated.
> Heaps of ashes were the stepping-stones, on which the passer-by,
> who cared in the least for cleanliness, took care not to put his
> foot. Our friends [Barton and Wilson] were not dainty, but
> even they picked their way, till they got to some steps leading
> down to a small area, where a person standing would have his

head about one foot below the level of the street, and might at
the same time, without the least motion of his body, touch the
window of the cellar and the damp muddy wall right opposite.
You went down one step even from the foul area into the cellar
in which a family of human beings lived. It was very dark inside.
The window-panes, many of them, were stuffed with rags,
which was reason enough for the dusky light which pervaded
the place even at mid-day. After the account I have given of the
state of the street, no-one can be surprised that on going into the
cellar inhabited by Davenport, the smell was so foetid as almost
to knock two men down . . . [Barton] had opened a door, but
only for a minute; it led into a back cellar, with a grating instead
of a window down which dropped the moisture from pig-sties,
and worse abominations. It was not paved; the floor was one
mass of bad smelling mud. It had never been used, for there was
not an article of furniture in it; nor could a human being, much
less a pig, have lived there many days. Yet the 'back apartment'
made a difference in the rent. (vi)

She can cope with Mrs Barton's death in childbirth in her second
chapter without seeming sensational or morbid; by the same simple,
candid manner she can unobtrusively suggest all the young singer
Margaret's terrors as she gradually goes blind, the conflicts of
loyalties of the striker committed to his course for his fellow-workers'
good, yet agonized by seeing his friend starve, and his friend's children
die. She can go on finally to present a reconciliation between a
murderer and the father of his victim, which falls into neither melodrama, nor sentimentality, nor religious transport; and she can make
all these as much the stuff of everyday life as the hesitations of the
inarticulate young workman Jem in love with an indifferent girl, the
humours of the scientifically-minded old Job Legh with a mania for
biological specimens, or the pathetic childlike ramblings of the dying
old woman Alice Wilson.

Naturally she does have some difficulties with her relations with
her reader. They arise from the nature of her subject, more than from
being unsure of her own narrative personality. She realizes that in
Manchester she is writing of a place unfamiliar to most: the mill-
workers and their families, a new class in 1848, confined to the
Northern English region, are a social class every detail of whose way
of life may be new. Hence the rather frequent and often unnecessary

footnotes of the earlier chapters, explaining the meaning and origins of dialect words. Plainly she is anxious not only that they be understood, but also that the reader shall not see them as signs of uncouth speakers; by the dignity of the derivation from Lydgate, Chaucer or Skelton, for instance, she wishes to establish the dignity of those who use them. She realizes that their springs of conduct, their religion, their morality and, still more, their view of society may be unknown and surprising. And, finally, she knows that with them she is on dangerous ground: that the troubles of factory workers, strikes, the relation between management and labour (or 'masters and men' as Elizabeth Gaskell prefers to term them) and the rising Trades Unions, are the subject of economists' and reformers' debates, of public disapproval, anxiety, and even panic, and that the novel has already been made to treat of them, notably in Disraeli's *Coningsby* (1844) and *Sybil* (1845).

Being conscious of these difficulties, she sometimes over-exerts herself to make the way plain for the reader. She intrudes as speaker when the action and characters can be left to speak for themselves. Occasionally descriptions of physical conditions can go on too long, or she makes a character the vehicle for too much or too detailed a set of moral or religious musings, and sometimes she feels compelled to state her position – a dispassionate one – on the subject of employers and employed, with unneeded emphasis:

> At all times it is a bewildering thing to the poor weaver to see his employer removing from house to house, each one grander than the last, till he ends in building one more magnificent than all, or withdraws his money from the concern, or sells his mill, to buy an estate in the country, while all the time the weaver, who thinks he and his fellows are the real makers of this wealth, is struggling for bread for his children, through the vicissitudes of lowered wages, short hours, fewer hands employed, etc. And when he knows trade is bad, and could understand (at least partially) that there are not buyers enough in the market to purchase goods already made, and consequently that there is no demand for more; when he would bear much without complaining, could he also see that his employers were bearing their share, he is, I say, bewildered and (to use his own word) 'aggravated'. . . . The contrast is too great. Why should he alone suffer from bad times?

> I know this is not really the case; and I know what is the truth in such matters; but what I wish to impress is what the workman feels and thinks. (111)

Though these are times at which she uses political terms of her day, such as Chartist, Communist, or radical, the general absence of jargon is another small but significant reason why her work does not date, compared with other writers with a social purpose, whose free use of such terms – now no longer meaningful except in their historical context – impedes and alienates the reader of a later age. It is not surprising that such insecurities happen: it is surprising that they happen so rarely.

Yet she is, for her time and with her aims, very sparing of addresses to her reader. She seems consciously to avoid haranguing him, even when she addresses him. She was known to her friends as a brilliant and exciting teller of tales orally, and the voice of the oral story-teller is her voice as narrator, essentially simple in expression, and with the inner eye entirely on the matter of the story. When she does intervene, it is because of the feelings her story arouses, and these are always legitimate, powerful ones. When Mary agonizes over realizing that her own father has, in fact, done the murder of which her lover Jem is accused, Elizabeth Gaskell perceives that

> in the desert of misery with which these thoughts surrounded her, the arid depths of whose gloom she dared not venture to contemplate, a little spring of comfort was gushing up at her feet, unnoticed at first, but soon to give her strength and hope.
>
> And *that* was the necessity for exertion on her part . . . It is the woes that cannot in any earthly way be escaped that admit least earthly comforting. Of all the trite, worn-out, hollow mockeries of comfort that were ever uttered by people who will not take the trouble of sympathising with others, the one I dislike the most is the exhortation not to grieve over an event, 'for it cannot be helped'. Do you think if I could help it, I would sit still with folded hands, content to mourn? Do you not believe that as long as hope remained I would be up and doing? I mourn because what has occurred cannot be helped. (xxii)

Whether we choose to remember or not at this point that Elizabeth Gaskell began to write as an escape from her own grief that 'could

not be helped' – her baby son's death – we realize the robust unsentimental attitude that recognizes the comfort of action, and demands it
of her characters even in the most desperate of crises. Elizabeth Gaskell may be gentle with her characters, but she is also uncompromisingly tough. Heaven in her novels never tempers the wind to the
shorn lamb; her own and the reader's pity never induce her to falsify
events, nor minimize distress, any more than moral indignation
induces her to exaggerate suffering.

The author's relations with his reader are closely bound to his
relation to his subject. Here again Elizabeth Gaskell is clearly working her way towards her own original method. Her previous writings
have plainly helped her. She began with descriptive writing and
sketches,[6] which are simple, unpolemic, faithful documentary accounts with a mere outline of story. She gradually introduces plot,
attaching this precise noting of situation and detail to a developing
narrative. Her habit of letting facts as she sees them speak for themselves is her natural and most precious power when she comes to a
full-length work in *Mary Barton*.

Her powers are perhaps best defined by a negative: she has the
ability of *not* passing judgement, or condemning. She simply selects
and presents events and characters so that the reader understands
them. This is one of the great powers of the nineteenth-century
novel, and one for which George Eliot, not to mention the greater
later Russians, is rightly admired. Elizabeth Gaskell's power here is
akin to Charlotte Brontë's, who writes alongside her; but they differ
in that Charlotte Brontë, in her social novel, *Shirley*, does rigid justice, despite her dislike, to uncongenial facts and characters, whereas
Elizabeth Gaskell's charity does not permit us even to give way to
dislike. Like George Eliot she requires and supplies justice and understanding for the admitted wrongdoer, felon or even criminal, like
John Barton himself, or the minor character, the intriguing scandal-
mongering Sally Leadbitter. But unlike George Eliot she presents
them from a Christian as well as a moral position. Her characters are
assessed finally for their whole life and ideas, not for a single act:
John Barton is so assessed, not condemned, because he has killed a
man; he is judged as sinner, not criminal. The murdered man's
father, Carson, is revealed as just as faulty, not only because he nearly
causes the wrong man, Jem, to be hanged for the crime, but because

6 Her first published work was 'Sketches Among the Poor', *Blackwood's Magazine*,
XLI (January 1837).

he has given his whole being up to the thirst for vengeance. By contrast George Eliot can seem naïvely orthodox, when for instance in *Adam Bede* she does not bring Arthur Donnithorne forward for judgement until he has actually committed his offence against Hetty, and, when he has done so, condemns him extremely harshly. There is a flavour of poetic rather than real justice when Arthur gives up the estate so dear to him, to go into the army, as though George Eliot contrives against probability that his punishment shall in some way equal Hetty's. She has neither Elizabeth Gaskell's generosity, nor the eighteenth-century honesty that enables Jane Austen to say:

> That punishment, the public punishment of disgrace should in a just measure attend *his* share of the offence is, we know, not one of the barriers, which society gives to virtue. In this world, the penalty is less equal than could be wished. (*Mansfield Park*, XLVIII)

Admittedly George Eliot matured, and handles sin and eventual inevitable retribution very much more surely when she comes to Mrs Transome, in *Felix Holt*, but it is fair to compare George Eliot's first full-length novel with Elizabeth Gaskell's.

Just as she will not rigidly judge or condemn, Elizabeth Gaskell will not impose any of the usual kinds of novelist's order on her material by her attitude to it. She uses her characters themselves, their eyes and thoughts, to reveal what happens. She does not use a narrator's personality as a lens, as Thackeray does, to impose unity and provide interpretation; she does not use the consciousness of one leading character, like Jane Austen or Henry James; nor does she adopt George Eliot's position of standing back and seeing more, and more wisely, than her characters. To the reader expecting a visible guide and shaping hand, such a narrator is disconcerting; and the consequence a sense of formlessness. As will be seen later, her novels are far from formless and her sense of form grows rapidly; they work by cumulation and juxtaposition. But the method, like all new methods, can be exhausting, when there are no easy distinctions between major and minor characters, and when any incident is required to be seen from many different views. Before Jem's trial for instance (XXXII) – one of the novel's greatest scenes – we are made to feel innumerable emotions in succession and at the same time: we feel pity for Mary and intense excitement under the suspense of wondering what will be the verdict; we feel irritation with Job for thinking Jem may be guilty, yet must realize that he (and Margaret) have just as good reasons as Mary for what they think:

> 'Who is to believe me – who is to think him innocent, if you, who know'd him so well, stick to it he's guilty?'
>
> 'I'm loth enough to do it, lass,' replied Job; 'but I think he's been ill-used, and – jilted (that's plain truth, Mary, bare as it may seem), and his blood has been up – many a man has done the like afore, from like causes.'
>
> 'O God! Then you won't help me, Job, to prove him innocent? O Job, Job; believe me, Jem never did harm to no one.'
>
> 'Not afore; – and mind, wench! I don't over-blame him for this. (xxII)

But we realize that on the evidence – that Jem had actually quarrelled with and struck the murdered man, his rival with Mary, who was found shot with Jem's gun – Job has grounds for his belief, and to think otherwise than he does would be worse than sentimental, it would be soft-headed. Such assessments from the points of views of different characters are not primarily to intensify the heroine's plight – though they do that – but to give the wholeness of the situation. Later, during the trial itself, Elizabeth Gaskell gives scrupulous attention to everyone concerned: to Mary and Jem, the key figures; to Jem's mother Mrs Wilson, miserably and inadvertently giving evidence against him while yet 'trying to check her sobs into composure, and (unconsciously) striving to behave as she thought would best please her poor boy, whom she knew she had often grieved by her uncontrolled impatience' (xxxII); to the murdered man's father, Mr Carson, who, seeing Mary, feels 'a kind of interest yet repugnance, for was she not the beloved of the dead' (xxxII):

> It never shook his belief in Jem's guilt in the least, that attempt at *alibi*; his hatred, his longing for vengeance, having once defined an object to itself, could no more bear to be frustrated and disappointed, than a beast of prey can submit to have his victim from his hungry jaws ... he seemed to *know*, even before the jury retired to consult, that by some trick, some negligence, some miserable hocus-pocus, the murderer of his child, his darling, his Absalom, who had never rebelled, – the slayer of his unburied boy would slip through the fangs of justice, and walk

free and unscathed over that earth where his son would never more be seen. (ibid.)

She can even register the reactions of the defence lawyer who puts Will on the witness stand,

> not so much out of earnestness to save the prisoner, of whose innocence he was still doubtful, as because he saw the opportunity for the display of forensic eloquence. (ibid.)

and of the jury,

> shaken and disturbed in a very uncomfortable and perplexing way, and almost grateful to the prosecution [for trying to demolish] evidence, which was so bewildering when taken in connection with everything previously adduced. (ibid.)

The proof of Elizabeth Gaskell's triumph here is to be seen in comparison. The scene has often been admired by readers, who respond to the excitement it generates. Any reader juxtaposing it with comparable episodes, like the trial of Felix Holt for the accidental killing of a rioter, or the trial of Sidney Carton in Dickens's *Tale of Two Cities*, will feel a fullness of response in Elizabeth Gaskell, a sense of a whole world involved, and of ultimate and universal values at stake. Yet this is merely the trial of a local engineer for a small-town manufacturer's son's death. Like Jane Austen, though not by Austenian methods, Elizabeth Gaskell reveals the universal significance of the apparently minor.

Towards her characters, Elizabeth Gaskell is very unlike most novelists before her. She readily treats all her characters by all the means she possesses: seriously, humorously, by speech, account of their actions or thoughts, favourably or with reservations; and she will use any of them at various points as a means of narration or focus. So it is difficult, even irrelevant, to classify them in the usual ways, as major or minor, 'flat' or 'rounded', comic, satiric, caricatured, grotesque, or heroic. From a single incident, it would often be impossible to say from the way Elizabeth Gaskell treats and regards him whether any character concerned were a leading or a secondary one. Major is distinct from minor not through the author's attitude, but through the material: the complexity of the character itself, or the circumstances which he undergoes or creates. The value of her method is one that novelists only gradually realize, for the enormous enrichment it permits. Trollope can be like her in recognizing that a stupid or even ludicrous person can respond and experience as intensely as a hero or heroine. In *Barchester Towers*, for instance, he can pause to perceive and analyse the conflicts and concerns of the feckless Stanhopes, who are at other times his butt. But Trollope is at all times a more leisurely teller of tales than Elizabeth Gaskell, without her driving moral impulse or overriding seriousness of intention. George Eliot develops the method, most notably in *Middlemarch*, where she can devote serious care to faulty, limited characters, and to apparently not very 'deep' ones, like the well-known example of Bulstrode, or the easy-going bachelor cleric Farebrother. Or, to compare her earlier work with Elizabeth Gaskell's, there is the clergyman Mr Irvine in *Adam Bede*, rector of Hayslope, a *bon-vivant* and an indifferent preacher:

> if that handsome, generous blooded clergyman had not had these two hopelessly-maiden sisters, his lot would have been shaped quite differently: he would very likely have taken a comely wife in his youth, and now, when his hair was getting gray, would have had tall sons and blooming daughters. . . . As it was, having with all his three livings no more than seven hundred a-year, and seeing no way of keeping his splendid mother and his sickly sister, not to reckon a second sister, who was usually spoken of without any adjective, in such ladylike ease as became their birth and habits, and at the same time providing for a family of his own – he remained, you see, at the age of eight-and-forty, a bachelor, not making any merit of that renunciation, but saying laughingly, if any one alluded to it, that he made it an excuse for many little indulgences which a wife would never have allowed him. (*Adam Bede*, v)

George Eliot preserves also at first the more usual attitudes to character, and so her excursions of this sort into secondary characters are generally, like this, author's analyses for which the action pauses; when it resumes, the character behaves in his usual way as a secondary character, coloured for the reader by the extra knowledge he has been given. In her later, larger novels too, she has problems of perspective larger than Elizabeth Gaskell undertakes, which demand some simplifying of the way characters and situations can be handled. She preserves too her narrative detachment from the situations in which her characters are placed, and so, as a wiser and often ironic and slightly wry commentator, she does not depend so fully as Elizabeth Gaskell on the method Elizabeth Gaskell pioneers. As is to be expected of one who is not an imitator but an original developer, she takes over what is useful to her, and amalgamates it with her own new and original forms. When she in her turn undertakes the trial for life – Hetty's for child-murder in *Adam Bede* – at a parallel stage in her development as a novelist, she concentrates her forces on Adam's response, and on the simple accounts of the witnesses, saving the fluctuations of Hetty's agony for the later scene of confession to Dinah. George Eliot's method is a simpler, more orthodox one, linked to Elizabeth Gaskell's by its aim at avoiding theatricality and melodrama, and by its wish to present the helplessness of the ordinary humble man caught up by the inexorable operation of social forces and laws upon him.

As a narrator Elizabeth Gaskell only gradually develops ironic detachment, as will be seen later in *Sylvia's Lovers* and *Wives and Daughters*, of her own original kind. Her strengths as a beginner are with the poignant and pathetic; what irony there is, contributes to them, and arises naturally out of the material itself rather than out of the way the author presents or views it. When, for instance, the prostitute Esther visits her niece Mary, with the paper in Jem's handwriting found on the scene of the crime, the irony of situation springs from Esther's unawareness that Mary loves, not the dead Harry Carson, but Jem, and wishes to save him; and the irony of relationships comes from Esther's pathetically pretending to be a respectable and prosperous married woman:

> Her words shot a strange pang through Mary's heart. She had always remembered her aunt's loving and unselfish disposition; how was it changed, if, living in plenty, she had never thought it worth while to ask after her relations who were all but starving! She shut up her heart instinctively against her aunt. (xxi)

This irony offers no surprises with new facts, only of new ways of seeing facts already known, like Job's remark that, to prove Jem's innocence,

> 'Best way, if you know'd him innocent, would be to find out the real murderer. Some one did it, that's clear enough. If it wasn't Jem, who was it?' (xxii, p. 288)

The reader knows it was Mary's own father; Job's question reveals both Mary's 'agony of terror' and the poignant irony of Job's own position, unaware of his own friend's guilt. This kind of pain of ironic circumstances looks forward to Thomas Hardy, who, without Elizabeth Gaskell's religious faith, is far more troubled than she by the helplessness of men in the grip of fates created by themselves, yet beyond their knowledge or control. Elizabeth Gaskell, unlike Hardy, saw this consequence not as her end, but as her fault. Hardy ends his novelist's career with his darkest work, *Jude the Obscure;* Elizabeth Gaskell, writing of Mary Barton, said 'I acknowledge the fault of there being too heavy a shadow over the book',[7] and ended her writing life with her wisest and most generous work, *Wives and Daughters.* Even so, Elizabeth Gaskell is always serious, and can be sombre. *Wives and Daughters* is no more a gay book than *Mary Barton* or the tragic *Sylvia's Lovers.* As her understanding deepens, she realizes that the seriousness of life does not involve sensational events, but is the very substance of everyday living, that though cheerfulness keeps breaking in, and though comedy is of the stuff of life, so also are distress, anxiety, frustration, sorrow, and the temptation to despair.

With such an attitude both to her readers and her material, Elizabeth Gaskell does not run into the difficulties that face other novelists who, like her, document a social reality, reveal a contemporary situation and intermingle historical and fictional material. Her fidelity to the actual, and her wish for complete and fair comprehensiveness, make it easy for her. Though her characters and their predicaments may be invented, she feels that they are also close to the actual, because they are representative of so much that happened historically. The circumstances and settings and details that attend them are vividly actual because they are those common to their kind. Her success in combining historical fact and documentary detail with her invented story is virtually complete, on both the greatest and most trivial levels. Probably the most important single incident she employs is the mill-workers' march and petition to Parliament of 1839. It is so completely worked into the fabric of the novel that the reader feels he would not know, from the texture of the narrative, that this event is of a different kind from the invented material. In a sense, it is not, for the hunger that gradually oppresses the Bartons, the fever that

[7] Letter to Mrs Greg, undated, written early 1849, letter 42 in *The Letters of Mrs Gaskell,* ed. J. A. V. Chapple and Arthur Pollard (Manchester, 1966).

attacks the Davenports, the accident that years before crippled Mrs Wilson when she 'cotched her side' in the spinning machine, are all actual happenings to many actual people of their time. On the other hand, the reader's awareness that the Chartist petition was a historical event gives substance to the fictional events because of the identical artistic effect made by it, and by what Elizabeth Gaskell invents elsewhere.

The petition is presented wholly through the participant's eyes, which are wholly adequate for the aspects of the political situation that Elizabeth Gaskell explores, since she has already created them as thinking, intelligent men hampered only by ignorance and the limited views their position has forced upon them.

> An idea was now springing up among the operatives, that originated with the Chartists, but which came at last to be cherished as a darling child by many and many a one. They could not believe that Government knew of their misery: they rather chose to think it possible that men could voluntarily assume the office of legislators for a nation who were ignorant of its real state. . . . So a petition was framed, and signed by thousands in the bright spring days of 1839, imploring Parliament to hear witnesses who could testify to the unparalleled destitution of the manufacturing districts. Nottingham, Sheffield, Glasgow, Manchester, and many other towns, were busy appointing delegates to convey this petition, who might speak, not merely of what they had seen and had heard, but from what they had borne and suffered. Life-worn, gaunt, anxious, hunger-stamped men were those delegates.
> One of them was John Barton. (VIII)

Elsewhere she presents, just as fairly, how the recession in trade affects the employers also, forcing them to lay off workmen and lower wages, even though in this novel she is not as anxious as she is in *North and South* to present the whole of the economic conflict. Her facts once stated, she has no need to go again further than her characters can see: the petition, its reception in London, and the consequences, form the substance of John Barton's magnificent and poignantly comic account in Chapter IX. The whole episode gains power by being intermingled with and juxtaposed to other happenings: George Wilson's sudden death, Mary's relations with her would-be seducer Harry Carson and his go-between Sally Leadbitter, and Job Legh's tale – a wonderful short story in its own right – of his own journey to London a generation before.

She copes equally with documentary fact. She knows and avoids the heavy thud usually made by statistical details in a story, for instance, when John Barton reports his discovery that, in factories and mills, 'by far th' greater part o' th' accidents as comed in [to the infirmary] happened in th' last two hours o' work' (VIII); the context is delightfully comic, for his only audience is Jem, who, since he came to court the unwilling Mary (who has coyly escaped to her bedroom), is not listening to him at all. She copes as equably with necessary horror, when her subject demands, for example, that she shall deal with the physically unpleasant. Her method neither mini-mizes nor melodramatically heightens. When (XVI) a brought-in workman is the victim of vitriol thrown at him by a striker, she wisely subsumes the incident by presenting it through one of the characters' own reactions. The sheer physical horror is minimized, so that the reader is able to respond with pity and judgement, rather than merely be sickened.

Her complete familiarity produces complete confidence, without any of the sense of strain or overwriting of Dickens's nightmare evocation of the steelworks in *Old Curiosity Shop*, and without resort-ing to imagery and symbolism as he does in *Hard Times* or, also in that novel, embarrassingly idealizing the virtuous workman bodied forth in Stephen Blackpool, whose reflections on his plight never get beyond the catchphrase 'It's aw a muddle'; and equally without any undigested sections like Disraeli's near-farcical account of a Union initiation[8] or of the iron-working community of Wodgate.[9]

Such use of contemporary or near-contemporary history is a necessary and fast-growing part of the nineteenth-century novelist's subject and, much more, of those who write from outside London. Though Dickens uses social conditions, he rarely uses events; but both Trollope and George Eliot, different as they are, follow Elizabeth Gaskell's lead in absorbing the historical and embodying it in the fictional. Though neither ventures to use an actual place as Mrs Gaskell uses Manchester, Trollope bases the Barchester con-troversy over the finances of the almshouses in *The Warden* on those of St Cross, Winchester; and George Eliot uses the Chartist riots and the 1832 Reform Bill, in *Felix Holt* and *Middlemarch*.

Just as confidently as she incorporates history into fiction Eliza-

8 *Sybil*, Book IV, 14.   9 *Sybil*, Book III, 4. .

beth Gaskell incorporates those parts of human existence which reach out towards the eternal: death, and religious belief. Both are essential elements in the world of *Mary Barton*, as they are, in even deeper and greater degrees, in the novels that follow. Generally speaking, before her, death is something extra, and strange to, the existence of characters and action in novels. Minor characters can die, for thematic reasons, or simply as a means of being got rid of; heroes and heroines are immortal, unless their dying is, like Little Nell's, the culminating excitement and climax for the reader. Death, for the novelist before Elizabeth Gaskell, is either a casual accident, or of momentous significance. Jane Austen notoriously avoids it; Scott's great characters die, in ways befitting themselves, and as emblematic as the characters themselves: like Fergus McIvor in *Waverley*, that embodiment of a lost cause and forsaken belief, whose execution is as brutal as the reality which crushes his Jacobite cause and the clan system, and as magnificent as the devotion and loyalty he both gave and inspired. Charlotte Brontë, whose *Jane Eyre* is but a year before *Mary Barton*, recognizes death as a part of life, but her characters' deaths – Helen Burns's and Mrs Reed's – though natural accidents of time and chance, are momentous and significant landmarks in the heroine's spiritual and moral voyage. Only rarely before Elizabeth Gaskell's novels is death a necessary inescapable eventuality within life and society as a whole. For her, sad and solemn though it invariably is, it is no subject for hysteria, for melodrama, for sentimentality, or for terror; it may even be recognized as a mysterious blessing or a welcome release; it is always accepted as the one inevitable fact of life.

More of the people who die in Elizabeth Gaskell's novels are in no way exceptional for doing so than is the case in most other nineteenth-century writers' works. Their deaths may be of the conventional novelist's sort, crucial to the plot, like Henry Carson's murder by John Barton; they may be the necessary thematic and moral end for a character who has no more life to live, like Barton's own; they may embody the social message, like the death of John Davenport, from starvation and disease, lack of work and vile living conditions. But these deaths never seem consciously contrived, or rigged to point a moral, still less adorn the tale. Besides these are other characters, whose deaths are much more an embodiment and acceptance of death as an inescapable element in life. Of this kind are most notably the Wilson twins, Mary Barton's mother, and Alice. The twins are ailing children – 'Who like many a pair of twins, seemed to have but

B

one life divided between them' (viii) – frail from their birth to a
crippled mother 'a cranky sort of body at the best of times' (i), 'little
feeble twins inheriting the frail appearance of the mother' (vii),
who, since their brother Jem is adult, obviously had them late in life.
It is no surprise to the reader then that, when typhus fever breaks
out in undernourished, unemployed Manchester, 'the twins, after
ailing many days and caring little for their meat, fell sick on the same
afternoon, with the same heavy stupor of suffering' (vii). It is
physiologically probable that they should die, and psychologically
right that their death should be both sad and yet secondary to the
main course of events. Elizabeth Gaskell recognizes the genuine
sorrow of their dying, but sees it entirely without sentimentality. It
is thus reported to their brother Jem:

> He would make his aunt speak: he would not understand her
> shake of the head and fast coursing tears.
>   'They're both gone,' said she.
>   'Dead!'
>   'Aye, poor fellows. They took worse about two o'clock.
> Joe went first, as easy as a lamb, and Will died harder like.'
>   'Both!'
>   'Aye, lad! both. The Lord has ta'en them from some evil
> to come or he would na ha' made choice o' them. Ye may rest
> sure o' that.' (vii)

The religious message, which comes in appropriately from Alice, the
character with the most simple faith in the ways of God, is not the
'message' of the scene, but simply an essential of its context. Elizabeth
Gaskell does with assurance what other novelists touch at their peril;
and in thus removing death from an aura of sentiment and sanctity,
begins to lay the way clear for Hardy's *Tess of the d'Urbervilles*,
forty-three years later. Tess's child is like the Wilson twins, a natural
element in his world, and a minor one, whose going is as arbitrary,
or as inevitable, as his birth. Though Hardy's infant has a symbolic
force in the novel as a whole quite different from that of Elizabeth
Gaskell's Wilson twins, the actual handling of the children within
the fabric of the novels, and the recognizable human world at the
basis of both, is very closely akin, and lies in a different area, and a
more realistic one, from any similar material in, say, Dickens, who can
never lose a child to death with such balanced and robust equanimity.
   Elizabeth Gaskell is equally secure with the mature and the old.

Mrs Barton, Mary's mother, dies in childbed in the novel's third chapter. One can see the death is useful, in leaving the heroine alone in her future trials; one sees also that the novel could have begun with Mrs Barton already dead, without any loss to the story [as does *Heart of Midlothian*, or *Emma*, or *Middlemarch*, or *The Warden*]. Mrs Barton's death, faced as unflinchingly, and as briefly, as the twins',[10] establishes that mortality and the chances of life are contingencies as inescapable for characters in the novel as for men and women in real life. Such events impress upon the reader that though Elizabeth Gaskell will adhere to the basic conventions of the novel, and will produce an artistic whole, she will not only not leave us before a conventional plot has been concluded, but she will adhere to natural probability and consciously and deliberately enforce it.

Alice's death is both more central, and more functional. Hers is neither sudden, unexpected, nor cruel. It does not need to be acknowledged as the workings of a providence the characters cannot comprehend, nor is it a necessary adjunct to the working out of the plot. To the modern reader, it may seem only too obviously functional, in reinforcing her life's simple Christian messages of faith and trust in the beneficence of God's will. But, apart from the fact that what a character believes is not necessarily what its author believes, Alice's own circumstances both in life and death are neither happy nor fulfilled. She lives on the edge of poverty, gradually loses her hearing and her sight, and dies after a stroke, in second childishness and mere oblivion, having never had her one wish, to go back to the Cumberland home she left as a girl. But Alice herself tries always to see her life as shaped by the hand of a kindly God:

> 'Yo're mourning for me, my dear! and there's no need, Mary. I'm as happy as a child. I sometimes think I am a child whom the Lord is hushabying to my long sleep. For when I were a mere girl, my missis always told me to speak very soft and low and to darken the room that her little one might go to sleep, and now all noises are hushed and still to me, and I know it's my Father lulling me away to my long sleep. I'm very well content, and yo mustn't fret for me. I've had well-nigh every blessing in life I could desire.' (XIII)

And in her dying ramblings she indeed believes herself back in her home and her childhood. However, though the characters recognize

10 Mrs Barton's death takes two pages, the twins', four.

that her death is a happy one, Elizabeth Gaskell does not expect her readers to swallow this draught of undiluted sweetness. The contrasts between Alice's resignation and her circumstances are ironically astringent, make the reader appreciate the cruel limitations of a life so restricted that she can never return the few miles from Manchester to her home, the rigours of a service that prevented her reaching a dying mother, the physical ills that prevent her seeing or hearing properly her beloved sailor nephew Will Wilson, and the ironically poignant comfort of her fancied return in her dying imaginings. Alice's life as seen in the novel is in effect a long dying, contrasting, by being the inevitable conclusion of old age, with the other deaths from age, agues, tyrannies, despair, law, chance, which threaten or occur. In this, her first full-length work, Elizabeth Gaskell shows herself able to see not only life but death steadily and see it whole, as few English writers before or since have done. She looks forward, though her scale is so much smaller, more to the Tolstoy of *War and Peace* than to any English writer, and is fortunate perhaps in her historical position, living at a time when death was so much more an inescapable fact and event of life, when a man must face the possible loss of a wife in childbirth, and of a child in infancy, and when death was not to take place concealed within a hospital, or shuffled off without any religious assurance. Though she handles death in all her novels, and, with increasing artistic power, she is assured from the first.

Alice is also the clearest voice in the novel of Christian moral precepts. Her voice runs through the novel with its gentle reflections on personal submission and duties, alongside that other afflicted character, the blind singer Margaret Legh. But though these two voices may be the clearest, they are not alone, nor to be taken as speaking for their author. Christianity pervades *Mary Barton*, but there are varieties within it, and Christian ethics can be and are challenged.

It is no more a didactic religious novel than it is a novel of social reform. It is untheological and unsectarian. From reading, it would be impossible to deduce that it is the work of a Unitarian by upbringing, who was the wife of a Unitarian minister. The beliefs are embodied, enacted, and voiced by the characters rather than the author, with comments that are almost always on the separate situation, not on life in general. It is nevertheless always clear – even though no character goes to church, and many do not read the Bible – that

Elizabeth Gaskell is writing of and in a world where ethical and moral principles are *ipso facto* Christian ones; that faith, hope, and charity are vital springs of action; that love to one's neighbour is the equivalent of love of God, and that life after death and reunion with loved ones are the compensations for a harsh and unjust world. Elizabeth Gaskell is perhaps the last novelist of real stature who not only possesses this security, but can, for her purposes as a novelist, assume it in her readers. The advantages to her of so doing are as great as, contrarily, are those to later writers, like George Eliot and Hardy, who neither have the faith themselves, nor can depend on any kind of faith or similarity in their readers, and so have to establish moral standards by re-examining conventional positions and beliefs. Elizabeth Gaskell shares her security with the eighteenth century, though in her questioning she is unmistakably nineteenth century. The personal questionings are mainly part of Mary Barton's story, who has the traditional dilemma in her own great crisis, of having to prove the innocence of one person, without committing a sin herself, in betraying her father; her dilemma recalls that of Jeannie Deans who, in Scott's *Heart of Midlothian*, has to save *her* sister's life without the sin of a lie; as with other moral tests in the novel generally, the later writer's is more severe and complex than the earlier. Elizabeth Gaskell herself is not so much concerned here with personal morals as in her later work; the ethical dilemma facing Mary is very simple compared with those in *Sylvia's Lovers;* nor is Mary so much in the grip of forces she cannot control, imposed by society and other personalities, as is Molly in *Wives and Daughters.* The public questionings, on the ordering of society, are less clearly put, but more germane, and though brief, far more startling and revolutionary.

'. . . God being our Father, we mun bear patiently what'er he sends.'
    'Don' ye think he's th' master's Father, too? I'd be loth to have 'em for brothers.' (vi)

As with her social problems, Elizabeth Gaskell does not see it as her duty as a novelist to provide revolutionary answers – she neither expects nor desires revolution. Her answer – the reconciliation in mutual goodwill, recognizing of wrongdoing, and attempts to amend – is virtually 'Go and sin no more'. As an answer, it means less to modern readers than to contemporary ones; since Elizabeth Gaskell's day, more revolutionary answers have been given, and tried. One must not, even so, dismiss Elizabeth Gaskell's. If it is both naïve and a cliché, it has the power of clear sight that *naïveté* can have, and the power (that has made clichés what they are) of universal truth.

When one comes to examine Elizabeth Gaskell's handling of characters, the problem is of selection and classification. While some few are undoubtedly major, like Mary and John Barton, it becomes very difficult to say which are minor, or even secondary. Her full serious gaze at every character she treats has various consequences, most of them tending to emphasize how original she is as a novelist, how much she pushes out the frontiers of the art of the novel, and its power to give an increasingly full view of life, and how she can offer ideas and opportunities for other writers. *Mary Barton* shows that her original handling of characters is not something she evolved, but something natural to her, the consequence not of self-conscious technique, but of her whole way of looking at life, and what she chose from it for her material. It is also a consequence of her moral and religious beliefs, embodying the principles in her form. Just as all men are equal in the sight of God, so all characters are equal in the sight of the narrator. Elizabeth Gaskell never subordinates by caricature, or by making a character an exclusive vehicle for humour (though most of her characters can be humorous); she does not divide characters into those whose thoughts she gives, and motives she analyses, and those whom she presents only by action and speech; nor does she operate a separation by moral approval and disapproval. She realizes that character can change, or that the elements of a personality, while remaining the same, may produce very different results in different circumstances, making good qualities into apparent vices, or neutral qualities into strengths. Examples from among the secondary characters abound. Among those who appear least is, for instance, Mrs Carson, wife of the manufacturer whose son tries to seduce Mary and is shot by John Barton. She has no part in the action and impinges on it only once, when her son's body is brought home; yet her fully-realized existence and personality bring out the nature of the relationships in the society of masters and men. The first reference to her comes when John Barton calls to get an order to commit the dying Davenport to the hospital, and, waiting in the kitchen, hears that 'she's very black this morning. She's got a bad headache'; the chat goes on:

'Missis will have her breakfast upstairs, cook, and the cold partridge as was left yesterday, and put plenty of cream in her coffee, and she thinks there's a roll left, and she would like it well buttered.' (vi)

The contrast of such self-indulgent and thoughtless plenty with the foodless, fireless, cellar-dwelling, fever-stricken Davenports is obvious. But Elizabeth Gaskell avoids any explicit condemnation, leaving the facts and the dialogue to make the point. The restraint is impressive here, and an asset thereafter. Mrs Carson has been, as her son reveals, a mill-girl like Mary in her youth, and the very elements that condemned her make her pitiable:

She was not well, certainly. 'Wind in the head,' the servants called it. But it was but the natural consequence of the state of mental and bodily idleness in which she was placed. Without education enough to value the resources of wealth and leisure, she was so circumstanced as to command both. It would have done her more good than all the ether and sal-volatile she was daily in the habit of swallowing, if she might have taken the work of one of her own housemaids for a week; made beds, rubbed tables, shaken carpets, and gone out into the fresh morning air. (xviii)

Naturally, then, when Harry Carson is brought home dead, she can become poignantly pathetic in her capacity for understanding (shock makes her imagine Harry is alive but pretending to sleep) and render her husband so, for having no one to share his own contrasting, fully-comprehending despair:

In a chair, at the head of the bed, sat the mother – smiling. She held one of his hands (rapidly stiffening, even in the warm grasp) and gently stroked the back of it, with the endearing caress she had used to all her children when young. (xviii)

Possibly the most unpleasant character in the novel is Mary's friend and fellow-worker Sally Leadbitter, 'who had been from the beginning a confidante in Mary's love affair, made so by Mr Carson himself' (viii). She is always troublesome to Mary, ironically incapable of real feeling, and comic in her incomprehension – as when her only concern with Jem's trial is that Mary, as witness, should appear to the best advantage by borrowing her shawl. Yet even her

Elizabeth Gaskell will neither condemn, nor allow the reader to dismiss. Her introduction is balanced, precise and incisive: she is

> vulgar-minded in the last degree; never easy unless the talk was
> of love and lovers. . . . Considerations of modesty never checked
> her utterance of a good thing. She had just talent enough to
> corrupt others. Her very good nature was an evil influence.
> They could not hate one who was so kind; they could not
> avoid one who was so eager to shield them from scrapes by any
> exertion of her own; whose ready fingers would at any time
> make up for their deficiencies, and whose still more convenient
> tongue would at any time invent for them. The Jews or
> Mohammedans (I forget which) believe that there is one little
> bone of our body . . . which will never decay and turn to dust,
> but will be incorrupt and indestructible in the ground until the
> Last Day: this is the Seed of the Soul. The most depraved have
> also their Seed of the Holiness that shall one day overcome their
> evil; their one good quality, lurking hidden, but safe, among all
> the corrupt and bad.
>   Sally's seed of the future soul was her love for her mother,
> an aged bed-ridden woman. For her she had self-denial . . .
> her spirits, in the evenings, never flagged, but were ready to
> recount the events of the day, to turn them into ridicule, and to
> mimic, with admirable fidelity, any person gifted with absurdity
> who had fallen under her keen eye. (VIII)

The passage, though long, is necessary, not only for the part Sally is to play, but as a key to Elizabeth Gaskell's attitude to all her characters, a confession of her faith as a novelist. This fair-minded assessment of secondary or minor characters is one of the rapidly-developing features of the novel, especially evident in George Eliot, and no less in Trollope. Exploring new social milieus and the characters in them, as they and Elizabeth Gaskell do, prevents any temptation to reproduce old types, or habitual techniques. George Eliot even in her first work, *Scenes of Clerical Life*, deliberately chooses, as Elizabeth Gaskell had done, the unworthy and the humble; Trollope resembles her in drawing in the Barset novels upon a social order new to the novel. George Eliot, with a wider range, is not so consistent as Elizabeth Gaskell, and uses flat type-characters, or those founded on a few traits, as well, but, as she develops, one finds throughout her work instances of a Gaskell-type gaze. The clergyman Irwin in

Adam Bede has already been mentioned. Among many others are Mrs Bulstrode, Bulstrode himself, and Mrs Cadwallader (all in *Middlemarch*), or the devious agent Christian in *Felix Holt*.[11] Trollope is an altogether more casual writer than either, who, while his novels have many excellences, is systematic neither by instinct nor design, and who is successful more by sympathy and the happy accident. He is likely to enter a character's consciousness to arouse sympathetic understanding unexpectedly, as the events of his story require.

In this, her first full-length novel, Elizabeth Gaskell is not as accomplished as she later became, and does not always succeed. Since she does not set up the usual signs for the reader about the amount of emphasis and importance characters will have, she sometimes lacks balance, and a sense of shape. We are given little guide, for instance, to the fact that Margaret and Job Legh, the blind singer and her insect-collecting grandfather, are to play a great part, and that Job is to be a mainstay at the trial; nor on the other hand, that the three Carson daughters (xviii), beautifully caught and differentiated, will never appear again. But this very uncertainty will come in her later work to be a strength, reproducing the feel of life, in which people appear and depart, and return, and form new and unexpected relationships and connections.

Although Elizabeth Gaskell is not a self-effacing narrator in the sense Jane Austen is, using wherever possible her characters rather than her own voice to direct the reader, she is yet an unobtrusive one. Despite occasional direct addresses to her reader, most of her narration (other than that retailing events) is devoted to telling what characters are, or feel, or think. Moreover, in so doing she rarely passes judgement, or gives the reader the impression that she is deliberately directing his judgement, but rather that she is presenting indisputable facts from which judgements may be drawn.

Moral judgements are not only *on* characters, but often provided *by* them, particularly where a variety of judgements may be held on a single situation. Elizabeth Gaskell is not an ironist, nor does she regard her characters with an ironical eye, but irony is nevertheless a power in her novels, arising out of action and juxtaposition and the

[11] One should contrast Aunt Pullett in *The Mill on the Floss*, who, comic-grotesque in the childhood sections, yet makes a dramatic and unexpected yet consistent moral stand to support Maggie in her distress and disgrace. But such a sudden change, without preparation, is a Dickensian development.

apparently natural interaction of personalities. To provide such juxtapositions is a large part of the functions of Job Legh and Margaret,
both of them intelligent, and of sound sense and morals. By so doing
they reveal their own limitations of personality, and also their limited
information. Even less intelligent and informed people may do the
same, like Jem's mother Mrs Wilson. The consequences of these
limited judgements from varied positions are to reveal how hard true
judgement is to come by, and how painful, or pathetic, or comic the
ironic consequences may be. Margaret is a wholly estimable character,
a model of resignation to her blindness, and an embodiment of
common sense. But she is no paragon, and Elizabeth Gaskell exposes
how even the pure in heart and intention may blunder:

> . . . she was surprised and disappointed by the disclosure of
> Mary's conduct with regard to Mr Henry Carson. Gentle,
> reserved, and prudent herself, never exposed to the trial of being
> admired for her personal appearance . . . Margaret had no
> sympathy with the temptations to which loveliness, vanity,
> ambition, or the desire of being admired, expose so many. That
> is, she had no idea of the strength of conflict between will and
> principle in some who were differently constituted from herself
> and . . . was strongly inclined to give Mary up altogether.
> (XXII)

Similar is Job's innocent remark to Mary, when she asks how to
prove Jem's innocence; *she* knows and must conceal her father's
guilt, and *he* believes Jem to be the murderer, but intensely pities
Mary:

> 'Oh God! Then you won't help me, Jem, to prove him
> innocent? O Job, believe me, Jem never did harm to no one.'
> 'Not afore; – and mind, wench! I don't over-blame him for
> this.' Job relapsed into silence.
> Mary thought a moment.
> 'Well, Job, you'll not refuse me this, I know. I won't mind
> what you think, if you'll help me as if he was innocent. Now
> suppose I know – I knew, he was innocent, – it's only suppos-
> ing, Job, – what must I do to prove it? Tell me, Job! Isn't it
> called an *alibi*, the getting folk to swear to where he really was
> at the time?'
> 'Best way, if you knowed him innocent, would be to find

out the real murderer. Some one did it, that's clear enough.
If it wasn't Jem, who was it?'

'How can I tell?' answered Mary, in an agony of terror.
(xxii)

Mary's ambiguously-worded reply intensifies the shock of Job's
unconsciously deadly question. More brief and more poignant, one
of the most powerful moments in the novel's most powerful scene,
Jem's trial, is his mother Mrs Wilson's evidence:

. . . the gun was produced in court, and the inquiry made –
'That gun belongs to your son, does it not?'
She clenched the sides of the witness-box in her efforts to
make her parched tongue utter words. At last she moaned
forth –
'Oh! Jem, Jem! What mun I say?' (xxxii)

At the core of the novel are two stories and five main personalities,
all interlinked. The conventional story of the girl, her true lover, her
would-be seducer, and her great moral test, are Mary's; the entirely
original story of the man who, for nobly-based motives, out of love
of his fellow-men, and loyalty to his union, commits murder, is John
Barton's. That the murdered man is his daughter's wooer, and that
the falsely-accused is her honest lover, is an easy and obvious join.
Both John Barton and his daughter are natural and congenial subjects for their author, calculated to draw on her best. That neither is
as fine as what she is later to do shows partly that though both are
congenial, they do not quite cohere – as if they belonged in two
separate novels – and partly that the story that contains them is both
too melodramatic, and neither grand nor simple enough. The John
Barton story – in which his conflicts of conscience and impulse, of
honest and deep feeling with normal standards of right, lead to disaster, to reconciliation and something like tragedy – looks forward to
Sylvia's Lovers, not only to Philip, but to Sylvia herself; on the other
hand Mary Barton – the girl of good impulses and fervent passions,
reaching maturity by way of many small and one great single test of
her fibre – leads forward through Ruth, and Margaret Hale in *North
and South*, to Molly Gibson in *Wives and Daughters*. As this later
development reveals, the melodramatic, more extraordinary events are
needed for tragic material – like John Barton's story, and *Sylvia's
Lovers* – while the more subdued matter is suited to and developed in

the Margaret Hale story of *North and South*, the two not-quite-novels *Cranford* and *Cousin Phillis*, and *Wives and Daughters*.

That the novel was originally and provisionally entitled *John Barton* shows how centrally Elizabeth Gaskell thought of him, even though the novel as it stands spends less time on him than on Mary. Such restraint is artistically powerful even though it may be that she is not yet capable of more. Since she does not retail much of his thoughts or his motives, and withdraws from him altogether once he is elected to his doom, he becomes a figure of mystery and terror – for the reader as for Mary – whose inner torment is the more powerfully felt for being guessed, not known. Before this, however, his presentation is splendidly balanced, and the gradual shaping of his nature by circumstance precisely laid down. His powerful sympathy and love for his daughter and for his fellow-men both endear him and account for his increasing bitterness: we see him driven to sympathetic rage by the little he can do to assist the destitute Davenport family, by his frustrated desire to understand the economic pressures that throw him and his fellow mill-hands out of work, by the complete failure of the petition to Parliament, then finally driven by starvation to the comfort of opium, which inexorably intensifies his mood by weakening his self control. Since his downward progress is completely intelligible, so is his deed when he kills Henry Carson. Elizabeth Gaskell reinforces the external pressures with the personality with which she endows him, of a man given to violence (he once strikes Mary), with a good mind cramped by lack of education and knowledge. He poses all the novel's unanswered and unanswerable questions, including that which re-echoes through the whole, in reply to Wilson's remark that Ben's letter

'. . . were as good as Bible-words; Ne'er a word about repining; a' about God being our Father, and that we mun bear patiently whate'er he sends.'

'Don' ye think he's th' master's Father, too? I'd be loth to have 'em for brothers.'

'Eh, John! donna talk so; sure there's many and many a master as good or better nor us.'

'*If you think so, tell me this. How comes it they're rich, and we're poor? I'd like to know that. Han they done as they'd be done by for us?*' (vi, my italics)

Elizabeth Gaskell cannot answer. She can only extenuate, and mercifully permit John Barton to die, reconciled with Carson the man and father whom he has wronged, but never at one with Carson the mill-owner and 'master' who brought about the crime. When, in *North and South*, she next tries to cope with the strife of masters and men, she changes her ground to a study of the master, in John Thornton. When, in *Sylvia's Lovers*, she next undertakes the man who is helpless in the face of overwhelming need, it is Philip Hepburn, helpless before things far more unalterable than social and economic necessity.

John Barton is the first appearance in a novel of a character who is the victim of economic necessity and also a man and a soul at strife, not merely an example whereby the novelist gets through to the public. After him come other men in the grip of such forces and of political belief, among the most notable being Kingsley's Alton Locke (1850). It is obviously not an easy or manageable subject, since examples are few, and not great – as witness Dickens's sorry achievement with Stephen Blackpool in *Hard Times*. Among secondary figures there are the mill-workers William Farren and Joe Scott in Charlotte Brontë's *Shirley* in 1849, who show how the novel is moving spontaneously in this direction – there can be no direct influence, as Charlotte Brontë had not read *Mary Barton* before she wrote *Shirley*. The type does not reappear again in a major novel outside Elizabeth Gaskell (who returns to it in *North and South*), until, eighteen years later, George Eliot's Felix Holt, who is Chartist and working-class by choice, and whose fate turns on his political commitment. But by this time there are many changes, the consequence of the passing of time, and the attitudes and the mental calibre of the writer. George Eliot is undoubtedly a more powerful and dispassionate political thinker than Elizabeth Gaskell, whose detachment affects the whole nature of her novel. But her springs of inspiration as a novelist do not necessarily lead her in the same direction as her processes of thought. Powerful though the novel *Felix Holt* is, its strengths and originality lie elsewhere than in the portrayal of the hero. Felix cannot engage the reader as John Barton does, partly from his circumstances, partly from the technique. George Eliot's novel is set back thirty years from the present in which she writes, giving her a perspective and scope not accessible to Elizabeth Gaskell, but robbing Felix's dilemmas of the sense of present and immediate peril that John Barton's reveal, set back as he is only a decade, and still a present reality. Secondly, Felix deliberately and

idealistically chooses to be a working man, rejecting a symbolic
starched neckcloth, and a course of training in medicine at Glasgow
University, in order to be a watch and clock repairer and a teacher.
He is young, strong and untrammelled by a wife and children.
Penury, much less starvation, is never a threat to him. He suffers no
mental torment comparable to Barton's, having only the rather more
elementary and traditional conflict between love (for Esther Lyon)
and his political commitment to his fellow-men. While, like John
Barton, he actually kills a man as a consequence of his political acts,
the deed is an accident; and George Eliot never faces, or brings her
reader to face, the dilemma of the political murderer. While one feels
that without the existence of John Barton, Felix Holt might not in
person have seen print, yet both the real powers and great originality
of the book lie elsewhere, in Mrs Transome's story, where, also, lie
the greater debts to Elizabeth Gaskell, as will be seen in more detail
later. Perhaps more akin, in a way both gentler and more modest,
are Trollope's interesting creations, and the situations in his very
first Barchester novel *The Warden*. Both the Warden Harding himself and the young doctor John Bold are men in the grip of forces
they cannot control: Harding of economic and political episcopal
jugglings that (like Barton) he cannot understand, but that he has to
change his life to escape; Bold of social beliefs that lead him into rash
action that affects both himself and those he loves. While Trollope
is not working on the same scale as Elizabeth Gaskell – no life is
ever at stake in his work, and in his world things work out always
more or less for the best – he clearly takes up her lead in realizing
that the most crucial and dangerous dilemmas, for potential tragedy
and disaster, belong not only to the young and the unmarried.
Obvious though this may seem now, it was plainly not so in the 1840s
and much after, when novels still in general tended to get their shape
from their young and unmarried heroes and heroines, and conclude
with their marriage. There are of course notable exceptions (not only
in the provincial novelists) like Dickens's *Dombey & Son*, but the
way pointed by Scott was still largely neither seen nor followed,
obscured by his habit of having a hero and heroine marry in the end,
even though his themes and greatest action and characters lie elsewhere, in historical and political and national dilemmas on which his
'heroes' barely impinge. Elizabeth Gaskell herself is no copier or
follower of Scott, but another opener of the road.

At an even greater distance from Elizabeth Gaskell is Hardy who.

with all his differences of outlook and belief, pushes farther along this way, and, in his greatest works, such as *The Mayor of Casterbridge*, takes a hero who like Barton is 'a man of character' (as Hardy subtitles his work), no longer young, whose tragedy comes about from outside pressures he cannot control.

But Elizabeth Gaskell has another tale to tell in *Mary Barton*, that of Mary herself – less arresting, less strikingly original, and more what the general novel-reader of the nineteenth century, and probably even of today, expects to encounter. Her conventional elements tend to obscure her power. Mary shows Elizabeth Gaskell's potential in the less obtrusive skills whose development is also her genius, and her contribution to the art of the novel. The honest but misguided girl like Mary, deluded by her beauty, vanity and ambition into not recognizing either what is right or her own real inclinations, is a stock-piece of the novel. But Mary is both more original and more complex than she seems. The details of her association with Henry Carson are not very important to her character; Elizabeth Gaskell realizes and demonstrates this by spending scarcely any space on scenes between them during its growth. This thread of narrative is important in that it provides Jem a rival and a possible motive for murder, and it is given extra thematic point by the story of Esther, the betrayed girl (Mary's aunt), who sinks into becoming a prostitute. But the story's main point comes with the events between Jem's arrest and his trial, which is also Mary's great test and the novel's climax, where it complicates still further Mary's distress, in that she, publicly supposed to be the lover of Henry Carson, not only suffers public shame and opprobrium, but also the private misery of her love and apparent disloyalty to Jem.

Mary is the first example of a kind of character and situation Elizabeth Gaskell is especially drawn to: that of the perceptive, intelligent, sensitive girl, who is put to a great public and spiritual test, partly by her own acts and partly by circumstances. Mary at the trial corresponds to Ruth rejecting Bellingham's offer of marriage, to Margaret Hale protecting Thornton from the rioters in *North and South*, and to Molly Gibson facing the blackmailer Preston. The resemblances to *Heart of Midlothian*'s Jeannie Deans, tempted to lie to save her sister's life, and then eventually gaining her pardon from Queen Charlotte, are plain. The increased complexity and subtlety are equally so. Jeannie is secure in her own innocence, and suffers no public shame (even unmerited) and is aided finally by the illustrious

Duke of Argyll. Elizabeth Gaskell does not permit her heroines so to rise above either their social level, their own intelligence or their own distresses. They may be less heroic: they are the more moving. Mary, left with the secret of her father's guilt, and the onus of proving Jem's innocence, has to battle against her own ignorance of the law and her lack of experience, and against the disbelief of even her friends. It is infinitely a stranger and more perilous journey for Mary to go from Manchester to Liverpool than Jeannie from Edinburgh to London, and the perils she encounters are more immediate, probable and real:

> Common as railroads are now in all places as a means of transit, and especially in Manchester, Mary had never been on one before; and she felt bewildered by the hurry, the noise of people, and bells, and horns; the whiz and scream of the arriving trains.
>
> The very journey itself seemed a matter of wonder. She had a back seat, and looked towards the factory chimneys, and the cloud of smoke which hovers over Manchester, with a feeling akin to 'Heimweh'. She was losing sight of the familiar objects of childhood for the first time. (xxvi)

Equally perilous is her predicament in pursuit of the *John Cropper* (the boat on which Will Wilson serves, who can prove Jem's alibi); 'rocking and tossing in an open boat for the first time in her life, along with two rough, hard-looking men' (xxvii). Elizabeth Gaskell's power to see and feel into ignorance, inexperience, and a nature pushed to its limit, and then to convey them to the reader, is assured even in this first work. Mary's greatest and final blow, in practical terms, is to lose herself. Elizabeth Gaskell, with perfect discretion, does not write it up, but down:

> Mary felt in her pocket for the card, on which was written the name of the street where she was to have met Mr Bridgnorth at two o'clock; where Job and Mrs Wilson were to have been, and where she was to have learnt from the former the particulars of some respectable lodging. It was not to be found.
>
> She tried to brighten her perceptions, and felt again, and took out the little articles her pocket contained, her empty purse, her pocket-handkerchief, and such little things, but it was not there.
>
> In fact she had dropped it when, so eager to embark, she had pulled out her purse to reckon up her money.

She did not know this, of course, she only knew it was gone. It added but little to the despair that was creeping over her. But she tried a little more to help herself, though every minute her mind became more cloudy. She strove to remember where Will had lodged, but she could not; name, street, everything had passed away, and it did not signify; better she were lost than found.

She sat down quietly on the top step of the landing, and gazed down into the dark, dark water below. (xxviii)

Pathetic though Mary is here, no concessions are made to heighten the pathos. Her losing the address is utterly probable, and telling of it here, for the first time, produces a shock for the reader similar to Mary's. The account of the effects of mental exhaustion is perfectly precise; other considerations are never lost: 'better she were lost than found' is no mere emotional utterance – the only way in which she can now, she thinks, clear Jem is by exposing her father, so, since she had certainly better not appear in court, death is a bitterly safe way of escaping both her moral dilemma and a court subpoena.

The physical and mental strains Mary endures before and during the trial make her subsequent breakdown entirely natural, even though 'brain fever' may not be an acceptable modern term for it. That she has hitherto been a capable girl makes it more so. Far from helpless in her normal life, she has been a competent housekeeper, who has coped with sorrow, shortage of money, death, illness, over-work, sleepless nights, and her own personal dilemmas, all over a long period, during which she has also had to act independently with-out help or confidante. It is entirely accurate psychologically that the sudden release from such a strain should result in collapse. Such study of mental and spiritual states over a long period is a growing pre-occupation, not only of Elizabeth Gaskell, but of the novel of her age. In *Villette*, five years later (1853), comes Charlotte Brontë's remarkable study of a woman who, attempting to evade suffering by withdrawing from life, only comes to terms with it and herself by being almost broken by it. Mary's delirium during the trial is remark-ably akin to Lucy Snowe's wanderings at the fête in the park.

Mary never let go her hold on the rails. She wanted them to steady her, in that heaving, whirling court. She thought the feel-ing of something hard compressed within her hand would help her to listen, for it was such pain, such weary pain in her head, to strive to attend to what was being said. They were all at sea, sailing on billowy waves, and everyone speaking at once, and no one heeding her father, who was calling on them to be silent, and listen to him. Then for one brief moment, the court stood still, and she could see the judge, sitting up there like an idol, so rigid and stiff. (xxxii).

The mingling of the cold fact, the hallucination representing the secret truth, and the heightened and distorted detail, all in their lesser way look towards Lucy Snowe in her drugged state (*Villette*, xxxviii), with the intensified response to the illuminations, her symbolic and hallucinatory sights of Paul Emmanuel, his sinister and grotesque companions, and the symbolic phantom of the dead past in 'Justine-Marie'.

While such close comparisons cannot be made with other writers, there is plainly a line of development here that passes through George Eliot to Hardy. In *Adam Bede* the crisis of Hetty's wanderings, and her extraordinary confession to Dinah of how she murdered her child, is followed, later, in *Daniel Deronda*, by Gwendolen's confession and recreation of how she refused to save Grandcourt from drowning. Hardy, even more interested in extremes of spiritual suffering, handles even greater crises: in *Far from the Madding Crowd*, Fanny Robin's dreadful journey (xl), at the end of her strength and in the beginnings of childbirth, to the workhouse at Casterbridge, extends such a study to even a minor character; while Tess's ordeals, though of less local intensity, show Hardy handling even longer periods of such heightened suffering, and consequent symbolic revealing of the significances of human existence and Lear-like 'wisdom in madness'.

Elizabeth Gaskell is a master of detail. Her wise use of it in the whole world she creates is extraordinarily vivid and precise. It extends to her means as well as her material – to dialogue, and all the varieties of her settings of scenes, in natural scenery, weather, and sense-impressions. Through such detail and its juxtapositions and accumulations, she shapes the larger sections of her work, and builds up her climaxes. Her structure is thus cumulative rather than episodic. There are rarely any sharp breaks, or dramatic changes of scene or mood. It is hard to say where scenes or events begin or end. Her work has thus the ebb and flow of life rather than the sharp division of drama –

which has always indirectly influenced the structure of the novel. Such structuring accounts in large measure for the difficulty of demonstrating Elizabeth Gaskell's unobtrusive art; it is even harder to catch her in the act of greatness than it is Jane Austen: we feel the consequences, but cannot promptly pick out the components.

Her use of speech is one of the more accessible. In *Mary Barton* she commits herself to one of its most difficult kinds, with characters who speak a dialect. She solves from the start the difficulties of representing sound without making phonetic transcript a formidable barrier for the reader, by representing only the more pronounced discrepancies from received English, and depending for the rest on her perfect ear for idiom.[12] After her faintly uneasy start, in which she feels she must justify dialectal forms by footnoted literary precedents, she proceeds with ever-increasing power and originality. The un-self-conscious and dignified Lancashire she writes is still easy on the tongue of a Lancashire speaker. Almost any example will show its power:

> So, one day, th' butcher he brings us a letter fra George, to say he'd heard on a place – and I was all agog to go, and father was pleased like; but mother said little, and that little was very quiet. I've often thought she was a bit hurt to see me so ready to go – God forgive me! But she packed up my clothes, and some of the better end of her own as would fit me, in yon little paper box up there – it's good for nought now, but I would liefer live without fire than break it up to be burnt; and yet it's going on for eighty years old, for she had it when she was a girl, and brought all her clothes in it to father's when they were married. (IV)

Alice, quoted here, is one of the broadest speakers; but even with more articulate and thoughtful characters Elizabeth Gaskell has no truck with the well-established convention (akin to that whereby Shakespeare's secondary prose-speaking characters change to verse at moments of crisis or heightened mood) that major characters speak more correctly than minor, or speak without accent at climaxes and crises. Her naturalistic honesty is a literary virtue; the power of

---

[12] An example of a writer with an equally perfect ear who almost ruins one of her richest creations is Emily Brontë, whose Joseph in *Wuthering Heights* is virtually unreadable on the page: most readers lose his humour through sheer exhaustion with deciphering it.

language is at its most intense at the points of intensest emotion. The dying John Barton confesses to Jem,

> 'Lad, thou hast borne a deal for me. It's the meanest thing I ever did to leave thee to bear the brunt. Thou, who wert as innocent of any knowledge of it as a babe unborn.' (xxxv)

The homely idiom of this makes it as impressive as the 'standard' speech of Mr Carson's terrible utterance:

> 'Let my sins be unforgiven, so that I may have vengeance for my son's murder.' (xxxii)

Both utterances gain by the contrast.

But there are lapses in *Mary Barton*, where her hold on her material is insecure, where the author gives way to conventional moral utterances, or presents situations not fully realized or apprehended. The most striking instance is in the prostitute Esther, who, as Mary's mother's sister, should speak like the rest of her family. Though decent and restrained compared with many of her kind in the novel, hers is nevertheless the standard English and stereotyped rhetoric of the fictional 'fallen woman':

> 'And do you think one sunk so low as I am has a home? Decent, good people have homes. We have none. No: if you want me, come at night and look at the corners of the streets about here. The colder, the bleaker, the more stormy the night, the more certain you will be to find me. For then . . . it is so cold sleeping in entries, and on doorsteps, and I want a dram more than ever.' (xiv)

Such lapses do not occur in her later work; she goes on to more assured gradations of language in *North and South*, and to her greatest achievement in speech, the rendering of what was not even native or familiar to her, the north-east Yorkshire of *Sylvia's Lovers*.

Elizabeth Gaskell does for dialect in the English novel what Scott had done for Scotland and its language. There can be no sense, however, in which she can be said to have imitated him. She learned from him ways in which local speech can be presented and employed in the novel, and she transmits these means for other provincial writers to develop therefrom their own opportunities. But she does not establish a 'type' – as Scott's Lowland Scots became a type, or as London Cockney was – which later writers go on using even after it has ceased to represent current idiom. George Eliot afterwards can employ the Midland English of Warwickshire for her own purposes, realizing its possibilities because Elizabeth Gaskell had seen those of Lancashire; and the new ground of local speech is plain and open by the time Hardy creates Wessex. Neither of these, however, uses local language so comprehensively as Elizabeth Gaskell in *Mary Barton* and *Sylvia's Lovers* but, as will be seen later, on principles closer to those of *North and South*.

Elizabeth Gaskell's own narrative is deceptively simple and never obtrusive. Yet details of setting, scenery, weather, and the sensuous apprehensions they convey to the reader, and reveal in the characters, are powerful elements. Much of the mood, and quality and depth of feeling, is conveyed through them. It is always with such matters of content, rather than questions of style, that Elizabeth Gaskell's genius can be defined.

Her descriptive detail creates delight as well as horror; there are perhaps more passages revealing the small pleasures and comforts of the characters than their distresses; such passages bring out clearly the degrees of prosperity among those whose wealth is never more than modest. The comforts of the Barton family are vividly defined by their house: 'the place seemed almost crammed with furniture (sure sign of good times among the mills)'; prosperity is witnessed by 'geraniums, unpruned and leafy' on the window-sill, and by

> a cupboard apparently full of plates and dishes, cups and saucers, and some more non-descript articles, for which one would have fancied their possessors could find no use – such as triangular pieces of glass to save carving knives and forks from dirtying table cloths. However, it was evident Mrs Barton was proud of her crockery and glass, for she left her cupboard door open. (1)

Elizabeth Gaskell never lets an artificial taste or the fastidiousness of another class intrude: she shares and lets the reader share her characters' delight:

> On [the table] resting against the wall, was a bright green japan-ned tea-tray, having a couple of scarlet lovers embracing in the middle. The firelight danced merrily on this, and really (setting all taste but that of a child's aside) it gave a richness of colouring to that side of the room. It was also in some measure propped up by a crimson tea-caddy, also of japan ware. (1)

Such details are not idle; they contrast within a few pages with Alice's much humbler one-room cellar:

> Two chairs drawn out for visitors, and duly swept and dusted; an old board arranged with some skill, two old candle boxes set on end (rather rickety, to be sure, but she knew the seat of old, and when to sit lightly; indeed the whole affair was more for apparent dignity of position than for any real ease); a little, a very little round table, put just before the fire, which by this time was blazing merrily; her unlacquered, ancient, third-hand tea-tray arranged with a black tea-pot, two cups with a red and white pattern, and one with the old friendly willow pattern, and saucers, not to match (on one of the extra supply the lump of butter flourished away); all these preparations complete, Alice began to look about her with satisfaction, and a sort of wonder what more could be done to add to the comfort of the evening. (IV)

The comfort takes the form of Cumberland oat-cake as an addition to the half-ounce of tea, quarter of a pound of butter and common loaf which have 'gone far to absorb her morning's wages' (ibid.). The Bartons by contrast provided for their tea for the Wilsons (seven people altogether) two pounds of Cumberland ham, an egg apiece, a penny-worth of milk, bread, butter, tea, and 'sixpenny worth of rum, to warm the tea' (I). As hardship overtakes John Barton, its growth is charted by the gradual disappearance of the tea-tray and caddy, and the selling of the furniture. After such an opening, the reader feels the pain, as well as the penury, involved in the loss of these treasures.

Elizabeth Gaskell is continually aware of the power of physical sensation over mood and personality.

> There came a long period of bodily privation; of daily hunger after food; and though he tried to persuade himself he could bear want himself with stoical indifference, and did care as little about it as most men, yet the body took its revenge for its uneasy feelings. The mind became soured and morose, and lost much of its equipoise. It was no longer elastic, as in the days of youth, or in times of comparative happiness; it ceased to hope. And it is hard to live on when one has ceased to hope. (XV)

John Barton's feelings for his fellow-workers and against the masters are thus intensified by his hunger, and his moral desperation by his resorting to opium, the common cheap remedy for the pangs of hunger. Similarly Mary is weakened and her moral crises made more dangerous by sleepless nights, spent helping Margaret sew mourning clothes, and by sitting up with the prostrated Mrs Wilson and the dying Alice. Physical as well as mental exhaustion thus causes her breakdown after the trial.

The relative importance of events can be registered by similar detail: when John Barton is about to leave with the Chartist petition to London, Mary's occupation was

> the same as that of Beau Tibbs' wife 'just washing her father's two shirts', in the pantry back-kitchen; for she was anxious about his appearance in London (the coat had been redeemed [from the pawn-broker's] though the silk handkerchief was forfeited). (VIII)

Climaxes are built up, and the novel's highest moments of intensity created, by constant use of such minutiae, and by the juxtaposition and accumulation of small events and smaller detail. This is Elizabeth Gaskell's most original and finest skill. It is also what makes her difficult to reveal in extract, or by quotation. The novel's most moving moments, like some of Shakespeare's most moving lines, are apt to look rather flat out of context. She has no power like Dickens's of creating the quotable or unforgettable moment in isolation. Nothing in her corresponds to Oliver's asking for more, or Sidney Carton's last speech, or Bill Sikes's death. But she has no need of them. No one can fault Jane Austen because there is no single memorable utterance in Wentworth's proposal to Anne Elliot in *Persuasion*, or Scott because there is none in Fergus McIvor's farewell to Waverley. Nor should one so fault Elizabeth Gaskell. The sequence from Jem's arrest to his acquittal is a superb piece of writing, taking its effect from the vast number of its elements, rather than from the heightening of individual ones. Alice's death, Mrs Wilson's despair, Margaret's disapproval, Job's interview with the lawyer, the various sensations of Mary's journey, the jarring contact with uncomprehending strangers – Mrs Jones, Will's landlady, who tells Mary she is too late to catch him before he sails, and her wild young son who guides Mary to the rough boatmen who take her on her nightmare sail down the Mersey, the boatman himself who gives her a roof over her head – all these, together with Job's interpolated comico-pathetic wait for Will and

Mary in the Liverpool lawyer's office, build up by their very variety
the extreme tension before the trial itself. Elizabeth Gaskell concentrates on no single mood or emotion, but works by contrast and by
cumulation of small tensions and abrupt changes. Mary reaches
exhaustion and despair when she has seen Will sail away over the bar,
despite his promise to return on the pilot-boat:

> She sat down quietly on the top step of the landing, and gazed
> down into the dark, dark water below. Once or twice a spectral
> thought loomed among the shadows of her brain, a wonder
> whether beneath that cold dismal surface there would not be a
> rest from the troubles of earth. (xxviii)

Rescued by the boatman, with '"Come with me and be d—d to
you!" replied he, clutching her arm to pull her up' (xxviii), Mary
is abandoned by her author, who moves to Job awaiting her, fidgeting
in the lawyer's office, then enquiring for her at Mrs Jones's, then
back to the lawyer, and back to Mrs Jones, then, finally, reaching his
own little climax of despair, when he lies to Mrs Wilson that Mary
and Will are safe and ready to prove Jem's alibi at the trial on the
morrow. Then comes the return to Mary, roughly cared for by the
boatman's wife, and sitting alone all night waiting for the wind to
change:

> And quietly, noiselessly, Mary watched the unchanging
> weathercock through the night. She sat on the little window-
> seat, her hand holding back the curtain which shaded the room
> from the bright moonlight without; her head resting its weari-
> ness against the corner of the window-frame; her eyes burning,
> and stiff with the intensity of her gaze.
>   The ruddy morning stole up the horizon, casting a ruddy glow
> into the watcher's room.
>   It was the morning of the day of trial! (xxxi)

So the chapter ends. The next brings its own shock, for Elizabeth
Gaskell turns our gaze upon one we had almost forgotten, 'the
father of the murdered man', Carson, and adds his burden of pain to
that of 'all the restless people who found that night's hours agonising
from excess of anxiety' (xxxii); and so she plunges into the trial itself,
with the cumulative intensities of Mrs Wilson's evidence and Mary's,
finally ended with Will's dramatic arrival. But even so there is no
melodramatic collapse of opposition, or improbable paean of triumph.

Will's evidence is doubted by the prosecution – 'Will you have the kindness to inform the gentlemen of the jury what has been your charge for repeating this very plausible story?' (XXXII) – and the verdict is, in essence, rather 'Not proven' than 'Not guilty'.

One can hardly fault Elizabeth Gaskell's art in this closing section, but one suspects that it is not only new to her, but her first discovery of it, for *Mary Barton* contains one other sensational scene of a quite different kind. This is the fire at Carson's mill. While it is the traditional material of heroism and hairbreadth 'scapes (Jem's rescue of his father and another man), and the all-too-traditional fainting heroine, though it advances the action by putting men out of work, and though it reveals the cynicism of the employer who would rather have insurance money than old outdated machinery, it serves very little structural purpose beyond its intrinsic excitement. As a first essay at a scene of violent action and men in the mass (the crowd is well handled) it serves Elizabeth Gaskell in good stead when she comes to write the attack on Thornton's mill in *North and South* and shows that her handling owes nothing there to Charlotte Brontë's mill-riot in *Shirley*.

In a final estimate, it has been generally agreed that *Mary Barton* is both a good and an important novel. It has always been considered so for its new subject matter, for revealing the industrial working-class of Manchester, for its penetrating and vividly realistic picture of social conflict, and for its deep understanding of the life and personal distresses of those caught up in strife and change. But these are as much the virtues of the social document as of the work of art. *Mary Barton* is undeniably valuable for these things; it is even more valuable for the qualities in it that are not of an age, that make it rewarding for those who care nothing for history or politics, which make it literature. It stands forth as the early, secondary work of a great writer, like *Northanger Abbey*, or *Guy Mannering*, or (to come into her own time) *Nicholas Nickleby*, *The Luck of Barry Lyndon*, or *Silas Marner*. It is not an ambitious work: the plot is not complicated, it does not have an unduly large number of characters (about twenty of any stature) nor a wide range of scene. It is the more a success because its reach does not exceed its grasp. It establishes its writer as a novelist of stature, though anonymously. It was reviewed by the influential and established organs, and read by the illustrious and influential, who thought enough of it to record their reactions. Through *Mary Barton* Elizabeth Gaskell becomes professional; she learns her strength, and advances on her way towards her greater work. But in her next novel *Ruth* she does the reverse of repeating herself, for she turns aside from the trodden way of Manchester, and ventures far more rashly into the unknown.

Ruth

Ruth is a problem novel, it is a good novel, and it is a valuable novel –
all of these in a wide variety of ways. Her second full-length novel,
separated from *Mary Barton* by five years, and by various shorter
writings like *The Moorland Cottage* and *Cranford*, it shows that
Elizabeth Gaskell has no intention of standing still, of ensuring
popularity by keeping to what she knows she can do, of repeating a
successful method, or even of improving on it. After the change from
the socially-motivated *Mary Barton* to the nostalgic social observation
of *Cranford*, *Ruth* at first sight does show a return to social commitment, in being a study of the problem of the unmarried mother.
But beyond any such very general statement very little comparison
of intention or material can be made. *Ruth* shows a different and
entirely new subject, different areas of experience, a new range of
emotions, new kinds of characters, and a greatly extended technique.
Shocking to the public at its first appearance, *Ruth* is probably the
least read and least successful of all her full-length novels; yet it has
some of her greatest writing in it, and stretches the art of the novel
far more than *Mary Barton*. The reasons are many and varied, and
all relate to its problems, its kind of excellence, and, indirectly, to
its value and influence to other writers. Ruth is the heart and the
ruling spirit of the novel which bears her name, in a way that Mary
Barton is far from being, and that John Barton (the original eponym-
ous hero) cannot be. From this fact come the problems.

The most obvious one is probably the least important. Girls have
had bastards in the novel before, and their authors have not been reviled

for it. The mid-nineteenth century was not so squeamish as is often made out; not all writers wrote primarily for the middle-class family reader, as Dickens and Trollope did, nor limited themselves only to those topics which are acceptable to the morally, socially and sexually naïve. Thackeray and his readers took illegitimacy and even adultery in their stride in *Vanity Fair* (1848) and *Henry Esmond* (1852), Charlotte Brontë makes a profligate the hero of *Jane Eyre* and a sympathetic minor character of his bastard daughter; Dickens produces prostitutes in *Oliver Twist*, and the bastard Esther Summerson in *Bleak House*, and Trollope has an illegitimate heroine in *Doctor Thorne*, to mention only a few examples. But there is no denying that there are literary conventions and expectations to be satisfied. Sexual irregularity is acceptable if it is history, or treated with reticence or humour, or secondarily; prostitutes can appear if idealized or good-hearted, or if they die; and almost any topic and its implications can be examined if the actual event does not happen (as Thackeray's Pendennis does not, actually, seduce Fanny Bolton) or if we are left in some uncertainty (as to whether Becky actually committed adultery with the Marquis of Steyne). One feels that the mid-nineteenth century in its fiction could stomach fallen women, illegitimate children, adulterers and profligates of both sexes, provided that there are not too many at once, and certain rules were observed: that, if present in large quantities, they are peripheral, that there is no reward for vice, or if there is, it is condemned, and that certain combinations are avoided. It is not so much prudery that is in question with either the major novelists or the serious intelligent reader. It is rather that it has not occurred to them that such subjects are especially useful or practicable in fiction as a central concern.

When something entirely new hits the reading consciousness, the consequence is always shock. *Ruth* is entirely new. Elizabeth Gaskell took the seduced girl and her child through the whole course of the girl's life from her seduction to her death, and the child's from birth to maturity, and made them her whole concern. *Ruth*, therefore, was inevitably a shock to its readers, and in one sense intended to be so. Elizabeth Gaskell requires first of all that her reader shall face a social problem, in the same way as she asked him to face the social problem of *Mary Barton*. To do so necessarily invited the kind of stir *Mary Barton* created, for which she was prepared. But for other reasons *Ruth* was an alarming work, and for some of these reasons it remains a disturbing one. These concern more the spirit and mind of the central character and its growth. The modern reader is not repelled by love outside of wedlock, or its consequences, yet *Ruth* continues to disturb the reader, as *Jane Eyre* continues to disturb, by the moral, emotional and spiritual progress that it compels him to experience. We may not share Elizabeth Gaskell's or Charlotte Brontë's ethics, feeling that Ruth has done no wrong in loving Bellingham, or that Jane Eyre need not have fled from a married Mr Rochester; or we may accept them only for the span of reading the novel; yet the heroine's progress of the soul keeps its validity. This progress of the soul, as well as the subject matter, makes *Ruth* valuable to other writers, and to readers who wish to assess their achievement. Without *Ruth*, one feels there would have been no Hetty (or a very different one) in George Eliot, no Tess Durbeyfield for Hardy, and no Esther Waters for George Moore. Elizabeth Gaskell did not invite them to imitate, but by stripping all the conventions away from a very conventional situation, as old as the institution of matrimony, she showed them where to look, and suggested how they should look.

As always with Elizabeth Gaskell (and with many other novelists) implicit artistic purposes go far beyond conscious intentions. In *Ruth*, as never in her other novels, they conflict. She intends, plainly, to write an honest 'documentary' history of the heroine from her original seduction, through all its consequences, to her death, the death being in itself the final consequence. She also intends to examine all the moral implications of her chosen story: to present what she believes to be the right moral position, and examine all the other current moral positions in all the degrees of the unthinkingly conventional, the bigoted, the weak and the misguided, and also the degrees of limitation of even the honestly held. Since Elizabeth Gaskell's morals are Christian, religion plays a much larger part in this novel than her others. She is thus by design committed to driving three horses: presenting a story and characters who will seem 'real' in the everyday contemporary world, examining moral values, and dealing with religious belief; of which the last two, though they overlap, are not the same. She must also come to a moral conclusion, not necessarily explicitly stated, but brought about incontestably as the action proceeds. This is much more than she attempted in *Mary Barton*, where she can, on a moral if not practical level, suggest how the problems she presents should be solved. There is a difference in kind between *Mary Barton's* statement that there should be better understanding and goodwill between masters and men, and *Ruth's* far more complex questions, which it is impossible to reduce to any formula, because they embrace so many more areas: they are questions of how far a sin done in ignorance is a sin, how far other men are justified in punishing a sinner, how long it is before sin is purged, how far the sins of the parents are to be visited upon the children, how one kind of sin weighs in comparison with others, what is the relative weight of private faults of character in comparison with wrong acts involving others, how one should judge wrong things done with good and unselfish intentions, and how far a man should weigh the salvation of his own soul against that of his neighbour's. Some of the problems cannot be defined in these terms because they are social and moral as much as religious; they cover social expediency, right and wrong, virtue and vice, sin and blessedness, all of them dealt with, and all kept separate; wrong, vice, and sin are not synonymous in Elizabeth Gaskell's language. These preoccupations determine the whole form of the novel and all that it contains – every scene, and character, and every detail bear on one or more of them. Ruth is the embodiment and presentation of many of them, particularly the most central, the sin committed in virtual ignorance, since she barely realizes what she is doing when she allows Bellingham to take her away to London. Through her Elizabeth Gaskell examines how long her penance should last. Her son Leonard is not only wronged by her in being conceived, but is also the source of her salvation through her love for him. In Leonard is studied the problem of how far or whether the child should suffer for what he cannot help, his bastardy, as well as the conventional notion that the child is the mother's punishment for her sin. The Bensons are the representatives of fault committed deliberately for good reasons, when they pass Ruth off as a widow. Mr Bradshaw embodies society's punishment of the sinner, and also the relative weight of private faults of character compared with a single wrong act like Ruth's, in which latter he is joined by his daughter Jemima, who is passionate and headstrong though right-principled, just as he is self-righteous and complacent though upright. His son, Richard Bradshaw, is a deliberate wrongdoer and social criminal (he embezzles money), the victim of his father's failings in bringing him up, as well as of his own weak character. The list could be extended through all of the major characters, who bear on the topic either by embodying a quality, or eliciting it in someone else.

To put it in such terms gives the work the sound of a moral tract.

It is its flaw that it does have some such features. But they are only peripheral, and confined to occasional minor incidents and characters. Another more valuable comparison would be with a Jane Austen novel, where there is no detail that does not contribute in some way towards the pattern and the development of the themes. Actually the social and moral examinations keep any element of religious 'preaching' well in check, since Elizabeth Gaskell is much more concerned with examining these difficult areas of the pressures of the world of her day, and of human personalities within themselves and upon each other, than with impressing the religious truths she takes for granted.

In *Ruth*, Elizabeth Gaskell has to choose her story, her plot and her setting. They are not decided for her, as *Mary Barton's* were, by the very subject she chose. Her heroine could have come from many walks of life, from town or country, could have been clever or stupid, pretty or plain, and still have been a 'fallen woman'. Elizabeth Gaskell chooses well, and handles skillfully. She begins with the conventional, and goes on to the utterly original and new. Even the young innocent girl, charmed and seduced by the young man above her station, is more than conventional, she is universal. She has the profound pull of her ancestry in centuries of ballad and folklore. Ruth Hilton, sixteen years old, the orphan neglected and at the mercy of the wealthy charmer, the unscrupulous seducer Bellingham, has the authority of her folklore and ballad ancestry, without any of the romance or un-reality. She is intelligent and sensitive, but never above her station like Richardson's Pamela; nor has she, orphan daughter of an unsuccessful farmer, apprenticed to a dressmaker, the charm of rusticity of the peasant girl, which Hardy will make such use of in Tess. Bellingham is not far enough above her to make his misbehaviour exonerable, like that of Pamela's Mr B: he is no nobleman, merely the spoilt son of the local wealthy middle-class gentry, and comes in for his own judgement in turn. Her desertion by Bellingham (borne off by his mother after a severe illness) leaves Ruth most credibly destitute, yet involves no melodramatic or villainous desertion. Nor can Bellingham be merely a heartless jilt, and cast Ruth off. If he were, though Ruth might go on loving him, the reader would not have much patience with her for doing so; and he must be such that he can later offer her the honourable matrimony Mr B. offers Pamela, which Ruth, with the more complex sensibility of a later era, rejects. Rescue by Mr Benson, the Dissenting minister, is just as probable as the desertion, and moves her to an even more limited milieu, of the small manufacturing town Dissenting community. Every choice of material proves an avoidance of romance, fantasy and escape, in favour of the probable and, as far as possible, the predictable. However, Elizabeth Gaskell has obviously to manipulate her plot because she is writing to a thesis. How she does so reveals clearly where lie her artistic concerns as well as her social and moral ones. To explore as she does Ruth's problems as an unmarried mother, the difficulties of those who help her, the attitudes of people to her situation – in the abstract, and when they face it in reality – and to cope with the plight of the bastard child, leaves little room for manœuvre. As an artist Elizabeth Gaskell has to select still further, choosing kinds of incident, situation and setting. She chooses to devote herself, and about three-quarters of the novel, to Ruth, not as betrayed girl, but as woman and mother. Ruth learns of her pregnancy in the eleventh of the novel's thirty-six chapters (the 108th of 454 pages in the Knutsford Edition). She also chooses that Ruth shall face all the conceivable likely crises of life, even the possible death of her son.[1] Elizabeth Gaskell's reasons are not in any way sentimental or sensation-hunting; she wants Ruth to be compelled to live to her fullest mental, emotional and spiritual power, not to evade life, but to use her potential in society, and to embody and examine the individual's social as well as personal responsibilities. A Ruth living peaceably retired, and only for her son, could be accused of being both escapist and selfish.

Elizabeth Gaskell's story deliberately faces another powerful issue – the one that called the storm about Charlotte Brontë's ears after *Jane Eyre* – the power of love of woman for man. Though the sixteen-year-old Ruth of the opening chapters is most convincingly innocent and sexually ignorant, author and reader are well aware of the nature of Bellingham's power over her. Ruth's passion may be unintelligible to herself, but it produces the dreams of Bellingham giving her 'flower after flower in that baseless morning dream' (11) and it rouses her sense of guilt at walking with him after church:

> she wished him back again, and found the day very dreary, and wondered why a strange, undefined feeling, had made her imagine she was doing wrong in walking alongside one so kind and good as Mr Bellingham. (111)

[1] This last would have been much more likely than it may seem to the modern reader, in an age of high infant mortality.

The reader sees clearly enough that the unease is not merely conscience (Ruth knows no reason why she should not meet Bellingham), but the stir of the dangerous and powerful force of physical passion. Ruth sins, not only out of circumstance, but for love. Elizabeth Gaskell does not forget or let the reader forget that Ruth did so, or that she continues to love Bellingham long after he has left her. There must, then, be the second meeting eight years later to reassess that love against her mature self-knowledge, her conscious moral standards, and her other great love for her child. This second meeting is the highest point, the most vital and crucial episode of the whole work, and one of its author's greatest, most original and profound creations. But to reach it entails a severe stretch of her powers of manipulation. The plot creaks under the strain of reintroducing Mr Bellingham (under another name, Donne, drawn from the property he has inherited) as the prospective Liberal candidate for Eccleston.

The theme requires that Bellingham shall appear yet once more, when Ruth meets her death by nursing him through typhus fever; but the coincidence of this return, to what is now his parliamentary constituency, is a much lesser one; that Ruth should then hear of his illness is natural, and that she should nurse him is a moral choice, a matter of character which requires no manipulation of plot. That Ruth should die, strained, overworked and exhausted by nursing during the epidemic is not only credible, it is all too probable. Charlotte Brontë among others felt that there was no good reason why Ruth should die; that she does is another proof of Elizabeth Gaskell's reliance on realistic probability. Literary heroines all too often bear charmed lives in peril; Ruth does not. Yet with her dying her author stumbles into that other literary convention of the pathetic death scene. Though one may feel that it was impossible to end *Ruth* in any way that avoided literary cliché, the way she has chosen allows her to make a last penetrating exposure of Bellingham, in his totally inadequate reactions, and to complete a cycle which leaves Ruth's son now free to face the world alone.

Elizabeth Gaskell's skill in preparing for the more startling developments of events is unobtrusive and skilful. The character sketches of Bellingham and his mother in Chapter 11, acute as they are, seem to account only for Ruth's seduction:

> He was old compared to Ruth, but young as a man; hardly three-and-twenty. The fact of his being an only child had given

c

him, as it does to many, a sort of inequality in those parts of the
character which are formed by the number of years that a person
has lived.

The unevenness of discipline to which only children are
subjected; the thwarting, resulting from over-anxiety; the
indiscreet indulgence, arising from a love centred all in one
object – had been exaggerated in his education, probably from
the circumstance that his mother (his only surviving parent) had
been similarly situated to himself . . . her income gave her the
means of indulging or controlling him, after he had grown to
man's estate, as her wayward disposition and love of power
prompted her . . . His boyish tricks annoyed and irritated her far
more than the accounts which reached her of more serious
misdoings at college and in town. Of these grave offences she
never spoke; of the smaller misdeeds she hardly ever ceased
speaking.

Still, at times she had the greatest influence over him, and
nothing delighted her more than to exercise it. (111)

These brief psychologically acute remarks, as well as accounting
wonderfully for the attractive but irresponsible Bellingham, prepare
the way equally effectively for us to understand how he can desert
and abandon Ruth completely. Having explained him here in general
terms, Elizabeth Gaskell has no need to explain him again after he
has left Llan-dhu, when all her concern, like the reader's, is with
Ruth in her despair.

It would be almost fair to say that *Ruth* has a story, a sequence of
events building up her 'progress of the soul' rather than a plot, or
plots. The areas which constitute sub-plots – the stormy courtship of
Jemima and Mr Farquhar, the downward career of Richard – are
better considered as parts of the moral progress of Mr Bradshaw,
the parent and 'moral man' who ironically parallels Ruth, the parent
and 'immoral woman'. The stories run concurrently, and mutually
illuminate rather than interact. Almost the only point at which
they can be said to interact is when Mr Farquhar, disappointed and
hurt by Jemima's perversity, considers Ruth as a possible wife.

As in *Mary Barton*, Elizabeth Gaskell shows that an ingenious or
elaborate plot neither interests nor serves her, that she has to work
out and discover her material for herself, without drawing on previous
models, and that, once her purposes are achieved, mere events, how-

ever well she could have done them, are of little interest. Hence she allows the married Jemima almost to vanish from our sight, while Ruth is so far from being, like Charles II, 'an unconscionable time a-dying', that she seems more likely to be, as Jane Eyre refuses, 'hurried off in a suttee'. Ruth's death leaves a final problem – Leonard, and his future. His adoption by the childless doctor is convenient, appropriate, and well prepared: as early as Chapter xxv the doctor has remarked, apropos of Leonard's illness, that

> 'he thought he was glad he had had no children; as far as he could judge, they were all plague and no profit.' But as he ended his speech he sighed . . . common report was true, which represented the clever prosperous surgeon of Eccleston as bitterly disappointed at his failure of offspring. (xxv)

He offers to undertake Leonard's schooling and his training as a surgeon (xxxiv), moved by sympathy for an illegitimate child, and by admiration for Ruth's courage as a nurse. A more brutal fate – though perhaps a no more realistic one – like that of Mme Bovary's child, is out of the question here, since *Ruth's* whole progress has been towards improvement, not futility.

Yet Ruth's story is hardly enough for a full-length novel. It might have been much more powerful if shorter – not much more than *Cousin Phillis* or *The Crooked Branch* – with some of the author's moral reflections, and the interpolations (like the servant Sally's magnificent comic tale of the proposals of marriage) omitted. It might have gained in intensity what it lost in elaboration. Elizabeth Gaskell still shows herself, in her grapplings with unmanageable material, a writer of both inexperience and integrity. She now sees that she must eschew the conventional and apparently safe, and go her own way, in her materials and plots as elsewhere.

Just as her theme could not decide her material for her, as *Mary Barton*'s did, neither does it decide her settings, physical or social. She has far more freedom of choice. How she uses it shows her powers, her predilections, and her originality. The uses of her settings direct response, and interpret events. Perhaps Elizabeth Gaskell's hardest task is to make the reader believe in Ruth's innocence. Her settings are a vital, though not the only, means of doing so. They reveal far more than mere analysis could do about the forces working within and upon an impressionable nature, by working also within and upon the reader. Ruth begins her career in a small assize-town whose grandeur is all in the past, where gentry's former houses have declined into shops, and whose high society is no more than a gathering for a ball in the shire-hall. Shadows of past and faded grandeur fall on the dressmaker's house where Ruth is an apprentice:

> people were occasionally surprised, after passing through a common-place looking shop, to find themselves at the foot of a grand oaken staircase, lighted by a window of stained glass, storied all over with armorial bearings.
>
> Up such a stair – past such a window (through which the moonlight fell on her with a glory of many colours) – Ruth Hilton passed wearily one January night, how many years ago. (1)

She works in 'an old drawing-room which must once have been magnificent' (1). The shire-hall, too, where she first meets Mr Bellingham at the ball, is a place of gothic windows, moonlight, indistinct brilliance, and illusion:

> Outside all was cold, and colourless and uniform – one coating of snow over all. But inside it was warm, glowing and vivid; flowers scented the air, and wreathed the head, and rested on the bosom, as if it were midsummer. Bright colours flashed on the eye and were gone, and succeeded by others as lovely as the rapid movement of the dance. (11)

In this place there is no new life, only the exhausted remnants of the romantic past, an exhaustion shared by the overworked dressmakers, and their struggling employer Mrs Mason – who, negligent despot though she may be, neglects them partly because she herself has to struggle to support her family. The echoes of Keats's 'Eve of St Agnes' in the opening are fortunate, since they place Ruth as an unconscious Madeleine, accessible to life and susceptible to change – though her rescuer is no Porphyro, and the consequence is her disaster.

No moral guidance or standards are offered, except what are also past and dying; Ruth's visit to her former farmhouse home is another exploration of the past's 'bare ruined choirs, where once the sweet birds sang'. The house is dust-covered and derelict, and the old man Thomas fails to give Ruth the warning he knows she needs; the standards and the culture are 'gone – all gone into the land of shadows' (IV). The vigorous natural life of the countryside and the blossoming year, to which Ruth so vigorously responds, make it inevitable that she should follow her natural impulses and act like a child of nature.

Elizabeth Gaskell next presents her as such, living with Mr Bellingham in the little village in North Wales, delighting in mountains and wilderness, and participating in every change of scene and weather:

> Even rain was a pleasure to her . . . she saw the swift-fleeting showers come athwart the sunlight like a rush of silver arrows; she watched the purple darkness on the heathery mountainside, and then the pale golden gleam which succeeded. (v)

If the town of Fordham was Keatsian, Wales is Wordsworthian, and despite Elizabeth Gaskell's casual and neutral use of names, one feels that Ruth's own may have been a conscious associative choice.[2] She reaches her apotheosis by a tree-girt mountain pool with 'speedwell in the shallowest water', where Bellingham crowns her with waterlilies.

> Down in that green hollow they were quite in harmony. Her beauty was all that Mr Bellingham cared for, and it was supreme. . . . She stood in her white dress against the trees which grew around, her face was flushed into a brilliancy of colour which resembled that of a rose in June; the great, heavy, white flowers drooped on either side of her beautiful head. . . . She pleased him more by looking so lovely than by all her tender endeavours to fall in with his varying humour. (vi)

The idyll is brief, and the isolation is promptly employed to intensify disaster.

When Bellingham is swept away, nature can give Ruth no support, only 'a bare table of moor' to epitomize her agony, and 'sloping turf by the roots of an old hawthorn tree' in a hedge-bank inadequately to hide her misery from human eyes. Human sympathy was irrelevant to her happiness; human indifference almost sends her to the natural end of her following of natural impulses – suicide.

The Bensons' help and intervention bring her to Eccleston, to a small manufacturing town, and to an enclosed community within it, of the Dissenting congregation. Here there is no romance, and no

---

2 The name may also be an echo from Crabbe's poem in *Tales of the Hall*, which she uses for the central incidents in *Sylvia's Lovers*.

idyll, but there is vigorous human life, both communally and individually. Ruth's progress in the rest of the novel is to be to spiritual knowledge, and to social reintegration. As this is no longer simply Ruth's concern, but must also deal with the society that is to accept or reject her, a vigorous, contemporary world is essential. The Bensons provide the spiritual standards; the merchants Bradshaw and Farquhar provide the material; and their individual detailed surroundings, their houses and ways of life, are significant extensions of themselves. The details of daily living, as precise as in *Mary Barton*, indicating income, standards, and way of life, are now far more varied and flexible. Attitudes to life as well as living standards are clearly implied, by the wearing out, for instance, of the Bensons' carpet, which, when it finally dies, is replaced by a home-made hearth-rug. Their standards and sensibilities are implied by the exquisite details of their daily living, in which domesticity and nature combine: their parlour, 'homely, pretty, old-fashioned', where

the window was open, to let in the sweet morning air, and streaming eastern sunshine. The long jessamine sprays, with their white-scented stars, forced themselves almost into the room. (xiii)

They clearly have a moral code which comprehends the influences of 'nature' that were revealed in the opening sections – many of the scenes between Ruth and Leonard take place in the garden, revealing him as a 'natural' child in more than the usual euphemistic sense.

The Bradshaws' rigid standards of conscious self-righteousness, on the other hand, are embodied in scenes that take place almost entirely indoors, interpreted and coloured by their chillily prosperous dwelling, 'square and massy-looking, with a great deal of drab colour about the furniture' where tea is served 'the equipage for which was as handsome and ugly as money could purchase' (xvii).

The chapel of which Benson is the incumbent symbolizes the unassuming, uncontroversial religious principles which pervade the whole. It draws together the forces in Ruth's life from the previous sections, adding their power to its own, and embodying in itself the reconciliation that Dissenting life will perform in her. It has the spell of the past that Fordham had, built 'a hundred and fifty years ago . . . about the time of Matthew and Philip Henry' (xiv) and the charm of the natural world of the mountains of Wales; but both are now domesticated:

A lilac bush or two, a white rose-tree, and a few laburnums, all old and gnarled enough, were planted round the chapel yard; and the casement windows of the chapel were made of heavy-leaded, diamond-shaped panes, almost covered with ivy, producing a green gloom, not without its solemnity, within . . . The walls [inside] were whitewashed, and were recipients of the shadows of the beauty without; on their 'white plains' the tracery of the ivy might be seen, now still, now stirred by the sudden flight of some little bird. (ibid.)

For the crisis of Ruth's life, a whole new setting is created: in the rugged coast and sands, and the storm-swept house of Eagle's Crag at Abermouth, richly realistic and atmospheric, and significantly fitting for the reunion of Ruth with Bellingham. The symbolic quality is not pressed, but powerfully implicit, as when Bellingham comes between Ruth and her view of the eastern end in church (xxiii), and when their great struggle takes place on the cold open sands, left bare by a receding tide; what Ruth sees while waiting there has perfect verisimilitude, but sums up her whole life, just when she is about to face her life's crucial struggle and decision:

She was perhaps half-a-mile or more from the grey, silvery, rocks, which sloped away into brown moorland, interspersed with a field here and there of golden, waving corn. Behind were purple hills, with sharp clear outlines touching the sky. A little on one side from where she stood she saw the white cottages and houses which formed the village of Abermouth, scattered up and down; and, on a windy hill, about a mile inland, she saw the little grey church, where even now many were worshipping in peace. (xxiv)

Here are the cornfields of the farming country which has bred her, the moors and hills of her period of love and despair, the village of the common human lot she has worked to rejoin, and the church and the religion which have guided and sustained her. Autumn here corresponds both naturally and significantly with action, as did rich summer with Wales, and winter, with its covering of 'innocent snow' (xv), with Leonard's birth.[3] Yet natural chronology is perfectly kept, and no violence done to natural probability.

[3] Elizabeth Gaskell's echo of Milton's 'Ode on the Morning of Christ's Nativity' is as deliberate, precise and unobtrusive as are all her many echoes of other writers.

Elizabeth Gaskell's natural symbolism is invariably delicate and unobtrusive, and can easily pass unobserved. Yet its power as a method is undeniable, and looks forward to a writer like Hardy, who makes it no mere accessory but a powerful element in his vision. Tess is his heroic, tragic and noble counterpart of Ruth; in her life also her physical surroundings partake of and symbolize herself. One needs only to remind oneself of what is so well known and much praised as Tess's own fruitful rich life under the summer sun of the lush and fertile valley of the dairies, her sufferings in the bleak bare windswept fields around Flintcombe-Ash, or her sublime and symbolic end amid the monoliths of Stonehenge. What Elizabeth Gaskell, liberated by her new, unexploited places and scenes, develops as a device, Hardy, finding his own still stranger country, elevates into a system, and view of the universe. Elizabeth Gaskell seeks only reconciliation and balance of the forces of the human spirit, one of her means being to relate man to his physical and temporal world; Hardy in *Tess* subdues not only his protagonist, but the whole of society, to the forces of nature, and beyond terrestrial nature, to an inhuman cosmos.

This use of setting not simply as background but as an organic part of the texture of the novel has other consequences, not least in rendering Ruth's sufferings more universal than particular, and making them far more than the social consequence of misdoing. That such details are generally in themselves interesting from their truth and sensuous appeal renders them precious in so sombre a tale.

For *Ruth* is a painful story, whose greatest events cause its protagonists not merely sadness, but torment amounting to agony, and whose lesser happenings entail anxiety, apprehension, or difficult choices. Elizabeth Gaskell never shirks the suffering, and is indeed at her finest on the small conflicts, strains and irritations of day-to-day existence. She offers no escapes from complete response – such as treating events as 'black comedy', or rendering unpleasant characters villainous or grotesque, or passing over unpleasant detail; and she is equally just on matters great and trivial. After Ruth's first great trial, Mr Bellingham's illness, and after the 'false dawn' of his recovery, the narrative, leaving Ruth with her hopes of seeing him again, and the reader with the certainty that she will not, devotes half a chapter (VIII – wryly entitled 'Doing the thing Handsomely') to Mrs Bellingham's discussion with her son on how conveniently to get rid of Ruth. Though *tout comprendre* is not in this case *tout pardonner* (the conversation does not excuse either of them) yet it compels serious consideration of the mother's point of view, and of the son's character which, already irresponsible, is unable, in physical weakness, to put up any resistance, even though he feels that 'it's a bad business, and I can hardly avoid blaming myself in the matter' (VIII). Ruth's despair, following, is the more poignant for having an intelligible human cause that is not mere villainous malignity. Equally, though, Elizabeth Gaskell completely avoids tormenting her reader. She realizes that to overwrite would be disastrous. Though she would not believe with Eliot that 'human kind cannot bear very much reality', she does not force upon him undiluted or long-continuing distress. She takes no morbid or sentimental pleasure herself in the sufferings she feels called on to retail, and offers her reader no chance to indulge himself either. Balance is Elizabeth Gaskell's artistic creed, with the minimum of heightening or distortion. Where-ever the load can be eased, she eases it, by contrasting and balancing incident, or detail within incident, producing humour, or irony, or simply proportion. She realizes that human experience comprehends many impressions, even at moments of extreme absorption or abandon: so Ruth, after her agonizing despairing effort to pursue the coach bearing Bellingham away

> threw herself down on the ling by the side of the road in despair. Her only hope was to die, and she believed she was dying. She could not think; she could believe anything... Yet afterwards – long afterwards she remembered the motion of a bright green beetle busily meandering among the wild thyme near her, and she recalled the musical, balanced, wavering drop of a sky-lark into her nest, near the heatherbed where she lay. (VIII)[4]

Other times of misery are reassessed or relieved, as practical necessity breaks in: Ruth, arrived at the Bensons' house, has to be established as a widow. Faith Benson gives her her mother's wedding ring, pointing out the 'posy' engraved on it – 'Thine own sweetheart till

---

[4] Everyone can recognize such truth; it is the same *aperçu* as that of Rossetti's poem 'The Woodspurge':

> From perfect grief there need not be
> Wisdom or even memory;
> One thing then learnt remains to me, –
> The woodspurge has a cup of three.

death do part' – the irony showing Faith's characteristic mixture of sympathetic sense and lack of sensitivity. Almost immediately afterwards, Sally, making her own, unsympathetic contribution to verisimilitude, chopping off Ruth's hair, and supplying coarsely-made widow's caps, provides briskly comic relief. Such as this is the author's consistent method, allowing acts or speech, or scene, or descriptive detail, to direct the reader's response.

Though the novel pleads a cause, the author's voice rarely does the pleading. She shows more and more confidence in what she tells and the way she arranges it, letting details and their juxtaposition do the pleading for her, without intervention of the author's voice. That she does occasionally intrude, and does occasionally miss out an aspect, may show that she is not yet fully her craft's master. That she does so less than in *Mary Barton* shows how she has progressed. Perhaps her most striking lapse is in dealing with the child. Apart from the inadequate portrayal of Leonard himself, which will be dealt with later, there is also the response of Ruth to the situation from its very beginning. Told that she is pregnant,

> 'She did not seem [says Faith Benson] to understand how it ought to be viewed, but took it just as if she had a right to have a baby. She said "Oh, my God, I thank thee! Oh, I will be so good!" ' (xi)

The reader may swallow this as a first reaction, but will find it impossible to accept that any child should be at every moment of its infant life a source of delight to its parent – one suspects that Elizabeth Gaskell has her own emotional block here, in the loss of her own son in babyhood. Even in this instance Elizabeth Gaskell's delicate art preserves a balance, with the poignant anecdote recalled by Sally, of

> 'Nelly Brandon's child as was left at our door, if I hadn't gone to th' overseer we should have had that Irish tramp's baby saddled on us for life; but I went off and told th' overseer, and the mother was caught.'
>
> 'Yes,' said Mr Benson sadly, 'and I often lie awake and wonder what is the fate of that poor little thing, forced back on the mother who tried to get quit of it.' (xiv)

In respect of authorial attitude, Elizabeth Gaskell is unique. Though only Jane Austen resembles her in avoiding using her own voice to discriminate and pass judgement, she is not like Jane Austen. The earlier writer depended on a central consciousness to convey judgement, whether directly or by ironic limitation, used action and dialogue as her other means and provided a minimum of description. Elizabeth Gaskell has a high proportion of narrative and description as well as speech and action, and depends greatly on telling the reader about the natures of her characters and their feelings, though always leaving him to pass the final judgement. No other writer of stature follows her mode in the nineteenth century, preferring in this respect to follow, in their various ways, the mode of Fielding, in projecting his views upon his material and his own personality upon the reader. This attitude is common to writers as unlike as Charlotte Brontë, who never forgets her reader and even apostrophizes him; George Eliot, who tends to expound her characters for the reader's benefit; and Trollope, who has the friendly man-to-man tone of the club-room, and openly admits the author's power to know and manœuvre his characters, though he treats them as real though inferior beings, not the specimens and 'puppets' of Thackeray's world. Hardy, like George Eliot, expounds his characters to the reader, but without her ironic detachment, and without any feeling of kinship between himself and the reader. Elizabeth Gaskell is as simple and self-effacing as may well be: her stance as author is so imperceptible that it is not imitable, because readers are scarcely aware of it. Its great virtue is that it seems to present so little barrier between the reader and the experience. Its great power and the art it entails go, therefore, unaccounted for. It is also one reason why other novelists found her so rich a source of ideas, since they feel as little as may well be the pressure and colour of the personality of the artist herself, in her transmutation of the stuff of life into art.

With *Ruth*, Elizabeth Gaskell's powers of characterization take a great leap forward. The novel gives her a different range from *Mary Barton*, and while it gives her by no means the freedom she requires, enables her to show even more power than she needs. Most noticeable are her increasing powers of organization and proportion. Whereas in *Mary Barton* one leapt from one character or group to another of equal interest — so that, along with a rich sense of community life, one was sometimes uncertain where the most central interests lay, and material conflicted with development and structure — here in *Ruth* there is no such conflict. Characters group themselves by emphasis, function and setting, and by what they reveal of themes and problems. Ruth is always central and passive, and (with a few important exceptions) others actively support, contrast with, or illuminate her, contribute to her development, or influence her fate. Immediately surrounding her are her greatest guides, comforters, and friends, the Benson household: the gentle, crippled Dissenting minister, Thurstan Benson, his lively and strong-minded sister, Faith, and their equally strong-minded servant Sally. Part of this household, though utterly separate in role and handling from any other character, is Ruth's son Leonard. The other main group is the merchant Bradshaw, Benson's patron, and his family, comprising his spirit-broken wife, two young daughters Mary and Elizabeth, his unsatisfactory deceiving son Richard, and, most most important, his eldest child Jemima, high-spirited and wilful. Along with this group is Mr Farquhar, connected with it as Bradshaw's partner, and as the intended husband of the wayward Jemima. Outside this central Eccleston community there is one important figure, the only person besides Ruth whose career covers the whole novel, her lover Bellingham. Numerous other characters appear only briefly, yet provide a rich sense of life and growth and change. Altogether, her groups of characters give the author in one respect more scope than any of her other novels, in that she has all ages, from children to the old, in many different relationships.

Socially, it is difficult to define the range within the novel, or to pin down these groups. There are no aristocrats, nor are there any 'poor', either of the kind who live permanently in penury (though some are mentioned from time to time), or who, like the mill-workers of Manchester, run the hazard of starvation in bad times. Socially, and no doubt financially, Mr Bellingham is the highest in the scale of any we meet – though we are made aware of a land-owning level in Eccleston society, represented by the Cranworths, the Tory family with whom Bellingham (Donne, as he is then called) contests the election. In the main group of characters, the Bensons' comparative poverty distinguishes them from the Bradshaws' comparative prosperity. But the Bensons feel no sense of inferiority to the Bradshaws, despite Bradshaw's patronizing: they are his equals in manners and intelligence, his superiors in sense, culture and taste. The provincial society with its changes of traditional social pattern, rendered by the non-conformist religious tradition, separating its members from the established church, and by the rising merchant and manufacturing interests, is an integral and invaluable element, so perfectly familiar to the author as as to cause her no problems, and so completely under her artistic control as to require no exposition or explanation to the reader.

By setting the cultural level higher than *Mary Barton*'s, the novel frees itself to show greater variety of perception and sensibility. Dialect need no longer be the norm for speech. We are aware that the Bradshaw's voices, for instance, are different from Mr Bellingham's 'measured, graceful way of utterance, with a style of pronunciation quite different to that of Eccleston' (xxii), yet though speakers thus have a regional accent, they do not have a regional language, and the main characters can then contrast more readily and vividly with the secondary ones, like the wonderfully vigorous and pithy servant Sally. In this mixture of classes, and variety of language and idiom, *Ruth* looks forward to the next novel *North and South*, with its far wider range of social, cultural, and regional variation.

Though Elizabeth Gaskell organizes by function and weighting, she does not use any of the more mechanical methods of showing subordination, by making characters 'flat', or comic, or caricatured, or even simply neutral. Yet her work abounds with men and women who make brief, more than adequate, appearances, and then are heard no more. Their author wisely makes no attempt to tie them in any way once their purpose is served, but, more important, she never scamps, or dismisses a person, however small his part. She contrives always to produce the impression that a character has a full life, though an invisible, because irrelevant, one, which he will go on living when the spotlight of the action passes from him. She uses no stock devices to make characters stand out with momentary exaggerated force – such as comic names, grotesque features, or mannerisms of speech – her great genius being to depict the interest of the ordinary, the humdrum, and the everyday. She distinguishes major from minor by the quantity and detail of attention, and the amount of space they occupy, not by different treatment. One feels that any character in the novel could be, with a shift of emphasis, himself the central character. An example is Jenny Morgan, the keeper of the inn where Ruth and Mr Bellingham stay in North Wales. Introduced absolutely neutrally, as the easy-going proprietrix who can be lorded over and bribed into 'many little lies' to give Bellingham the best room, she impinges again during his illness and Ruth's distress, with a sharply-observed mixture of limited, inattentive, insensitive good sense and kindliness, as when reporting Bellingham's illness to Ruth:

> 'Mr Jones said tonight was a turning-point; but I doubt it, for it is four days since he was taken ill, and whoever heard of a sick person taking a turn on an even number of days? It's always on the third, or the fifth, or seventh, or so on. . . . I don't think he will get better myself, though – Gelert does not howl for nothing. My patience! what's the matter with the girl – Lord, child, you're never going to faint, and be ill on my hands?' (vii)

The entirely natural way she sees only her own point of view makes her kindness equally natural and convincing, as it is the little observation following upon her bringing Ruth some tea:

> the scolding Mrs Morgan gave her when she found the buttered toast untouched (toast on which she had herself desired that the butter might not be spared), did Ruth more good than the tea. (vii)

Though circumstances are bitterly cruel to Ruth, Elizabeth Gaskell will not let us convict individuals of such cruelty, even when Mrs Morgan scolds Ruth again for speaking to and angering Mrs Bellingham:

> 'Did I not give you a room last night to keep in, and never been seen or heard of; and did I not tell you what a particular lady Mrs Bellingham was, that you must come out here right in her way? Indeed, it was not pretty, nor grateful to me, Jenny Morgan, and that I must say.' (vii)

Though Jenny is Welsh, Elizabeth Gaskell wisely avoids representing her speech except by such unobtrusive turns of phrase as her last sentence here.

It is not surprising that few novelists attempt such universally full characterization as this. Together with the increase in material, it makes the organization of the whole work truly formidable. George Eliot makes her own refinements upon it, and Trollope too has his variations. George Eliot is prepared to use the full attention at key points, on characters who have hitherto or elsewhere been minor, flat or even comic; Trollope is much more like Elizabeth Gaskell, in moving his gaze to a character who has featured little, and giving him the serious attention and opportunity to function, momentarily, as major characters do. This is because he is in the habit of not having a main character, but of working with groups, all of whom have their parts in the development of events, parts whose size varies as the events progress.

Since *Ruth* covers a long period of time – about thirteen years, of which twelve are set in Eccleston – characters must grow, or age, or develop. Some earlier writers have dealt with the changes wrought by time and circumstance. Scott showed his power in *Old Mortality*, with Balfour of Burley; in *Heart of Midlothian*, where he created both the young and feckless Effie Deans and the Lady Stanton whom she becomes; and even finer the brilliant romantic Young Pretender of *Waverley*, who is the ageing tarnished relic of his former glory in *Redgauntlet*. But in these Scott only produces a 'then' and 'now', and does not have to show how the one turns into the other. Elizabeth Gaskell is not only one of the first to show such changes actually taking place, but one of the masters, not only with young and central characters, but with others of all ages. Indeed the alterations are more obvious in the latter, for, whereas a girl like Jemima may change from young womanhood into the early years of marriage, she does not feel the ache of mortality; a woman in her fifties, like Faith Benson, will, and does. One of the gayest, yet most pregnant scenes in the novel is that in Chapter XIX (entitled 'After Five Years') in which Faith Benson considers her advancing years:

'Sally!' said Miss Benson, 'my hair is nearly white. The last time I looked it was only pepper and salt. What must I do?'

'Do – why, what would the wench do?' asked Sally contemptuously. 'Ye're never going to be taken in, at your time of life, by hair-dyes and such gimcracks, as can only take in young girls whose wisdom teeth are not cut.'

'And who are not likely to want them,' said Miss Benson quietly. 'No! but you see, Sally, it's very awkward having such grey hair, and feeling so young. Do you know, Sally, I've as great a mind for dancing, when I hear a tune on a street-organ, as ever; and as great a mind to sing when I'm happy. . . . But an old woman with grey hair ought not to have a fancy for dancing or singing.'

'Whatten nonsense are ye talking?' said Sally roused to indignation. 'Calling yoursel' an old woman when you're better than

ten years younger than me; and many a young girl has grey
hair at five-and-twenty.'
    'But I'm more than five-and-twenty, Sally – I'm fifty-seven
next May!'
    'More shame on ye, then, not to know better than to talk of
dyeing your hair.' (XIX)

Enchanting though this is, it makes very serious points: it is the
wiser woman who feels most sensitively, the simpler one who has
the more robust attitude. Through them the amused reader has to
consider life and time; the effect is almost poignant, and the result
from such scenes is that Elizabeth Gaskell's characters are inescapably
moving, like ordinary humanity, towards their graves. Some of them
may live happily, but none will live 'happily ever after', with the
kind of assumed immortality of so many fictional creations. As the
novel goes on Sally grows deaf, Mr Benson gets more delicate and
uncertain, and all around them move with them, inevitably, to old
age and the grave and eternity.

    This handling of time is one of the tremendous extensions of the
novel's range. George Eliot avails herself of it, and makes it central to
Felix Holt, in Mrs Transome, who is verging on old age when the
story begins, and descends painfully into it as retribution comes upon
her. George Eliot's time-scale is more complex than Elizabeth
Gaskell's, since it involves stretching back into the past, as well as
marking an ever-changing present. We must see and understand the
young Mrs Transome, the gay girl with warped principles, who
produces the married woman who will bring up her child by her
lover as the legal heir, who has to live in daily contact with the man
for whom her love and power have turned to revulsion and fear, and
endure the conflict between him and the son who knows nothing of
the relationship. George Eliot's achievement here is superb, and Mrs
Transome touches tragedy in her great culminating utterance, 'If I
have sinned, my punishment went before – that I should sin for a
man like you.' Yet the marking of change and time within the
actual time-span of the action owes much to Elizabeth Gaskell. Mrs
Transome, having just met her son after several years' absence,

stood before a tall mirror, going close to it and looking at her
face with hard scrutiny, as if it were unrelated to herself. No
elderly face can be handsome, looked at in that way; every little
detail is startlingly prominent, and the effect of the whole is lost.

She saw the dried up complexion, and the deep lines of bitter discontent about the mouth.

'I am a hag!' she said to herself (she was accustomed to give her thoughts a very sharp outline), 'an ugly old woman who happens to be his mother. That is what he sees in me.' (*Felix Holt*, 1)

That she is overstating the case at this point renders her situation less immediately painful – she is still the upright autocrat who rules her own life and lands; but her increasing age renders her increasing powerlessness more agonizing, and makes her final despair harrowing. In answer to Harold's question (when he has discovered the truth) 'Who is my father?'

She was mute: her lips only trembled. Harold stood silent for a few moments, as if waiting.

'*He* has said it – said it before others – that he is my father.'

He looked still at his mother. She seemed as if age had struck her with a sudden wand – as if her trembling face were getting haggard before him. (*Felix Holt*, XLVIII)

Trollope too commits himself to advancing time and the coming on of years in many of his novels, particularly in the Barchester series, where writing a sequence with the characters reappearing compels him to it. The Warden, Harding, is aged by his conflicts in the first, the novel named after him; so that in *Barchester Towers* when, five years later, the deanship of Barchester is offered to him, he proclaims himself too old to accept it and the duties pertaining to it. But Trollope is more merciful to his favourite creations, through being less high-principled in his art, and makes very little change in Harding's personality. His more skilful and subtle changes are with younger creations, with Eleanor Bold for instance, transmuted delicately from the unmarried dutiful daughter, to the independent widow with a fortune of £12,000, who can choose her society, defy her brother-in-law Archdeacon Grantley, and choose her second husband, Mr Arabin, without influence or consultation.

Hardy, at a greater distance, often handles an extended time-span in his work, and is deeply concerned with the grip of circumstances on his characters' lives, as in *Jude the Obscure*; and also, in *The Mayor of Casterbridge*, and *Tess of the D'Urbervilles*, with the later consequences of deeds committed earlier. Of these Henchard, the mayor of

Casterbridge, is the one who comes closest to Elizabeth Gaskell's kind, since he, being middle-aged in all but the first chapters, travels the downward road towards death without interruption or gaps in narrative. Hardy watches and delineates how his drinking impairs his intelligence, how age and suffering render his spirit less resilient, and finally brings all together in Henchard's symbolic departure when he realizes that Elizabeth-Jane, the girl whom he had believed to be his daughter, will marry the young Scotsman Farfrae, the rival merchant who has ruined him:

> During the day he had bought a new tool-basket, cleaned up his old hay-knife and wimble, and set himself up in fresh leggings, knee-naps and corduroys, and in other ways gone back to the clothes of his young manhood, discarding for ever the shabby-genteel suit of cloth and rusty silk hat that since his decline had characterised him in the Casterbridge street as a man who had seen better days. . . . [Elizabeth-Jane] watched his form diminish across the moor, the yellow straw basket at his back moving up and down with each tread, and the creases behind his knees coming and going till she could no longer see them. Though she did not know it Henchard formed at this moment much the same picture as he had presented when entering Casterbridge for the first time nearly a quarter of a century before; except, to be sure, that the serious addition to his years had considerably lessened the spring of his stride, that his state of hopelessness had weakened him, and imparted to his shoulders, as weighted by the basket, a perceptible bend. (*The Mayor of Casterbridge*, XLIII)

Hardy, using similar means to Elizabeth Gaskell, reaches different ends. Since his characters are not in the hands of any benevolent deity, or even an ordered universe, he gains in tragic power, yet loses the plangency and pathos that Elizabeth Gaskell so often has when she, with her complete and implicit Christian faith, reproduces time and mortality.

Characters' functions and handling cannot be conveniently schematized, since all characters have many functions, and numerous interrelationships. Elizabeth Gaskell is more aware of than most novelists, and better able to suggest, the innumerable ways in which any single individual responds to and influences all the others whom he knows, however small a part he may play in the main story. The younger Bradshaw girls, Mary and Elizabeth, are a pleasant instance.

They are too young for the author to give them much part in the
action – though Elizabeth's illness is the cause of Bradshaw's taking
the house at Abermouth, and so, indirectly, of Ruth's great encounter
there with Bellingham – but they are deftly portrayed – inexperienced
as they are in life or suffering – as innocently comic and unconsciously ironic commentators; the following page-long exchange, of
apparently desultory chat, has no irrelevant word. It is Elizabeth
Gaskell's equivalent to Jane Austen's classic examples of idle chat, all of
which is vital (such as Miss Bates's magnificent monologues in *Emma*):

'Lizzie, did you see how the tears came into Minnie's eyes
when Mr Farquhar looked so displeased when she said good
people were always dull? I think she's in love.' Mary said the
last words with grave emphasis, and felt like an oracle of twelve
years old.

'I don't,' said Lizzie. 'I know I cry often enough when papa
is cross, and I'm not in love with him.'

'Yes, but you don't look as Minnie did.'

'Don't call her Minnie – you know papa does not like it?'

'Yes, but there are so many things papa does not like I can
never remember them all. Never mind about that; but listen to
something I've got to tell you, if you'll never, never tell.'

'No, indeed I won't, Mary. What is it?'

'Not to Mrs Denbigh?'

'No, not even to Mrs Denbigh.'

'Well, then, the other day – last Friday, Minnie – '

'Jemima!' interrupted the more conscientious Elizabeth.

'Jemima, if it must be so,' jerked out Mary, 'sent me to her
desk for an envelope, and what do you think I saw?'

'What?' asked Elizabeth, expecting nothing else than a red-
hot Valentine, signed Walter Farquhar, *pro* Bradshaw, Farquhar
& Co., in full.

'Why, a piece of paper, with dull-looking lines on it, just like
scientific dialogues: and I remember all about it. It was once
when Mr Farquhar had been telling us that a bullet does not
go in a straight line, but in a something curve, and he drew some
lines on a piece of paper; and Minnie – '

'Jemima!' put in Elizabeth.

'Well, Well! She had treasured it up, and written in a corner,
"W.F., April 3rd." Now, that's rather like love, is not it? For

Jemima hates useful information as much as I do, and that's saying a great deal; and yet she had kept the paper, and dated it.'

'If that's all, I know Dick keeps a paper with Miss Benson's name written on it, and yet he's not in love with her; and perhaps Jemima may like Mr Farquhar, and he may not like her. It seems such a little while since her hair was turned up, and he has always been a grave middle-aged man ever since I can recollect; and then have you never noticed how often he finds fault with her – almost lectures her?'

'To be sure,' said Mary; 'but he may be in love, for all that. Just think how often papa lectures mamma; and yet, of course, they're in love with each other.'

'Well, we shall see,' said Mary. (xx)

From this nicely and delicately humorous creation of the twelve-year-old female mind Elizabeth Gaskell reveals Mr Bradshaw and his disciplinarian yet futile influence on his family; the sisters' relationship to each other and their affection (moderated by the age-gap between them) for Jemima; Jemima's own pitiable condition, alone with her confused emotions yet spied on by everyone, even her sympathetic little sisters; the unconsciously accepted close love between them and Ruth (Mrs Denbigh), who can be told any of their thoughts, even the most private and childish; the obstacles besetting Jemima and Mr Farquhar, not least the age-gap, emphasized by the child's-eye view of the sister who has only just put up her childish long hair, compared with the 'grave middle-aged man' who can only be thought of, even on a valentine card, as partner in the business of Bradshaw, Farquhar & Co.; the passage can even glance outward, *via* their brother Richard, to Miss Benson; and finally, it makes the point (that will be the saving of all) that though Bradshaw and his wife may not be 'in love' they are in their way a devoted couple, and that the family is a united and affectionate one, so that, when disaster strikes in Richard's ruin, the family will not fall melodramatically, improbably and miserably apart, like Dickens's Gradgrinds in *Hard Times*.

Such a method, so like Jane Austen's, of using dialogue of minor characters for all sorts of purpose beyond mere characterization, has the Austenian assets of economy and concision and humour. After such a passage as this, there is no occasion to describe and define in author's narrative the situation within the Bradshaw household.

Elizabeth Gaskell is free to concentrate where her purposes require, on Ruth and the Benson ménage, and to devote her time and space spent on the Bradshaws to Bradshaw himself, and to Jemima, whose spiritual progress is to parallel and contrast with Ruth's.

Mr Bradshaw, Jemima, and to a later and lesser extent Richard, affect Ruth, and the story, most and are therefore the most important. Bradshaw himself is primarily the representative of the public opinion with whom Ruth, as the representative of fallen virtue, must contend for her place in society. As a thoughtful and an honest and religious man, he is no ogre to be easily dismissed; by the time he comes to make his judgement, very late in the action, when Ruth's story becomes public, Elizabeth Gaskell has established him as a force to be taken seriously. The reader has learned to acknowledge him as a man both of judgement and principle, though of faulty practice. His judgement permits him to recognize Ruth's potential and employ her, and having done so, to recognize her worth; his principles prevent him from continuing to see her worth when he finds out her past, and cause him to dismiss, because she has 'exposed his innocent children to corruption' (xxvii), the woman whom he previously asked to influence his elder daughter's conduct. Alongside this role he has another, as the conventionally respectable parent – contrasting thus with Ruth herself – who fails in the nurture of his son, where Ruth succeeds with hers. The two roles come together when Richard Bradshaw is revealed as an embezzler. Bradshaw, standing by his principles again, and disowning his son, nearly tears himself apart, and has a stroke. His redemption comes from within the character with which Elizabeth Gaskell has endowed him, not from juggling with events, or with moral or social theory.

He is presented with a sure hand. Influential though he is, he is not omnipotent, nor all-serious. Elizabeth Gaskell has a light touch, and a humour in his representation which is honest and precise, and leads to understanding not ridicule. His main public trait, his love of patronage, is challenged almost as soon as it appears, when he sends Ruth a length of muslin 'in aid of any preparations Mrs Denbigh might have to make' (i.e. for baby clothes), which Ruth intuitively wishes to reject, because Mr Bradshaw, not a friend and scarcely knowing her, has no right to give. She is overcome by Mr Benson, and accepts, with, in Benson's words, 'only the very cool thanks which [she] felt' (xv). Ruth has established her independence, Elizabeth Gaskell the extent of Bradshaw's power. His patronage and self-esteem continue to receive checks which make the reader sympathize as well as smile – as when he feels his household standard fails to impress the political agent and the intending candidate Mr Bellingham – 'Mr Donne asked Mrs Bradshaw, with quiet surprise, if she had no pinery, as if to be without a pinery were indeed a depth of pitiable destitution' (xxii) – so that, when disaster does strike, Mr Bradshaw, broken by the disgrace of his son, is a psychologically convincing and moving figure.

As a character whose faulty principles and psychological limitations contribute to his disaster, he has connections both within Elizabeth Gaskell's work and outside her. He has obviously close connections with John Barton before him, and prepares in some degree for John Thornton in the next novel *North and South*, in whom also there conflicts a combination of personal honour and falsely-based principles. The line stretches out beyond these, to, ultimately, though very differently handled, Hardy's Angel Clare.

His eldest daughter Jemima also is an important figure in the novel, of the kind Elizabeth Gaskell does best, though here Jemima is not as successfully worked in as her father. Close to Ruth in age, she contrasts with her as the young woman, brought up in a normal family and right principles, who equally has conflicts with social pressure, and with impulses within herself. Lively, vigorous, unwilling to acknowledge authority, she is the personal antithesis of the submissive Ruth. In that the authority over her is unfairly administered, her circumstances contrast also: the Bensons advise Ruth rightly, and protect her; Bradshaw tries to coerce Jemima into advantageous marriage with Farquhar. Her personal distress arises from the conflict between her natural urge to rebel against her father's materialism, and her equally natural and genuine love for Farquhar – personal distress intensified still further when Farquhar turns from her to Ruth as a possible wife. Elizabeth Gaskell always does well with young girls. Although Jemima's history is not very exciting – a girl's conflicts with her parents and in courtship cannot rank very high against the greater ills of life – Elizabeth Gaskell is as usual psychologically acute in their rendering, particularly of how Jemima feels towards Ruth. Her problems with Jemima are not of execution, but of the role she has to play, in that there is not enough for her to do in the action of the novel as it stands. Her author cannot prudently give her more, without taking too much of the emphasis and interest away from Ruth herself; yet as the novel stands, Jemima barely enters

the action until Chapter xx; then, once she has drawn away from
Farquhar, revolted by her father's heavy-handed intervention, and
estranged herself from Ruth because she considers her to be in league
with her father, she has after Chapter xxi nothing to do until in
Chapter xxvi she accidently hears the milliner's anecdote of Ruth
Hilton of Fordham, and connects her with Mrs Ruth Denbigh of
Eccleston.

Richard is the third important element in the Bradshaw story. He
takes up little space, since if he did, he would be a distraction from
the main concerns, but, despite this and his very conventional role as
the deceiving and unsatisfactory son, he is a fully realized portrait,
emerging from a few small scenes, and from the comments of others,
such as, for instance, Faith Benson's, the first in fact that we hear of
him:

> 'But remember,' said Mr Benson, 'how strict Mr Bradshaw
> has always been with his children. It is no wonder if poor
> Richard was a coward in those days.'
>
> 'He is now, or I'm much mistaken,' answered Miss Benson.
> 'And Mr Bradshaw was just as strict with Jemima, and she's no
> coward. But I've no faith in Richard. He has a look about him
> that I don't like. And when Mr Bradshaw was away in Holland
> last year, for those months my young gentleman did not come
> half as regularly to chapel, and I always believe that story of his
> being seen out with the hounds at Smithiles.'
>
> 'Those are neither of them great offences in a young man of
> twenty,' said Mr Benson, smiling.
>
> 'No! I don't mind them in themselves; but when he could
> change back so easily to being regular and mim when his father
> came home, I don't like that.' (xvii)

Such material as this, which forms part of a discussion on a parent's
role between Ruth and the Benson's, is invariably worked into the
fabric of the scene in which it appears.

The young heir who runs into debt and disgraces his family is no
uncommon literary figure; the chief striking thing about Richard,
and the whole Bradshaw family, is how close their roles are to those of
the Gradgrinds in *Hard Times*, published only one year later. The
dominant father bringing up his children according to his own fixed
principles, negative mother, rebellious daughter offered a *mariage de
convenance*, and deceiving, embezzling son, are too close in situation

to be coincidental, even though the handling and technique, and the individual personalities are very different.

The last appendage to this part of the novel is Mr Farquhar, Bradshaw's forty-year-old partner, destined husband for Jemima. He is a problem for his author, necessary as an admirer for Ruth (it would be unlikely that Bellingham should be the only man ever to be attracted), and as the upright yet not bigoted man of business who gives proportion to Bradshaw. The problem is that his motives and reactions seem at odds with his supposed right thinking. Though half in love with Ruth, he sighs with relief when he hears her true story and discovers that she is not an honourable widow, and moves his heart back to Jemima, congratulating himself on a lucky escape, even though Ruth, as he acknowledges, is just as virtuous as she seemed, and he has no reason to think she would be a bad wife. Elizabeth Gaskell scuttles over the problem, merely noting:

> the unacknowledged bond between [Mr Farquhar and Jemima] now was their grief, sympathy and pity for Ruth; only in Jemima these feelings were ardent, and would fain have become active; while in Mr Farquhar they were strongly mingled with thankfulness that he had escaped a disagreeable position.
>
> (XXVIII)

Again Elizabeth Gaskell's failure is of organizing the parts of her whole. She cannot give the space needed to a full portrait of Farquhar without destroying the balance of the whole, nor has he enough actions to perform to merit such attention.

The heart of the novel lies elsewhere, with the Benson household – a wonderful instance, like *Cranford*, of Elizabeth Gaskell making, out of limited and modest materials, an original and delightful creation. The Bensons and Sally, like the ladies in *Cranford*, are people to whom very little happens, who are yet full of life and delight. They show also her power of creating both individuals, and a sense of a household, which absorbs and transcends idiosyncrasies and class. Sally, Faith Benson, Thurstan Benson and Ruth form a unit, bound by their life together, their mutual affection, their way of life and the principles behind it. That they all also share Ruth's secret is not the cause of the unity, merely an addition to it.

Thurstan Benson is a difficult undertaking, superbly achieved. To define his function gives no idea of his effect, or the extent of his power. He comes within the great nineteenth-century group of clergymen involved with sexual standards and destiny of the hero or heroine, and within the sub-group of those who rescue or reclaim the woman in trouble, of which other notable instances are Charlotte Brontë's St John Rivers in *Jane Eyre*, and George Eliot's Mr Tryan in the second story from *Scenes of Clerical Life*, 'Janet's Repentance'. Though Benson belongs to a group and though Elizabeth Gaskell never loses sight of his function, she does not conceive him as a type. He has his own failings and conflicts, which make him into another instance of moral failure, in that he touches pitch and is defiled. Through lack of moral courage he permits the lie of pretending that Ruth is a widow; the lie involves all of them – Faith, Sally and Ruth herself – but haunts the conscience of him alone, the others being prepared to justify it by its obvious expediency and happy consequences. His motives for deciding to lie separate him from his type, and distinguish his author from others; he does so, not so much to protect Ruth as to save her child from the social trials of bastardy, rejecting indignantly Faith's stock reaction when she terms it 'this disgrace – this badge of her shame' (xi). Elizabeth Gaskell does well to contrast him with his practical and pragmatic sister Faith, and the unanalytical Ruth. It is a skilful move also to make him a Dissenting minister. Being outside the social hierarchy of squire and parish of a Church of England clergyman, he is thus given more freedom of moral choice to decide for himself on ethical points, with more serious consequences in so choosing; for when his deception comes to light, and Mr Bradshaw leaves the congregation, Benson's income falls accordingly, as a Church of England rector's stipend would not.

Elizabeth Gaskell wisely gives him weaknesses and numerous foibles. His physical deformity is a brilliant stroke. It prevents any hints of super-perfection, because, making him dependent on others, it makes his high ideals go along with doubts, diffidence, and uncertainties; it unites him to the sister and the servant who have shared their lives with him; it makes him a touchstone for the physically robust – Bradshaw condemns himself by despising Benson's physique; it sets him totally outside the physical relationships in which so many of the other characters are involved, and prevents any suggestion of such an attraction between him and Ruth. Since the idea never occurs to the reader, it is easy to deny Elizabeth Gaskell credit for the skill with which she has rendered it impossible, yet emotional attachment between the penitent or sufferer and the spiritual adviser is, in the novel in general, the norm rather than the exception. In *Jane*

Eyre, six years before, St John Rivers dominated Jane, and though he is no parallel to Benson in role, since he offers Jane temptation to avid self-denial which she has to resist, he is a parallel in his function of rescuer from despair and likely death. Elizabeth Gaskell's Mr Benson clearly owes nothing to him, but those who follow owe something to both, and in a lesser degree and at a further distance, to Hester Prynne and Dimmesdale in Hawthorne's *The Scarlet Letter* (1850), even though that strange work, set apart by its unique subject, by its American orientation, and by its historical and social setting, is less accessible as quarry for later writers. George Eliot's Dr Kenn in *The Mill on the Floss* (1860) has recollections of Rivers and takes similar practical steps, employing Maggie in her disgrace as governess to his children; but George Eliot descends to a sense of social pressure so crude as to invite the charge of cynicism. Admittedly George Eliot must compress here: Dr Kenn is one small unit in Maggie's end, and neither needs nor requires detailed attention. What is more, the conclusion of *The Mill on the Floss* is not its best part, and George Eliot's achievement should not be condemned because she occasionally slips. Even so Elizabeth Gaskell is incapable at any point of anything approaching so near moral irresponsibility as this, when the parishioners speculate upon Dr Kenn succumbing to Maggie's charms – 'Would he be so lost to propriety as to marry her before the year was out? The masculine mind was sarcastic, and thought *not*' (Book VII, IV). George Eliot moves still further in Daniel Deronda, who is the natural ultimate development for her – the non-Christian writer – of the non-Christian pastor, where the element of spiritual and sexual attraction latent in the precursors becomes an explicit element in Gwendolen's feelings towards her rescuer.

Foil to Benson, and balance to him in relation to Ruth and Leonard, is his sister Faith, one of Elizabeth Gaskell's many lively and original sympathetic portrayals of middle-aged and elderly characters, not intelligent or extraordinary, with no outstanding foibles, nor even any momentous acts to perform, who are yet indispensable to the story. Her immediate precursors are the single ladies in *Cranford*; one can find no earlier ancestry for her in the main stream of the novel unless it be the idiosyncratic and formidable Scotswomen of Susan Ferrier, who, however, exist primarily for the comedy they provide, extraneous to theme or plot, and who, though they offer much delight, rouse no sympathy within the reader. She is like the Cranford ladies also in being not alone, but part of a relationship of sister, or

brother and sister, or friend and friend, who share experience, and
interact in combination. She works alongside Benson in exploring the
making of the decision on which the bulk of the novel rests – to pass
Ruth off as a widow. Their first conversation on the subject reveals
how they interact throughout:

> 'The poor child!' said she at length – 'the poor, poor child!
> what it will have to struggle through and endure! Do you
> remember Thomas Wilkins, and the way he threw the registry
> of his birth and baptism back in your face? Why, he would not
> have the situation; he went to sea, and was drowned, rather than
> present the record of his shame.'
> 'I do remember it all. It has often haunted me. She must
> strengthen her child to look to God, rather than to man's
> opinion. It will be the discipline, the penance, she has incurred.
> She must teach it to be (humanly speaking) self-dependent.'
> 'But after all,' said Miss Benson (for she had known and
> esteemed poor Thomas Wilkins, and had mourned over his
> untimely death, and the recollection thereof softened her) –
> 'after all, it might be concealed. The very child need never
> know its illegitimacy.'
> 'How?' asked her brother.
> 'Why – we know so little about her yet; but in that letter, it
> said she had no friends; – now, could she not go into quite a
> fresh place, and be passed off as a widow?' (xi)

Each of them expresses compassion, and a different kind of grasp of the
situation, from which conclusions emerge which are the combined
thoughts of the two of them. Vigorous and entertaining, Faith is a
welcome feature, arriving after the harrowing scenes in Wales, full
of the spontaneous life that makes her indulge in masculine tricks like
'whistling a long low whistle when surprised or displeased' (xi), and
full of the minutiae of the life of Eccleston. She is more closely
involved with this life than any other person, having relations with
everyone – Ruth, Leonard, Sally, and all the Bradshaws – and providing pithy and entertaining commentary. She responds to life with
disarming gusto, shocking her brother and delighting the reader with
her honest responses, when, for instance, reproached for inventing a
surgeon husband for Ruth, she declares

> 'I do think I've a natural talent for fiction, it is so pleasant to
> invent, and make the incidents dovetail together, and after all,

if we are to tell a lie, we may as well do it thoroughly, or else it's no use. A bungling lie would be worse than useless.' (xiv)

She is a creation with far more power than the novel requires, and is capable of a much larger role; Elizabeth Gaskell shows not only her potential as a novelist, but also her discretion, in not letting Faith Benson run away with her. Such characters are always a delight in Elizabeth Gaskell, and recur even more successfully in *Sylvia's Lovers* and *Wives and Daughters*, of other classes and both sexes, extended and developed to make them partake of grief and hardship as well as the everyday hazards of life. They are part of Elizabeth Gaskell's extension of the secondary areas of the novel, and the extended uses of secondary characters. In this she is followed conspicuously by Trollope, who with his wide ranging eye, relishes the varieties of human nature, and, though he has his own types, and no equivalent to Faith Benson, can portray similar interactions to this in, to give only one example of many, Mrs Grantly, who influences her husband the archdeacon with unobtrusive common sense, as Faith does her brother.

Though Elizabeth Gaskell creates a powerful sense of the Benson household as pre-existing Ruth's entry to it, in fact it revolves around her for the whole of its time-span in the novel. Ruth herself, however, has an existence within the novel before she impinges on it. To create and delineate Ruth, rendering her sympathetic without sentimentality, faulty without being criminal, ignorant without being unintelligent, so that she can develop into maturity and awareness, and even to modest heroism, such is Elizabeth Gaskell's primary undertaking. Her degree of achievement is more surprising than that she does not entirely succeed. One of her biggest problems is her earliest, to create a girl who can be seduced without actually realizing her plight, who is yet not stupid, or insensitive, or corrupt. Ruth is, simply, innocent by nature and vulnerable by circumstance. To accept her is undoubtedly hard for the mid-twentieth-century reader; it cannot have been automatic even for the 1850s, which knew that young girls were just as likely to be as practical and sensible as Mary Barton, or Cynthia of *Wives and Daughters*. Elizabeth Gaskell knows Ruth is exceptional, and devotes the opening chapters to her careful delineation, showing how circumstances have made her so: giving her a country upbringing, a mother who died when she was twelve, a senile father who dies also, leaving her at sixteen to an unprotected and unrewarding life in the dressmaker's establishment, where her one friend Jenny the forewoman is ill and has to leave. Elizabeth Gaskell contrasts her inexperience and immaturity with the far from childish beauty of her 'tall slight figure and rich auburn hair' (II). To these facts and comments Elizabeth Gaskell adds the whole atmosphere that she creates for Fordham and for Wales (already discussed), which ally Ruth to nature and natural responses to the world, to her own emotions, and to other people. Ruth is therefore, in the first flush of her love for Bellingham, not idealized, nor painful, nor even especially an object of pathos. She is given her time of innocent delight in her natural feelings, which author and reader share. Her distresses begin only with the end of her idyll, when she has to encounter the world of men around her and their social conventions, and has to realize the moral consequences of her acts. These distresses are rightly mental, not physical; Elizabeth Gaskell is not here concerned to chronicle the penury, destitution and degradation she glanced at with Esther in *Mary Barton* – the progress to prostitution is a rightly ignored cliché – so there is no melodrama in Ruth's progress.

Her spiritual education coincides with intellectual development, and the widening of sensibility. As well as being compelled to think about her own and her son's future, Ruth becomes educated in order to teach Leonard. Elizabeth Gaskell realizes that the unthinking response of sixteen is unlike the informed decision of twenty-six. She creates both equally accurately. Ruth can reject intuitively Mrs Bellingham's £50, or Bradshaw's present, feeling that, in the first case, 'it seems as if he could comfort me, for being forsaken, by money' (XII), and, in the second, 'Mr Bradshaw's present hurt me, instead of making me glad' (XV). Even though such instinctive morality is rightly not very different in its expression from her later informed decisions, such as the way she rejects Bellingham's proposal – 'If there were no other reason to prevent our marriage but the one fact that it would bring Leonard into contact with you, that would be enough' (XXIV) – or decides to take up nursing – 'At any rate it is work, and as such I am thankful for it' (XXIX) – or goes to nurse the typhus-stricken Bellingham at the end – 'I don't think I should love him, if he were well and happy – but you said he was ill – and alone – how can I help caring for him?' (XXXIV) – yet a world of felt and thought experience lies behind these later choices.

Elizabeth Gaskell is equally good at less climactic emotion, recognizing and depicting, for instance, the stages of Ruth's post-natal depression, when the excitement of the birth is over, and the decision has been made to make no attempt to find work for a year:

> She fell into trains of reverie and mournful regretful recollections which rendered her languid and tearful . . . [she] had taken Miss Benson's share of the more active and fatiguing household duties, but went through them heavily – as if her heart was far away. (xvi)

But it is undeniable that there are some awkwardnesses in the delineation of Ruth, and some discrepancies, which suggest romanticizing. Since Elizabeth Gaskell writes with verisimilitude as her habitual mode, departures from probability jar in a way they do not with writers who do not have 'truth to life' as their norm. A small example occurs when Ruth washes up the breakfast things:

> they were done in so quiet and orderly a manner, that neither Miss Benson nor Sally, both particular enough, had any of their little fancies or prejudices annoyed. (xiv)

Anyone who has washed up in a strange house, or had it done for them in their own, knows such perfection is impossible. Such romanticizing usually centres upon her relationship with Leonard, which, despite the occasional attempt to suggest infant wakefulness or childish naughtiness, is over-sweet. The section needs an injection of Sally – the only one with practical experience – to remind the reader of the elementary facts and hazards of baby-care; Elizabeth Gaskell not only knew them herself (she had three daughters) but could put her experience to literary use, as in the delightful chapter of *Cranford* called 'Old Letters'. Needless romanticizing suggests itself as the reason for her failure in Ruth. Other failings of inspiration are indicated by the absence of dialogue and dependence on description for Ruth's behaviour and relationships within the Bradshaw family. Elizabeth Gaskell tells of Ruth's influence on the children and on Jemima, but presents few scenes or dialogues which realize them. Part of her difficulty here is that having committed herself to a passive heroine, who experiences and suffers, but rarely takes the initiative, she cannot contrive enough incident without overmuch shifting of emphasis.

Ruth, though she may not be perfectly realized at every point, rises to greatness at her own greatest moments of conflict and decision.

Emotionally and structurally the novel's climax is the great crisis of Ruth's life, when action, resolution and choice are required of her in the dilemma she has to face entirely alone – when she meets Bellingham again. Here she is offered the chance that society and conventional morality would rejoice to see her accept: to marry the man who seduced her, and to give her child an assured and prosperous future by legitimizing him. The whole episode – covering two long chapters (xxiii and xxiv) – is superb, and rendered almost wholly through what Ruth feels and perceives. Elizabeth Gaskell makes Ruth's shock, when she recognizes Bellingham, the same as the reader's, with emotions rendered through their physical consequences:

> The sands heaved and trembled beneath Ruth. The figures near her vanished into strange nothingness; the sounds of their voices were as distant sounds in a dream, while the echo of one voice thrilled through and through. She could have caught at his arm for support, in the awful dizziness which wrapped her up, body and soul. That voice! No! if name, and face, and figure were all changed, that voice was the same which had touched her girlish heart, which had spoken most tender words of love, which had won, and wrecked her, and which she had last heard in the low mutterings of fever. It seemed as if weights were tied to her feet – as if the steadfast rocks receded – as if time stood still; – it was so long, so terrible, that path across the reeling sand. (xxiii)

Ruth's conflict continues thus to be not described, but recreated, as the duties of common life intrude and torment her, and as she struggles with a far from simple emotional situation: her revived love for the Bellingham of years before, the comparison with the man he is now, and the realization that he is a danger to her and her child, and that, though she must resist and reject Bellingham, because she does not love him, because he is morally irresponsible and because he could do only moral harm to Leonard, yet he can expose and ruin her, can (she believes) take Leonard legally away, and yet can equally offer valuable worldly advantages to them both. To quote their conversation would sound trite and conventional, even in their final confrontation, because the significance and the force of feeling is not only in the conversation itself, but in all that has led up to it, in the total awareness of the scene as a whole, and of the strange setting, 'near the fisherman's nets which the receding tide was leaving every moment barer and more bare, and the posts they were fastened to more blackly uprising above the waters' (xxiv). When Ruth has finally repulsed Bellingham and finally triumphed, her exhaustion expresses itself similarly through the physical:

> her soul had lost the power of throwing itself forward, or contemplating anything beyond the dreary present, when the expanse of grey, wild, bleak moors, stretching wide away below a sunless sky seemed only an outer sign of the waste world within her heart, for which she could claim no sympathy; – for she could not even define what its woes were, and, if she could, no one would understand how the present time was haunted by the terrible ghost of the former love. (xxiv)

Ruth is not a creation of the same stature as *Jane Eyre*, but there is some similarity in the handling here of the extreme state of spiritual exhaustion, which corresponds to Jane's own during her wanderings on the moors above Morton, when she has fled from Thornfield Hall. After her Hardy finds the same use of natural setting to interpret Tess, who, like Ruth, has not the powers of self-analysis within her to define the responses that the reader must understand.

There remains the single isolated figure of this interconnected work, Mr Bellingham – or Donne, as he later becomes. His part need not be, and is not, large; but it is not easy to delineate, and shows a great advance on the comparable figure in *Mary Barton*, young Mr Carson. He is not a detailed portrait, for we need to see little more of him than the imperceptive Ruth sees. Elizabeth Gaskell has no need or desire to present a detailed study of a seducer (as George Eliot has with Arthur Donnithorne in *Adam Bede*), but only to give an adequate and convincing impression of the nature that can charm and desert Ruth. But he is no simple villain (any more than Ruth is a mere sinner). Elizabeth Gaskell has learned discretion, and wisely gives us, when he persuades Ruth, very little actual speech, such as was very improbably done with Carson, concentrating on Ruth's responses and on the turns of events to throw them together. The sketch of thoughtless self-indulgence is a good one, with the emphasis on his youth – 'old compared to Ruth, but young as a man; hardly three-and-twenty' (111) – the spoilt only child of a widowed mother. Such youth makes it easy and probable for him to reappear, changed into the disillusioned Mr Donne of Chapter xxiii, where the change is effectively and economically suggested, through Ruth's reaction:

He was changed, she knew not how. In fact, the expression, which had been only occasional formerly, when his worst self predominated, had become permanent. He looked restless and dissatisfied. But he was very handsome still. (xxiii)

He is kept in the reader's mind, through his long absences, by naturally-introduced remarks (such as the mention of his broken engagement) until his last appearance of all, which has a superb mixture of poignancy and brutal realism. Recognizing Ruth as his fever leaves him, he recalls their last blissful moment in the Wales of years past:

'Where are the water-lilies? Where are the lilies in her hair?'
(xxxv)

But his last words of her, after seeing her body laid out for burial, admitting to Benson his part in her life, and being turned out of the house, bring him firmly back to his nature:

'I have done my duty, and will get out of this abominable place as soon as I can. I wish my last remembrance of my beautiful Ruth was not mixed up with all these people.' (xxxvi)

It is the bitter antithesis of romance, and of the Lady of Shalott's epitaph from Lancelot:

'She hath a lovely face
God in his mercy lend her grace
The Lady of Shalott.'

Although it is rarely possible to discuss a writer's content and his art and technique without considering the language he uses, it is all too easy in Elizabeth Gaskell's case to underestimate or even wholly ignore the power and efficiency of her style. It is so simple, lucid, and candid that one often registers it only in its effects, of tone, or mood, or attitude. It is as close as possible to a private account given by one person to another. It has lost the occasional impulses to explain itself that produced little passages of instruction, or the occasional self-consciousness that made her explain herself or her own language in *Mary Barton*. It is again easier to define by what it is *not*: it has no elaborate sentence structure, no difficult or erudite vocabulary, very few changes of register, very little imagery, and that of the plainest. It is naïve in the best sense, and Wordsworthian in that it is, as he claimed himself in the Preface to the *Lyrical Ballads*, 'the very language of men'. This no more robs her of power and range than it does

D

Wordsworth. Examples and analyses of her range in dialogue and description have already been examined, when discussing the purposes which they served; but one area in which *Ruth* makes a notable advance on *Mary Barton* is in description of nature, scenery and the weather. Here as everywhere, Elizabeth Gaskell's power is that of accuracy and fidelity, not merely to appearance, but to the total sensuous response. She can tackle both the grand and the modest. Examples of the former have been given in discussion of the sense of place and in the climaxes of the novel. But it would be easy and unfair to underestimate Elizabeth Gaskell's power with the wholly unassuming:

> It was a beautiful day; the sky of that intense quivering blue, which seemed as though you could look through it for ever, yet not reach the black, infinite space which is suggested as lying beyond. Now and then, a thin, torn, vaporous cloud floated slowly within the vaulted depth; but the soft air that gently wafted it was not perceptible among the leaves on the trees, which did not even tremble. Ruth sat at her work in the shadow formed by the old grey garden wall; Miss Benson and Sally — the one in the parlour window-seat mending stockings, the other hard at work in her kitchen — were both within talking distance, for it was weather for open doors and windows; but none of the three kept up any continued conversation; and in the intervals Ruth kept up a low brooding song, such as she remembered her mother singing long ago. Now and then she stopped to look at Leonard, who was labouring away with vehement energy at digging over a small plot of ground, where he meant to prick out some celery plants that had been given to him. Ruth's heart warmed at the earnest, spirited way in which he thrust his large spade deep down into the brown soil, his ruddy face glowing, his curly hair wet with the exertion. (x x v)

Few details here are unusual (only perhaps the 'black infinite space'), the details are homely, the language not beyond a child. Yet one would call the total effect pre-Raphaelite were it not that its effects are much more than visual, that movement is in the essence, and that so much of it draws on senses other than sight; warmth breathes through the whole, Ruth sings, Leonard's 'curly hair wet with exertion' is tactile, while one cannot think of celery without recalling its smell.

So far discussion has concentrated on the strengths of Elizabeth Gaskell's technique and her positive achievements, but it was originally admitted that there were problems in *Ruth*. Many of these problems and the ways in which Elizabeth Gaskell copes with them have been dealt with, especially those springing from the nature of the subject and the material she has chosen: they do not entirely suit her, or give full scope to her powers. These are the faults of one still not at the peak of her powers. There are occasional troubles with her style, both in the author's narrative and in speech. These occur where Elizabeth Gaskell feels impelled to make generalizations about her moral purpose, or about religion. Here she becomes either over-simple or slightly rhetorical, or an uneasy mixture of both. Such passages are not frequent, and occur least in the later stages of the novel, most frequently when the greatest number of moral points have to be dealt with, when Benson and Faith first undertake to care for Ruth. Then Benson's own language exemplifies these qualities:

> It is better not to expect or calculate consequences. The longer I live the more fully I see that. Let us try simply to do right actions, without thinking of the feelings they are to call out in others. We know that no holy or self-denying effort can fall to the ground vain and useless; but the sweep of eternity is large, and God alone knows when the effect is to be produced. We are trying to do right now, and to feel right; don't let us perplex ourselves with endeavouring to map out how she should feel, or how she should show her feelings. (XII)

Until the final sentence, which, suddenly becoming concrete, becomes equally homely and vivid, the language here is trite and vague. Author's narratives can lapse in the same way:

> . . . she dreamt that the innocent babe that lay by her side in soft ruddy slumber, had started up into man's growth, and, instead of a pure and noble being whom she had prayed to present as her child to 'Our Father in heaven', he was a repetition of his father; and, like him, lured some maiden (who in her dream seemed strangely like herself, only more utterly sad and desolate even than she) into sin, and left her there to even a worse fate than that of suicide. (x v)

Though one does not doubt her sincerity or the honesty of her purpose, Elizabeth Gaskell has not the stylistic equipment for such heightening or rhetoric. After this, she never tries to be Dickens again, and rises, as will be seen in *Sylvia's Lovers*, to her great, even her visionary, moments in her own absolutely original way.

It would be fair to say that the sum of the parts of *Ruth* is greater than the whole. It is perhaps Elizabeth Gaskell's least read work; those who do read it may well share Charles Kingsley's reaction:

> read only a little (though of course I know the story) of the book, for the same reason that I cannot read 'Uncle Tom's Cabin' or 'Othello', or 'The Bride of Lammermoor' – it is too painfully good, as I found before I had read half a volume.

It created the greatest stir in its day, for its subject; it has had great influence on and opened up great opportunities for the novel that followed it, and contains some of her greatest and never-repeated writing. It marks the end of her probation in the novel. After it she never writes again for a social cause – even though *North and South* is based upon the same social problems as *Mary Barton* – and after it she writes as a fully professional creator, with her own way, in full possession of her own powers.

3

North and South

'The good end happily and the bad end unhappily: that is what fiction means,' said Wilde's Miss Prism. The idea behind Miss Prism's remark is of course that of 'poetic justice', and also includes its antithesis, the idea of the conventional 'sad' ending, like the death of Richardson's Clarissa, or of Dickens's Little Nell. She was behind the times; forty-four years earlier Elizabeth Gaskell struck the death-blow at this convention of the novel, with *North and South*. Despite the superficial fact that a small part of *North and South* seems to adhere to this view in the shape of the novel, the vital and original parts are those that, while not merely documenting life, do represent man's experience as difficult and recalcitrant material, for which any neat or obvious moral or social pattern, with obvious moral or social lessons to be drawn, or solutions to its difficulties, are both hard to find and difficult to achieve. When one has said that the heroine Margaret Hale eventually marries the man she eventually loves, John Thornton, one has said virtually all that conforms to the usual expectations of what will happen in such a story, to such a range of characters as Elizabeth Gaskell creates. Nowhere else is there any correlation between virtue, worth, strength of character and material worldly reward or happiness. Margaret's brother Frederick is never cleared of the charge of leading a mutiny. Even John Thornton him-self, man of honour, worth, and strength though he is, has more hardship than happiness, and his final success, in being put financially on his feet with Margaret's money, is good fortune rather than reward. It could be put more positively conversely: that every character of any value, who is capable of suffering, suffers, from chance, or economic pressure, or physical sickness and death, or the misfortunes of loved ones. Virtually the only exception is Margaret's cousin Edith, happily married to her Captain Lennox at Corfu, who, after her wedding in the first chapter, does not appear again until the end, though news of her, and letters, recur like a shining thread in the dark rich pattern of the story proper.

Elizabeth Gaskell has never been afraid of death in her novels. In *North and South* there are more deaths than in any of her other four – a feature of the story that has always brought protests from readers.[1] Margaret's mother dies, then Bessy Higgins, her lungs ruined by the dusty air of a carding shop, then the desperate weaver Boucher (by killing himself), then Mrs Boucher, then Mr Hale, and finally Mr Bell, Margaret's guardian: it is a weighty as well as lengthy list, since most are important and valued characters, and none of them, except Mr Bell, old. The excellent ways in which she handles the topic will be dealt with in due course, and her reasons for it. But it must be noted here as one of the most striking features of this very striking and original work. Equally striking is the extent of characters' helplessness in the grip of economic necessity, money and its want, the causes of which are not only immediate and personal, like the crisis of faith which compels Mr Hale to give up his living as a Church of England clergyman, but much wider, like the recession in the international cotton trade which ruins Mr Thornton, or the slow insidious decay of the agricultural system which rots the idyllic life of New Forest Helstone.

Elizabeth Gaskell has never had a wider range than in this novel: more characters than ever before, drawn from all classes from just below the aristocracy downwards, of all shades of political and religious belief, experiencing all the conceivable likely crises of human existence, in London society, the rural south of England and the industrial North Midlands. All are in the grip of this very severe fate, which seems as far as possible from being the author manoeuvring events, rather the inevitable outcomes of personality, or of economic pressure, or of the operation of an extra-human agency before which the individual is helpless. There are no villains and no heroes, apart

[1] She herself commented with some humour that 'a better title than *North and South* would have been "Death and Variations". There are five deaths, each beautifully suited to the character of the individual' (letter to Charles Dickens, 17 December 1854).

from Margaret herself, whose heroism is as much that of her place in events as a matter of personal qualities. All characters are mortal and fallible, compounded of mixtures of deficiencies, blindnesses and weaknesses with good or useful qualities.

Yet such a summary of some of the undoubtedly most striking and original features of *North and South* in no way adequately suggests either its full flavour or Elizabeth Gaskell's purposes. *North and South*, though a hard and disconcerting work, is not a gloomy one. It is harder than *Ruth* in its view of life, and even more disconcerting. It shares with *Ruth* the great power to recognize and recreate the sources of joy – ranging from extreme delight to small sensuous pleasures – which is one of its author's greatest gifts; and it has also a source of vigour, if not of joy, rising from its concern with courage, both physical and moral. Almost every event is in some way a study of an individual being put to the test, whether it is as mundane and minor as when Margaret is left to organize all the practical details of moving house from Helstone to Milton, or as apparently great as when she throws herself in front of Thornton to defend him from the mob of strikers. Fairly early in the novel (xv), an exchange between Margaret and Mrs Thornton stands out for the emphasis it places on bravery. Milton, says Mrs Thornton, 'is not a place for cowards . . . if you live in Milton, you must learn to have a brave heart'. Margaret's reply plainly thinks only of physical courage (her courage in other matters, moral and mental, is already proven), 'I do not know whether I am brave or not until I am tried', and anticipates her defence of Thornton in the riot. Along with Bessy's speculation 'I wonder how she'll sin', it points forward also to her other great test – the one she fails – when she denies having been at the station with her brother Frederick, too frightened to stand on the truth when Frederick's life may be at stake. Tests of courage – of physical bravery, of moral choice, of physical or mental endurance – are put before every character over and over again. They are faced in all sorts of ways; the failures are those who cannot rise to them. We are moved to admire both Bessy Higgins's acceptance of death, and Mrs Thornton's noble gesture when, preparing to accept Margaret as a daughter-in-law, she begins to pick out her own initials worked on the household linen to replace them with her son's; we are even required to recognize the degree of courage of the man whose despair leads him to suicide, Boucher, who drowns himself in the few inches' depth of a polluted dye-stained stream: 'he was a determined chap. He lay with his face downwards. He was sick enough of living, choose what cause he had for it' (xxxvi). The only characters rejected are those who are so feeble as to avoid all challenges, and these are very few, the only one of note being Fanny, Thornton's sister. Elizabeth Gaskell presents so many different kinds of courage, and so many different kinds of adequate response, with nothing schematized or mechanical in the rendering, that the emphasis on fortitude becomes more a matter of the total tone and view of life of the novel, than a theme.

This is an almost non-Christian attitude operating alongside the Christian ethos of the novel. Such an attitude, though present in English literature from Old English heroic poetry onwards, also traditionally characterizes the dogged north-country Lancashire and Yorkshire breed to which Elizabeth Gaskell herself belongs. It looms even larger in *Sylvia's Lovers*, owes nothing to the novel of civilized or cultured society, and reappears with tremendous strength in the novels of Hardy, epitomized in Michael Henchard's response to misfortune – 'I am to suffer, I perceive' — and is at the root of the kind of admiration called up by Hardy's characters. It explains the unwilling admiring way we regard Henchard even when he is being ridiculous, making his own greeting to the king, in his frayed and threadbare formal clothes 'waving the Union Jack to and fro with his left hand, while he blandly held out his right to the Illustrious Personage' (xxxvii). We admire Eustacia Vye in *The Return of the Native* for defying her circumstances – even when doing wrong in meeting Wildeve – at the same time as we admire her wronged husband Clym Yeobright for grappling with his blindness and becoming a furze-cutter to keep his self-respect.

Such a mood will not make a light-hearted work, but it will certainly not produce a depressing one; it is such a mood that prevents *North and South*, for all its sombre story, from being so.

As with her first novel, *Mary Barton*, the reader feels that Elizabeth Gaskell is not creating a 'world' – as Dickens does, whose characters are stamped with his own personality; or as Thackeray does, where all the happenings are tinctured by his view of life – but rather that she is rendering the substance and texture of actual life, in all its complexity and detail, with the absolute minimum of selection or distortion. Her authorial control of her material is the more excellent for being so unobtrusive.

She shapes her material in ways that are more varied than she has done before, because her purposes and the themes are greater in number and more complex. *North and South* is a novel of conflicts; public ones, like *Mary Barton's*; conflicts of the individual and society, and of man and his beliefs, like *Ruth's*; and even more pervasive here, of individual men and women at odds with one another, both deliberately and involuntarily, in personal relationships, even with those closest and dearest to them. *North and South* resembles *Mary Barton* in the obvious way, that it deals with the same conflict of 'masters and men', of mill-owners and mill-workers, in the same place, Manchester (here disguised as Milton Northern), the setting for thirty-nine of the novel's fifty-two chapters. The same types of characters reappear again in the oppressed mill-workers who strike for the wages to which they feel entitled, but which the owners, owing to recessions in trade, cannot pay. There is no repetition however; the Higginses and the Bouchers here are completely and distinctly unlike the Bartons, the Wilsons and the Davenports. They are opposed in this much fuller delineation of Manchester by John Thornton and his fellow mill-owners, who counterbalance the workers far more evenly than did Carson and his colleagues in *Mary Barton*. The owners' views are as cogent and pertinent as the workers', and as fully set forth, while their attitudes to each other, and the nature of both their conflict and their mutual misunderstandings, is more deeply revealed. It is not just to say that whereas *Mary Barton* presented the conflict from the point of view of the workers, *North and South* presents it from that of the employers. To do so is to over-simplify, and to be misled by Thornton's dual role, as representative master, and as the lover of Margaret. Margaret and Higgins between them are the great exposers of the sources of strife. This conflict is rendered both in more detail, and in more general terms, than in *Mary Barton*. Milton Northern at an unspecified date, in *North and South*, is not the same as the Manchester of the Chartist Petition in *Mary Barton*, although it uses many of the same kinds of incident, and similar material. A change in the author's purpose is clearly revealed. She is more concerned now with bringing out the universal human issues, of conflicts of groups and pressures of society within itself, and pressures upon the individuals who compose it.

Although Elizabeth Gaskell's social concern is clearly evident here, she is now no longer writing with a social purpose as her primary explicit motive. Margaret moves in both of the two Manchester

worlds, as the outsider who does not fully understand either of them.
She brings to the action the other worlds of London and of Helstone,
of both of which she partakes. Yet she is alien to London, and,
though she regrets, longs for, and idealizes Helstone, does not fully
understand that either. So a complex situation is set up, whereby
Margaret reveals, responds to and interprets (not always consciously)
for the reader the societies in which she moves; while these societies
themselves form a setting for Margaret's progress to maturity and
wisdom, marking her development as Fordham, Wales, and Eccleston did Ruth's. Thus in this novel for the first time the influence of
the Jane Austen type of novel is clearly seen in its theme, with
Elizabeth Gaskell employing a central heroine as a narrative medium.
Margaret, handsome and clever like Jane Austen's Emma, is the
chief means whereby her author shapes and interprets the action,
which in its turn shapes Margaret and moulds her personality.
Elizabeth Gaskell still regards her material with a sympathetic eye,
more concerned with giving full understanding than with passing
judgement, whether on social issues, or individual characters, but she
has greatly advanced in the means whereby she does so. Margaret is
the chief of these. The explanation in *Mary Barton*, of mill-workers'
positions and motives, which were expounded to the reader by the
author herself, are now wrought in with the action, when Higgins
explains them to Margaret, in dialogues such as this:

> 'My lass,' said he, 'yo're but a young wench, but don't yo' think
> I can keep three people – that's Bessy, and Mary, and me – on
> sixteen shillings a week? Dun yo' think it's for mysel' I'm
> striking work at this time? It's just as much in the cause of
> others as yon soldier – only m'appen, the cause he dies for is
> just that of somebody he never clapped eyes on, nor heard on
> all his born days, while I take up John Boucher's cause, as
> lives next door but one, wi' a sickly wife, and eight childer,
> none of 'em factory age; and I don't take up his cause only,
> though he's a poor good-for-nought, as can only manage two
> looms at a time, but I take up th' cause of justice. Why are we
> to have less wage now, I ask, than two year ago?' (xvii)

The speaker's passion rises naturally and dramatically, from the urge
to convince the uninformed and doubting listener Margaret. Situated
as she is, she is equally the recipient of the employer's views, expressed

with comparable, though different passion, which she equally doubts:

'I maintain that despotism is the best kind of government [for the workers]; so that in the hours in which I come in contact with them I must necessarily be an autocrat. I will use my best discretion . . . to make wise laws and come to just decisions which work for my own good in the first instance – for theirs in the second; but I will neither be forced to give my reasons, nor flinch from what I have once declared to be my resolution . . . the time is not come for the hands to have any independent action during business hours . . . And I say the masters would be trenching on the independence of their hands, in a way that I, for one, should not feel justified in doing, if we interfered too much with the life they lead out of the mills. Because they labour ten hours a day for us, I do not see that we have any right to impose leading-strings on them for the rest of their time.' (xv)

Margaret is not however the single consciousness, used in the novel to the exclusion of all others, that Jane Austen's Emma virtually is. Elizabeth Gaskell never uses this method; it would be crippling for her to do so. Her habit has been, and continues to be, to enter into and explain the nature and motives of any of her characters as need requires. Margaret's progress to maturity and wisdom is one theme; Thornton's parallel progress is another. Elizabeth Gaskell therefore treats him in the same way, though not so extensively.

The conflict between Margaret and Thornton is as central as the social conflict. Its working out and its resolution is the form of the work, which ends when their opposition ends, with Margaret purged of her social prejudices and her ignorance, and Thornton purged of his over-arrogant independence. Alongside these two central oppositions are others that affect every character, and cover every aspect of life. Though every family group in the novel is united within itself by mutual affection, every family is at odds with itself. The novel proper opens with Mr Hale's personal dilemma, in being compelled by his conscience to withdraw from his ministry in the Church of England, which in turn reveals the hopeless opposition of himself and even his dearly loved and loving wife. Dixon, Mrs Hale's maid, the other permanent member of the household, is divided from Mr Hale by her possessive devotion to his wife, whom she sees always as the beautiful Miss Beresford who threw herself away upon the humble clergyman, and whose youthful glories she can never forget. In the Thornton family Mrs Thornton despises her ineffectual daughter Fanny, yet even in her powerful love for her powerful son, cannot help hurting him. She can make the effort to yield her place to Margaret when she thinks Thornton will marry her, but cannot comfort him when he is rejected:

> 'Mother!' said he hurriedly, 'I cannot hear a word against her. Spare me – spare me! I am very weak in my sore heart; – I love her yet; I love her more than ever.'
>
> 'And I hate her,' said Mrs Thornton in a low fierce voice. 'I tried not to hate her, when she stood between you and me, because – I said to myself – she will make him happy; and I would give my heart's blood to do that. But now I hate her for your misery's sake.' (xxvi)

The Higgins family also has its hopeless oppositions. Higgins cannot help distressing his dying daughter, by undermining her pathetic over-emotional faith which clings to the apocalyptic and visionary comforts of the Revelation of St John – 'leave a' this talk about religion alone, an' set to work on what yo' see and know' (xi).

Elizabeth Gaskell, generous and gentle though she always is in her own voice, is yet exceptionally tough in her view of life. Though she asks the reader for honesty and compassion for all her characters, she never distorts those characters themselves, or manœuvres their fates, out of any sense of pity. She is at the opposite extreme from sentimentality; her verisimilitude can even seem harsh. The dying Mrs Hale begs the only woman she knows, Mrs Thornton, to be a kind friend to Margaret. But there is no weakening or softening of Mrs Thornton's position. She promises neither kindness nor affection, only what she honestly can:

> '. . . in any difficulty in which Miss Hale . . . comes to me for help, I will help her with every power I have, as if she were my own daughter. I also promise that if ever I see her doing what I think is wrong . . . such wrong not touching me or mine, in which case I might be supposed to have an interested motive – I will tell her of it, faithfully and plainly, as I should wish my own daughter to be told.' (xxx)

Most of the conflicts in the novel are, like this, unresolvable. Just as in *Mary Barton* she saw her duty to pose the problem honestly, but not to provide the answer, if she saw no practicable answer, so here she goes further, presenting problems that are not even reducible to questions. She sees her action in relation not only to time, but to eternity. The novel constantly pushes up against religious belief, though it poses no questions of doctrine, and has no theology. Elizabeth Gaskell is not concerned with doctrine or theology, only with how such beliefs affect human life and human nature. Bessy's visionary 'Methodistic' (as her father calls it) Christianity offers her an escape from her present suffering, but repels Higgins because it is no help to him in the problem besetting him, as the man who cares for the troubles of his fellow-men, and what he can do about them. When faced with her death, his creed fails him:

> 'If salvation, and life to come, and what not, was true – not in men's words, but in men's heart's core – dun yo' think they'd din us wi' it as they do wi' political economy? . . . Think o' her lying theere, after the life hoo's led; and I think how yo'd deny the one sole comfort left – that there is a God, and he set her life. I dunnot believe she'll ever live again . . . I dunnot believe in any other life than this, in which she dreed such trouble, and had such never-ending care; and I cannot bear to think it were all a set o' chances, that might ha' been altered wi' a breath o' wind.' (xxviii)

The opening episode therefore, in which Mr Hale finds himself unable to acknowledge the authority of the Church of England, or to make his declaration of conformity to the Liturgy, is quite intelligible and acceptable, despite many readers' uneasiness because he never defines the nature of his doubts. The nature of his doubt is not germane to the novel; the state itself of doubting is. In any case, it would be both misleading in an opening section to give the reader the notion that argument was to be the tendency of the novel, and inappropriate for either Margaret or her mother to enter into doctrinal debate. Even the exiled brother Frederick in becoming a Roman Catholic is linked in with the action in this respect, by being 'himself inclined to give up the form of religion into which he had become baptized, only that his opinions were tending in exactly the opposite direction to those of his father' (xx).

To embody argument in this way in action and character is artistically and dramatically more effective than to present it through the author's voice, but in this case has an adverse effect on the tone and mood of the whole. Where so many doubts and differences are expressed, not counteracted by any positive statements, uncertainty and despondency predominate over faith. One is sure that Elizabeth Gaskell herself shares the confidence of those of her speakers who believe in a divine order, in the prospect of improvement on earth, and reunion after death in heaven, but the positives, though understood, are not prominent enough to dispel the helpless melancholy of much of the work.

She does much to relieve the sadness with the material available to her, of humour in personal relations, of cheering incidents, and by her always happy response to weather, natural scenery, and sensuous delight in the small accessories of daily living. Yet whereas her next novel, *Sylvia's Lovers*, is a novel composed uncompromisingly of unhappy events leading to personal tragedy, while *North and South* leads to eventual fulfilment, *Sylvia's Lovers* is shot through with passionate commitment to life, and full-blooded response to it, while *North and South* is a long succession of deadly and enervating distresses. Her range of emotions also contributes to the mood of the whole. They are both more complex and more varied than before, but lean more to the anxious and distressing than the joyful, arising more from states of helplessness and suspense than from opportunities for action. She distributes her time and space equally between the strife of the workers, and the personal conflict of Thornton and Margaret. The new and original ground here is in the analysis of the lovers, nearly all of which comes after Thornton proposes to Margaret (XXIV), spurred on to believe that she loves him because she has protected him from the rioters. He is wrong, and rejected. Thereafter he suffers under his doubts of her honesty when he mistakes her brother Frederick for her lover, whom she denies meeting; while her love for him grows gradually at the same time as she suffers from knowing that he misjudges her, thinks that she has lost his regard, and never has the chance to explain. Alongside this personal relationship each has to endure other distresses, fundamentally more serious than those of thwarted affection. Thornton sees the ruin of the prosperity he has so painfully built up from penury, and becomes bankrupt; while Margaret faces the loss, one after another, of all the supports and objects of affection in her life.

Elizabeth Gaskell's mood and emotional impulses are clearly moving her away from the vigour and delight of the early works, which throbbed vigorously even in *Ruth*, towards the deeper, sterner achievement of *Sylvia's Lovers*, even while she is still working with the familiar subject matter of *Mary Barton*, *Ruth* and *Cranford*.

The sternest and perhaps the most intractable subject any writer can engage upon is, probably, death. Elizabeth Gaskell has never shirked it. Even in *Cranford*, whose gentle pace and nostalgic mood might suggest its evasion, she introduces both the slowly dying invalid Miss Brown and the sudden death of her father, Captain Brown, in the railway accident, and the death of Miss Deborah Jenkyns. Even though the need to provide exciting and unusual incidents in each episode could have been why they were introduced, the handling and the attitudes reveal rather that, as in *Mary Barton*, they are seen as necessary and inescapable contingencies of even the quietest lives and most decorous communities. Moreover even in sketches of the gentle unmomentous Cranford, Elizabeth Gaskell will not permit time to stand still, nor permit us to forget that *tempora mutantur: nos et mutamur in illis*. It moves equally for all characters, who are all subject to its rule, changing their lives, and their natures, and moving them perceptibly towards their end. She is the first writer to use time and change thus consistently. Before her, Charlotte Brontë in *Shirley* (1849) had shown all characters in its grip, but had moved forward to prophecy – as in the long passage foretelling Jessie Yorke's death – and had had characters who surveyed their own lives as a terminating span, as in Caroline Helstone's painful cry 'What am I to do to fill the interval of time which spreads between me and the grave?' (*Shirley*, x). Yet how to convey the unobtrusive but unchanging pace of time through day after day is Elizabeth Gaskell's own discovery. Her sense of time passing intensifies in *North and South*, to a degree that perhaps seems almost excessive for the purposes of the story. While one realizes that, practically, all the deaths in some way illuminate themes, or are necessary to further Margaret's development, or, simply, the plot, they even more reveal Elizabeth Gaskell's sense of how time must operate within the novel, and how it can be handled. The general assumption of novelists hitherto that some kinds of characters can stand still, minor characters being fixed and unchanging, and heroes and heroines, though maturing, incapable of ageing and dying; that death may conveniently dispose of an inconvenient life (like that of Mrs Churchill in Jane Austen's *Emma*) but that no secondary character can experience all the power and dignities of death – all these assumptions give way; and the whole response to the novel changes. When Scott, for instance, faces Effie Deans with the threat of execution, it remains no more than a threat, because the reader confides, rightly, in the conventions that will make Jeannie save her. By the mid-nineteenth century one can trust no more to such conventions. Death is no longer merely a peril and a threat, it is a dreadful promise. Bessy Higgins can no more be saved from dying from the accumulation of dust and fluff in her lungs, by any kindness of Margaret's, or any pity from her author, than could her equivalent in life. And though her death may be accounted for as an example of the social consequences of factory conditions, and irresponsible employers, Mrs Hale's death cannot be, yet is equally inexorable and inescapable, from (presumably) cancer, with no cause whatever in human agency. With such deaths as these preceding, one feels no sense of contrivance when Mr Hale dies suddenly on his visit to Oxford, of heart failure. Mrs Gaskell recognizes the connection between physical and mental character here, even though the death is rightly a shock to the reader as much as to Margaret, and even though we recognize Mr Bell's sound common sense – 'you spare thin men are always tempting and always cheating Death! It's the stout, florid fellows like me, that always go off first' (XLI) – nevertheless the reader sees by hindsight that such mental diffidence as Mr Hale's may well accord with a weak physique. Mr Bell's comment prepares us for his own death also. The result is that, while, when the reader looks back on the novel after shutting it, there may seem an unconscionable amount of dying, in the actual experience of reading, deaths come in with the inescapable movement of felt life, not the evident contrivance of art.

Death is perhaps the topic on which the contrasts between the metropolitan and the provincial novelists are most striking. Elizabeth Gaskell's handling and attitudes are taken up and explored with, if not increasing, yet ever-varied power. Trollope, like her apparently gentle as well as unassumingly tough, recognizes mortality. Though more sparing of death, he recognizes it, and the threat of it, as part of life. *Barchester Towers* opens with the death of the bishop, and concludes with the consequences of the death of the dean. The delineation of how Archdeacon Grantly, the bishop's son, thinks and behaves is one of the finest moments in all of Trollope. Dr Grantly hopes to take his father's place, and will do so if the bishop dies before the present government goes out of office, in five days. Grantly is not a sympathetic character, the bishop has been a lovable one; yet the

just balance of sympathy is perfectly held, and the reader is forbidden
to sentimentalize over the bishop, or dislike the archdeacon, musing
by his father's bedside, more than is just:

> He was already over fifty, and there was little chance that his
> friends who were now leaving office would soon return to it. No
> probable prime minister but he who was now in, he who was so
> soon to be out, would think of making a bishop of Dr Grantly.
> Thus he thought long and sadly, in deep silence, and then he
> gazed at that still living face, and then at last dared to ask him-
> self whether he really longed for his father's death.
>
> The effort was a salutary one, and the question answered
> in a moment. The proud, wishful, worldly man, sank on his
> knees by the bedside, and taking the bishop's hand within his
> own prayed eagerly that his sins might be forgiven him. (*Bar-
> chester Towers*, 1)

Equally just is the way Trollope handles Grantly when, a few
moments later, the bishop is dead:

> He had brought himself to pray for his father's life, but now
> that that life was done, minutes were too precious to be lost. It
> was now useless to dally with the fact of the bishop's death –
> useless to lose perhaps everything for the pretence of a foolish
> sentiment. (*ibid.*)

The fact of the bishop's death is necessary to the plot: the way in
which Trollope presents it is far more subtle than mere plot can
demand. The same is true of the dean's death. No personal feelings
are involved for so minor a character, but Trollope weaves it in with
the numberless goings-on of life, in this case the finest-wrought
episode of the novel, the magnificent Ullathorne Sports:

> The bishop of Barchester said grace over the well-spread
> board in the Ullathorne dining-room; and while he did so the
> last breath was flying from the dean of Barchester as he lay in
> his sick-room in the deanery. When the bishop of Barchester
> raised the first glass of champagne to his lips, the deanship
> of Barchester was a good thing in the gift of the prime minister.
>   (XXXVIII)

This is far from being, as it would be in Dickens, a heavily cynical
comment on man's inhumanity to man, it is an honest statement of

the way of the world. Trollope is equally good and equally unobtrusive about the fear of death, which lurks below the surface of all
the quarrels between Mrs Gresham and the Doctor himself in *Dr
Thorne*.

George Eliot's handling of death tends more to the conventional
and is less secure in its tone but, were it not for this ever-growing
sense of death in the midst of life in the novel in general, Hetty, in
Adam Bede, would be a far less poignant figure. Though George
Eliot may be soft-hearted enough to save her from the extreme
penalty for child-murder (and though the modern reader may think
transportation but little mitigation of it), she handles Hetty's own
death-wish with all the simplicity of complete assurance, in her
magnificent confession to Dinah of how she came to desert her baby:

> 'I didn't kill it – I didn't kill it myself. I put it down there and
> covered it up, and when I came back it was gone. . . . It was
> because I was so very miserable, Dinah. . . . I didn't know where
> to go . . . and I tried to kill myself before, and I couldn't. Oh,
> I tried so to drown myself in the pool, and I couldn't.' (xlv)

By contrast her earlier rendering in authorial narrative is much less
poised:

> She sits down on the grassy bank, against the stooping stem of
> the great oak that hangs over the dark pool. She has thought of
> this pool often in the nights of the month that has just gone by,
> and now at last she is come to see it. She clasps her hands round
> her knees and leans forward, and looks earnestly at it, as if trying
> to guess what sort of bed it would make for her young round
> limbs.
> No, she has not courage to jump into that cold watery bed.
>   (xxxv)

Its *faux-naif* attitude leads to false diction and unnecessarily emotional
vocabulary, to the use of the present tense, of the verb form 'she is
come', the emotive adjectives of 'young round limbs' and the cliché
'cold watery bed'. Though very unlike Dickens, George Eliot is
plainly closer here to him than to either Trollope or Elizabeth
Gaskell.

In the whole of this episode of Hetty's dreadful journey to Windsor,
fine though it is, she is writing in the established way, which makes

time move slower in times of great agony or intensity, which creates the intensity by the amount of space and emphasis it receives. For Elizabeth Gaskell, and those like her, 'time and the hour runs through the roughest day'. The point links with her handling of great moments in general, but also reveals a way of seeing life in terms of the novel. Both attitudes justify themselves by the excellence of their results, but Elizabeth Gaskell's reveals a new and fruitful presentation of life within the bounds of a narrative. It links directly with her discovery that the traditional machinery of plot and sub-plot, and interweaving of them, is not for her; that she is better served by a flow of interwoven incidents, 'the numberless goings-on of life'. The substance out of which, in *North and South*, she makes her plot, like her material, is a mixture of what she has tried and knows, with what is new. The new is the whole story and events concerning Frederick, Margaret's brother, who, as a mutineer, faces hanging if he returns to England. His own personal story, of courage in resisting injustice, the failure to clear him of the charge, and his new life in Spain, is important only as it affects Margaret's story and the main themes of the novel. His secret visit to Milton, to see Mrs Hale before she dies, gives new zest when the action is flagging, and life and warmth to relieve gloom. When he is seen at the station leaving with Margaret, and he throws from the platform the man who recognizes him, he sets off the long mis-understanding between Thornton and Margaret, and puts her in the position of having to tell a lie for his sake. He directly affects the conclusion, for he draws Margaret together again with Henry Lennox, the lawyer who tries to clear his name, and so separates her even longer from Thornton. This plot however is a minor element in the whole, and a curious last survival of Elizabeth Gaskell depend-ing on conventional material of the stock kind for her novels.

Apart from Frederick and his doings, this work, like *Ruth*, is a series of events taking place in chronological sequence. Elizabeth Gaskell shows increasing power of shaping and proportioning her material, of varying its speed and intensity, and handling climaxes. She still adheres to her own methods, and is now confident of her skill in dispensing with great excitements or momentous events. Thematic importance, and significance for the person concerned, decide her climaxes rather than the intrinsic excitement of the event itself. In a summary of action Chapter xxxii sounds like a climax, when Margaret and Frederick are seen by Mr Thornton walking to the station, Frederick is recognized by the ne'er-do-well Leonards, throws him off the platform, and leaves on the train in the nick of time. In fact Elizabeth Gaskell deals with all this in four taut pages. Far more significant are the consequences, when Margaret has to face the police inspector (xxxiv), decide on the spot to deny all knowledge of the event, face the moral implications of her lie, and on top of this discover (xxxv) that Mr Thornton knows of it, and has protected her from the ordeal of a public inquest on how Leonards met his death. It is the self-realization in Margaret that is thematically vital here: first that she is not morally irreproachable – 'where was now her proud motto, "Fais ce que dois, advienne que pourra"?' (xxxvi); second that Mr Thornton's knowing of her failure is almost as dreadful to her as the fault itself:

> If she had but dared to bravely tell the truth as regarded herself, defying them to find out what she refused to tell concerning another, how light of heart she would now have felt! Not humbled before God, as having failed in trust towards Him; not degraded and debased in Mr Thornton's sight. She caught herself up at this with a miserable tremor; here was she classing his low opinion of her alongside with the displeasure of God.
>
> (xxxvi)

Elizabeth Gaskell feels and renders not only such crucial realizations, but also the full inescapable flow of life, with its interminglings and juxtapositions, just as she did in *Mary Barton*, but here on a much more extended scale. This crisis of self-realization in Margaret is interwoven with the additional anxiety of Frederick's having to wait in London two days longer than expected (in order to see the lawyer Lennox); the episode gives due weight and space to the funeral of Mrs Hale, and Margaret's efforts to help and comfort her father; so that the reader endures like Margaret a multiplicity of strains which, far from detracting from the shock of the inspector's call, intensify it. The author does not confine her attention only to Margaret, but deals in its place with Thornton's agony of mind as well, which has a parallel growth.

Her own previous work is her only model for her method, which is far more complex here than before. Under her hand the movement of the novel comes increasingly to reproduce the sense of the flow of life, slow or rapid, with time spent on dealing with it reproducing the actual sense of the passage of time, as well as the intensity of experience, the nuances of thought and feeling, and the trivia of life, that make up the whole. Such handling continues to evolve after her, developed variously by later writers. It produces ultimately the fine and elaborate detail of Henry James, and the stream of consciousness of James Joyce. It accounts for the increasing absence of big and dramatic isolable scenes in the work of George Eliot and Thomas Hardy. The high points of the novels become, increasingly, spiritual and emotional crises rather than exciting events, crises whose power is increasingly dependent on what leads towards them, and on apparently minor or even distracting attendant circumstances, whose consequences are as vital as the crises itself. In *Middlemarch*, to take an example, Dorothea's relationship with Casaubon drags on its way through small but increasing realizations that each has married the other for the wrong reasons, until they learn that Casaubon is under sentence of death. When the doctor, Lydgate, has left Casaubon, Dorothea comes to him,

> and might have represented a heaven-sent angel coming with the promise that the short hours remaining should yet be filled with that faithful love which clings the closer to a comprehended grief. His glance in reply to hers was so chill that she felt her timidity increased; yet she turned and passed her hand through his arm.
>
> Mr Casaubon kept his hands behind him and allowed her pliant arm to cling with difficulty against his rigid arm . . . it is in these acts called trivialities that the seeds of joy are forever wasted, until men and women look round with haggard faces at the devastation their own waste has made, and, say, the earth bears no harvest of sweetness – calling their denial knowledge.

Dorothea's reaction comes next like the final word, the culmination and climax, resting not in the event, but the spiritual realization:

> She was in the reaction of a rebellious anger stronger than any she had felt since her marriage. Instead of tears there came words: –
>
> 'What have I done – what am I – that he should treat me so? He never knows what is in my mind – he never cares. What is the use of anything I do? He wishes he had never married me.' . . . If he had drawn her towards him, she would never have

surveyed him – never have said, 'is he worth living for?' but
would have felt him simply as part of her own life. Now she
said bitterly, 'It is his fault, not mine' . . . In such a crisis as this,
some women begin to hate.

Yet we do not rest even here, for the scene continues:

She did hear the library door open, and slowly the light advanced
up the staircase without noise from the footsteps on the carpet.
When her husband stood opposite to her, she saw that his face
was more haggard. He started slightly on seeing her, and she
looked up at him beseechingly, without speaking.
    'Dorothea!' he said, with a gentle surprise in his tone. 'Were
you waiting for me?'
    'Yes, I did not like to disturb you.'
    'Come, my dear, come. You are young, and need not to
extend your life by watching.'
    When the kind quiet melancholy of that speech fell on
Dorothea's ears, she felt something like the thankfulness that
might well up in us if we had narrowly escaped hurting a lamed
creature. (*Middlemarch*, Book IV, XLII)

Even here, in the larger span, the relationship does not rest, for
Casaubon continues his hold over Dorothea's fortunes, by the disposi-
tions of his will, even after his death.
    Hardy's methods and effects are different, but show the same
movement away from dramatic climax in action, towards spiritual
culminations, realizations, and consequences. In *The Return of the
Native* one of the most crucial acts committed is Eustacia's, when,
because Wildeve is with her, she refuses to open the door to her
husband's mother, Mrs Yeobright. Clym Yeobright himself, in
exhausted sleep, does not hear his mother's knock. She goes away,
convinced that Clym has rejected her – 'Clym, how can he bear to
do it! He is at home; and yet he lets her shut the door against me!'
(*The Return of the Native*, Book Fourth, 'The Closed Door', VI).
However, Hardy has filled in all the reasons for the other characters'
acting as they did: Wildeve, naturally unwilling to be discovered, has
slipped out the back door; Eustacia has felt that 'it was possible
that her presence might not be desired by Clym and his mother at
this moment of their first meeting, or that it would be superfluous',
and has wandered about in the back garden. Such details of motive,

like those of Elizabeth Gaskell and George Eliot, rob Mrs Yeobright's situation of most of its dramatic impact, but, instead, while
creating compassionate understanding, enormously increase the sense
of the complexity of life, and create the almost intolerably painful
irony of arbitrary events. Like George Eliot's and Elizabeth
Gaskell's, the scene does not stop or rest on its climax, but drags on
through Mrs Yeobright's journey back, her meeting with the child
Johnny Nunsuch, her snake-bite, sickness and death. The repercus-
sions of all continue through the rest of the novel.

Since Elizabeth Gaskell works with less material than either
George Eliot or Hardy, she has more chance to exploit the effects of
variation in intensity, rather than of variety of subject. This determines her organization over the larger sweep of the whole. Changes
of mood within the novel are not artificially created by a change of
scene, or area of interest, but are such as seem to happen out of the
sheer nature of human experience, the motion of the human mind,
and the discrepancy between the human tongue and what it wishes
to convey. Such changes both intensify impressions, and relieve
them, by the contrasts produced, whether of essential difference, or
partial resemblance. They are always relevant to character or theme,
never merely arbitrary. Margaret, for instance, having learned from
the doctor that her mother is dying (xvi) goes out to recover from
the shock: disliking the prospect of 'a long walk through these streets,
before she came to the fields which she had planned to reach' (xvii),
she changes her mind and visits the Higginses, where she hears of the
coming strike; thus the new topic gives relief from her personal
misery, but when she attempts to cheer Bessy – 'you're only looking
on one side, and there is another and a brighter to be looked to' – her
own miseries get the painful jolt of unconsciously ironic comment:

> 'It's all well enough for yo' to say so, who have lived in pleasant
> green places all your life long, and never known want or care,
> or wickedness either, for that matter.' (xvii)

Elizabeth Gaskell makes no attempt to weigh one kind of trouble
against the other: the juxtaposition alone is sufficient. Other juxtapositions are wryly comic, such as the interruptions of Fanny's vapid
concerns into the powerful dialogues between Mrs Thornton and
her son. Or they can be naturally and profoundly true of the way
human nature works, a particularly fine instance being Frederick's
secret visit. Margaret has agreed to it only as her mother's dying wish,

and thought only of the danger to Frederick if he is possibly recognized (as he is) and arrested; but she experiences in it the unexpected comfort of sharing her troubles with one who has an equal part in them as a child of the same parents, and the delight of consanguinity and their shared childhood at Helstone:

> The brother and sister arranged the table together, saying little, but their hands touching, and their eyes speaking the natural language of expression, so intelligible to those of the same blood.
>
> (xxx)

Trouble can even produce comedy, when expression is inadequate or inept in comparison with what it wishes to convey. Such is Margaret's exchange with Dixon, when they learn that Mrs Hale's illness will be fatal. Mutual strain produces a near-quarrel, and a comic resolution. Dixon is angry that Margaret knows, recalls Mrs Hale's prosperous and enchanting youth, and contrasts mother and daughter, in words that express her feeling while falling amusingly short of her meaning:

> 'You'll never be like your mother for beauty – never; not if you live to be a hundred.'
> 'Mamma is very pretty still. Poor mamma!'
> 'Now don't ye set off [weeping] again, or I shall give way at last' (whimpering). 'Go out and take a walk, and come in something like. Many's the time I've longed to walk it off – the thought of what was the matter with her, and how it must all end.'
> 'Oh, Dixon!' said Margaret, 'how often I've been cross with you, not knowing what a terrible secret you had to bear!'
> 'Bless you, child. I like to see you showing a bit of spirit. It's the good old Beresford blood. Why, the last Sir John but two shot his steward down, there where he stood, for just telling him that he'd racked the tenants, and he'd racked the tenants till he could get no more money off them than he could get skin off a flint.' (xvi)

Few though the chances are for comic relief in *North and South*, and few the chances for happiness, 'cheerfulness keeps breaking in'. Elizabeth Gaskell has the wry ironic north-country palate of that other north-countrywoman Charlotte Brontë, as well as of the characters she creates. Amid the seriousness of the loom-smashing

on the moors, in *Shirley*, comes the rescue of the men who should
have brought them back, and Yorke's account of it:

> 'I said, "is there aught wrong anywhere?" – "Deed is there"
> somebody says, speaking out of the ground like. "What's to do?
> Be sharp and tell me," I ordered – "Nobbut four on us ligging
> in a ditch," says Joe, as quiet as could be. I tell'd 'em, more shame
> to 'em, and bid them get up and move on, or I'd lend them a
> lick o' the gig-whip; for my notion was, they were all fresh –
> "We'd ha' done that an hour sin'; but we're tied wi' a bit of
> band," says Joe.' (*Shirley*, 111)

Elizabeth Gaskell has the same sure hand with Lancashire idiom and
dialogue as Charlotte Brontë has with Yorkshire; the two share the
same power of saying the apparently obvious with the wry unexpected
twist, such as Higgins's aphoristic comments:

> 'Meddling twixt master and man is liker meddling 'twixt man
> and wife than aught else: it takes a deal o' wisdom for to do ony
> good.' (XXXVIII)

or

> 'I'm not one wi' two faces – one for my measter, and t'other
> for his back.' (XLI)

Having plunged into a wholly dialect work in *Mary Barton*, and
eschewed it entirely in *Ruth*, Elizabeth Gaskell returns in *North
and South* to a position apparently like the common one, of using
dialect for secondary characters. Yet, as for Charlotte Brontë and
for Hardy, dialect is a true language far from being a mere rendering
of accent for merely comic ends, or for subordination. Much of what
is most moving is put forth in the local speech, as well as what is most
powerful. As with Hardy also, one could make the statement that the
most impressive parts of the writing are the interior analyses of what
the major characters experience in their minds (rather than what they
say), and what the lesser characters actually speak of that belongs not
only to their own minds, but to those of all men. Elizabeth Gaskell's
dialect speakers are far from being the choric commentators on
human destiny that Hardy's become, yet they do tend to speak from
positions of greater extremity than others, on deeper subjects, with
more pith and point, and with almost poetic insight:

> 'I used to think once [says Bessy] that if I could have a day of
> doing nothing, to rest me – a day in some quiet place like that

yo' speak on – it would maybe set me up. But now I've had many days o' idleness, and I'm just as weary o' them as I was o' my work. Sometimes I'm so tired out I think I cannot enjoy heaven without a piece of rest first. I'm rather afeared o' going straight there without getting a good sleep in the grave to set me up.' (xiii)

This is the true language of feeling, devoid of sentimental intensifying from the writer, and looks forward to Hardy's more generalized method, in for instance, Mrs Cuxom's account to the neighbours of Susan Henchard's death in *The Mayor of Casterbridge*:

' "... there's four ounce pennies, the heaviest I could find, a-tied up in bits of linen for weights – two for my right eye and two for my left" [said the dying Susan] ... and Martha did it, and buried the ounce pennies in the garden. But if ye'll believe words, that man, Christopher Coney, went and dug 'em up, and spent 'em at the Three Mariners. "Faith," he said, "why should death rob life o' fourpence? Death's not of such good report that we should respect 'em to that extent," says he ... Well, poor soul; she's helpless to hinder that or anything now ... And all her shiny keys will be took from her, and her cupboards opened; and little things a' didn't wish seen, anybody will see; and her wishes and ways will all be as nothing!' (*The Mayor of Casterbridge*, xviii)

Elizabeth Gaskell is showing increased power with the language of her characters in general, and especially with local speakers. The degree of dialect varies not only between speakers, but in different contexts. Higgins is at his broadest, not only with his family (as one would expect) but when in his role as 'man' to Thornton as 'master':

'Stop a minute measter.' Then going up confidentially close, he said, 'Is th' young gentleman cleared? ... Master Frederick, they ca'ed him – her brother as was over here, yo' known.'
    'Over here!'
    'Aye, to be sure, at the missus's death. Yo' need na be feared of my telling; for Mary and me, we knowed it all along, only we held our peace, for we got it through Mary working in th' house.'
    'And he was over? It was her brother?'
    'Sure enough, and I reckoned yo' knowed it, or I'd never ha'

let on . . . I've maybe gotten them into mischief already, for they kept it very close. I nobbut wanted to know if they'd getten him clear.' (L)

His language here is much broader than when on his best behaviour with Mr Hale, for instance, after Bessy's death:

'I ax your pardon if I use wrong words; but what I mean by belief, just now, is a-thinking on sayings and maxims and promises made by folk yo' never saw, about the things and life yo' never saw, nor no one else. Now, yo' say these are true things and true sayings, and a true life. I just say, where's the proof?'

(XXVIII)

This unobtrusive power here will come to the fore in *Sylvia's Lovers*, which is certainly Elizabeth Gaskell's, and probably the English novel's, *tour de force* in the handling of non-standard speech.

North and South, like *Ruth*, uses geographical setting as an element of its organization. It does so with even greater complexity and subtlety, and with more daring. Here for the first time in a full-length novel Elizabeth Gaskell moves out of her north-western England native ground. The four places in which the action takes place are, in the order in which we see them, London, Helstone in the New Forest, Milton, and Oxford (which though only briefly visited, yet has its own importance). In order of importance, Milton must take first place, as most of the events take place there, but all the others have their power and purposes, as do even remoter regions only glanced at with reference to other characters – Spain, where Frederick lives, South America, and Scotland. Elizabeth Gaskell is using a wider area than in any of her other novels, with increased assurance and skill, yet without any need to develop a different attitude or methods from those she has already tried and proved. Helstone and Milton are both 'invented' in that they have neither the names nor all the attributes of actual places, and are therefore more representative than an actual southern English village, or actual Manchester, could be. They bear the same relationship to the actual that George Eliot's Middlemarch, Trollope's Barchester, or Hardy's Casterbridge do to their originals, giving the author the freedom to develop their significance and symbolic qualities, alongside the sense of reality of an actual place with which the reader can have some familiarity. London does not require the same handling, because it has in itself so many aspects that selection can be made without any sense of distortion.

Whereas in *Ruth* the settings were used once only, as Ruth passed through the phases of her life with which they were connected, in *North and South* the pattern is more elaborate, with a design of departures and returns, with the ending a balanced coming-together of the aspects of life that each place presents and explores. Over-simplifying severely, one could say that London revealed conventional upper-middle-class standards and behaviour; Helstone the natural life of the country and the old rural standards; Oxford the life of the mind – 'sitting still, and learning from the past, or shaping out the future by faithful work done in a prophetic spirit' (xl) as Mr Bell puts it; and Milton a new world still in the process of creating itself, full of the troubles of adolescence, but with the power to develop and grow which the others lack.

Around these centres Elizabeth Gaskell suggests a much wider world than she has done before, of places which exist, and affect life in the most retired or self-absorbed provincial places. Edith's letters from Corfu, where her husband is stationed, Frederick's new and strange life in Spain, Thornton's business connections on the continent, even the consciousness of Glasgow and the Scottish universities, as the rare and only possible education for a Milton manufacturer's scion, all render the work and the reader aware of the whole contemporary world. The idea is one that Elizabeth Gaskell could have absorbed from Charlotte Brontë's *Shirley*, with its rather different handling of half-Belgian characters, and the effect on the lives and fates of mill-owners of the political events of the Napoleonic period.

We meet Margaret first in London, in the comfort and ease of her aunt's house, a dependent without cares or responsibilities, at the opening of her adult life, a looker-on at her cousin Edith's wedding. Elizabeth Gaskell firmly sets down here the main considerations of her novel; aesthetic and sensuous qualities, the emotions, and worldly success and honour. They are all present in an amorphous condition, with no sense of their relative importance, or of their implications. She does justice to them all, recognizing the genuine family affections of the Shaws and the Lennoxes; the genuine delights of a life containing Indian shawls with their 'spicy Eastern smell' and 'their soft feel and brilliant colours' (1); and the pressures of personal ambition and the need for money, which make Henry Lennox, the rising lawyer, unwilling to yield to the attractions of the near-penniless Margaret. It takes its tone from the inhabitants we meet, their life and standards: they are all, though not unprincipled, partly enslaved to the comfortable and the worldly: Edith dislikes the idea of going to Corfu with her soldier husband:

> Yet had anyone come, with a fine house, and a fine estate, and a fine title to boot, Edith would still have clung to Captain Lennox while the temptation lasted; when it was over it is possible she might have had little qualms of ill-concealed regret that Captain Lennox could not have united in his person everything that was desirable. In this she was but her mother's child; who, after deliberately marrying General Shaw with no warmer feeling than respect for his character and establishment, was constantly, though quietly, bemoaning her hard lot in being united to one whom she could not love. (1)

The handling is done with immense tact and economy, since Elizabeth Gaskell has to indicate that this opening chapter is merely a preface to what is to happen elsewhere. She avoids superbly any suggestion that London could provide a norm from which to judge the rest, since she carefully reveals that there are no standards in *this* London; and Margaret, plainly the main character, is an outsider, whose own world is elsewhere. Indeed Elizabeth Gaskell employs London here as Thackeray employs the country at the opening of *Pendennis*, as the place which the hero has outgrown, and from which he sets off on his real career in life, as Pendennis, after his amorous fiasco with the ageing Irish actress Miss Fotheringhay, departs for the university and for London.

Elizabeth Gaskell's delicately neutral attitude to London in Chapter 1 contrasts sharply with the impression she creates when Margaret returns, three years later, a woman, wise, independent, wealthy, and desolately alone in the world, for whom the round of daily comforts, family affairs, trivial occupations and dinner-givings falls into insignificance beside the sterner standards of life in Milton. She can judge 'a shade or two of coarseness' in Edith's finding her 'an attraction to the house' because 'ever so many men will be glad to visit here next year for your sake' (XLVIII), and can find her own life in social work among the needy. It is a pity that Elizabeth Gaskell, cramped by the serial form in which *North and*

South was originally written,[2] was unable to develop the final London section as she obviously wished. Her intentions are clear, but she has not room enough for their execution, particularly that of its new aspect, which is as a neutral meeting-ground for the reconciling of the conflicts she has explored, and for the final coming-together of Margaret and Thornton in whom they are embodied.

The action proper opens at Helstone, the place Margaret thinks of as home. Her brief stay there, before she is ousted by Mr Hale's giving up his living and leaving the Church of England, renders its enchantment through the eyes of the enthusiastic and enchanted Margaret, and allows it both to exist in its own right, and to function as an extention of her nature. Because it does so, it can reveal and establish her connections and disunities with others. It is 'the place where Margaret grew to what she is', as Thornton says (11); Lennox is clearly seen as no possible husband for her because he is out of tune with the place; Thornton becomes so when he has visited it: roses from Helstone have their part in his proposal and acceptance. Barely five chapters though there are of this first Helstone (its revisiting is a different world) Elizabeth Gaskell establishes it as a point of reference and contrast on a number of levels. All are seen through Margaret's eyes, and accepted by the reader as valid even though at a later stage Margaret's mature eyes, and the passage of time, create a different scene, and a different judgement. Helstone thus contrasts in impressions with London, where reservations were presented by the author herself. Helstone is both realistic and idyllic. Elizabeth Gaskell presents sensuously and faithfully the physical details of the countryside, 'the broad upland, sunstreaked, cloud-shadowed' commons, the forest trees which were 'one dark full dusky green; the fern below them caught all the slanting sunbeams; the weather sultry and broodingly still' (11); and recreates equally faithfully the domestic minutiae of house and garden that she delights in. Her purely descriptive passages are brief and enchanting, and, while seeming to exist for their own sakes, always have a structured purpose. When Mr Lennox visits them, lunch ends in an *alfresco* dessert of pears gathered and eaten in the garden:

> Margaret made a plate for the pears out of a beetroot leaf, which threw up their brown-gold colour admirably. Mr Lennox

[2] It appeared in *Household Words*, which Dickens edited, from September 1854 to January 1855.

looked more at her than the pears; but her father, inclined to cull fastidiously the very zest and perfection of the hour he had stolen from his anxiety, chose daintily the ripest fruit, and sat down to enjoy it at his leisure. (111)

He continues to do so during the climax of the chapter, when Lennox proposes to Margaret and is refused. Both are disturbed and chagrined:

> It was well that having made the round of the garden, they came suddenly upon Mr Hale, whose whereabouts had been quite forgotten by them. He had not yet finished the pear, which he had delicately peeled in one long strip of silver-paper thinness, and which he was enjoying in a deliberate manner. (111)

Such passages, which are many, act by transference to give the reader the sense of near-unconscious delight of the characters who share them. They render all the complexity of human experience: we register here Mr Hale's rest from his hidden trouble (whose nature has not yet been revealed) and feel also how, whatever startling changes have taken place in Margaret and Henry Lennox, the life of the rest of creation goes on at its own unregarding pace. The method is powerful in the very opposite way from the 'romantic' novel, where, to take an extreme like *Wuthering Heights*, all creation and nature participates in, or is seen as an aspect of, the characters themselves. Hardy can develop such techniques to his own ends, which drive home for him the bitter indifference of the universe to humanity. Elizabeth Gaskell may be less powerful, but she is wiser, in accepting such things as contingencies which, simply neutral, may be comfort as well as torment.

During Margaret's stay in Milton, Helstone is recalled in contrast, by allusion and recollection. Bessy Higgins sees it in imagination from Margaret's descriptions, and connects it in her mind with the Heavenly Jerusalem of the Apocalypse. Thus Helstone becomes more remote and idealized, even though Margaret occasionally acknowledges its drawbacks, such as that Higgins would be unable to stand the hardship of field labour there.

Three years later (XLVI) Margaret goes back to Helstone, for a single day, with Mr Bell. Elizabeth Gaskell treats it with the same honest and minute fidelity, through Margaret's now mature vision. Helstone has changed, both to reveal the changes in Margaret that make her see it now with a wiser perception, and in itself, so that it

demonstrates its author's constant theme, the operation of time. The
new clergyman and his wife have altered the vicarage – deliberately,
by changing Mr Hale's study into a nursery, and unconsciously:

> The garden, the grass-plot, formerly so daintily trim that
> even a stray rose-leaf seemed like a fleck on its exquisite arrange-
> ment and propriety, was strewed with children's things: a bag
> of marbles here, a hoop there; a straw hat forced down upon a
> rose-tree as on a peg, to the destruction of a long, beautiful,
> tender branch laden with flowers, which in former days would
> have been trained up tenderly, as if beloved. (xlvi)

The change may pain Margaret, but there is nothing wrong about
it: Elizabeth Gaskell's tone suggests that the signs of 'merry, rough
healthy childhood' are an intrinsic improvement. On the other hand,
Margaret interviews the old woman whose cat has been stolen by
her neighbour (who has roasted it alive, in accordance with a local
superstition that to do so would bring back clothes stolen by a gipsy);
the comic-macabre account and the woman's conclusion leave no
choice but to believe that change and education are all to the good:

> 'it were very cruel for sure, and she should not like to do it; but
> that there were nothing like it for giving a person what they
> wished for; she had heard it all her life; but it were very cruel
> for all that.' (xlvi)

The nostalgia remains of rural enchantment in woodland walks,
and the delights of washing in spring-water scented by 'fresh-gathered
roses plunged head-downward in the water-jug' (xlvi), or lavender-
scented towels, or a lunch of strawberries and cream, brown bread,
and jug of milk, and Stilton cheese – but it is nostalgia firmly put in
its place.

Milton, which occupies the main body of the novel, is equally a
balancing of qualities valuable and reprehensible, or both at once,
depending on the attitude and degree of understanding, and the social
or aesthetic bias of the beholder. Milton is the symbol and embodiment of industry and of all the social issues between 'masters and men'
that were at the heart of *Mary Barton*. It is also the catalyst for the
working-out of the personal and spiritual progress of Margaret and
Thornton, who change in relation to each other and to the place
itself, and it is finally indicated, are beginning to change Milton.
Elizabeth Gaskell has thus a more exciting as well as a more difficult

area than George Eliot in *Middlemarch*. Middlemarch is inert or
even destructive; it leads Lydgate into compromising his principles,
trammels him, and ultimately, through its small-town politics and
pressures and through Rosamund, its representative, destroys him;
it offers no outlets for Dorothea's ideals, who can fulfil herself
eventually only by escaping altogether with the aid of the outsider
Ladislaw. No single reforming character changes *Middlemarch* which
'moveth all together if it move at all', to the great vague outside
pressures (such as Garth's railways project) of time and the era. Those
who succeed personally are those who, like Mary Garth, Fred Vincy
and Celia Brooke, contrive to maintain their personal integrity within the confines of the society and its *mores*.

Elizabeth Gaskell, neither idealistic nor unrealistic, is not as unconsciously defeatist as George Eliot. Before the end of the novel,
she not only suggests that improvement is possible, but how it may
be brought about, and how it may be done by individuals, as well as
by groups. Thornton is both a representative of the masters and a
'man' who has risen from those 'men' whose representative is
Higgins, the mouthpiece of the unions, who as man to man can
communicate and work with Thornton. Elizabeth Gaskell rests her
faith on the position given in the crucial exchange between Thornton
and Margaret:

> 'A man to me [he says] is a higher and completer being than a
> gentleman.'
> 'What do you mean?' asked Margaret. 'We must understand
> the words differently.'
> 'I take it that "gentleman" is a term that only describes a
> person in his relation to others; but when we speak of him as
> "a man", we consider him not merely with regard to his fellow-
> men, but in relation to himself – to life – to time – to eternity.'
> (xx)

Higgins and Thornton are both men, in this sense; once they communicate, Thornton sees his way to providing for his workers' needs:
the provisions are slight ones, not much more than allowing employees some self-organization within the factory – such as the
canteen they run – and the more general hints of the penultimate
chapter:

> 'I have arrived at the conclusion that no mere institutions,
> however wise, can attach class to class as they should be attached,

E

unless the working out of such institutions brings the individuals of the different classes into actual personal contact. Such intercourse is the very breath of life.' (LI)

Elizabeth Gaskell undoubtedly intended something more precise, but was, as we know, painfully short of space at her conclusion. However, it is clear that Milton, no less than Helstone, is not only a changing place, but one that can be changed by those within it.

She has thus set herself a hard and elaborate task, to show change in action and also to show changes of attitude in her observers towards Milton itself, in its essential being. She succeeds superbly in her task, of moving by way of observers and interpreters with several extreme positions, to a balance, partly of opposites, and partly of those who grow to see that qualities must have the defects of their virtues. Any method other than justice and fidelity in representing Milton is thus impossible for her. She avoids the unconvincing extreme delineations of Disraeli or Kingsley, while making many of the same points as they do about the enormous, fundamental, and horrifying problems in the new, fast-growing world based on the factory-city.

To do so she needs a variety of viewpoints: she uses Margaret and Thornton as those who are young, wise, and responsive enough to achieve the balance, and a variety of others, of whom the chief are Mrs Hale and Mrs Thornton, to state the unchanging extremes. It is Mrs Hale who is most troubled by the physical unpleasantnesses of Milton, who suffers from the cold and fog, who cannot come to terms with its new and alien class-structure, in which the prosperous and proud mother of a prosperous and proud manufacturer can boast of her son's having risen from penury by his own exertions. Mrs Thornton herself embodies the courage, the inaesthetic hardness, the strong sense of right, and proud self-respect of the Milton character. Through her, her house, and the way of life she embodies, Elizabeth Gaskell presents the private and domestic life of Milton. It is a hard but far from unfeeling life, governed by high and rigid standards whose satisfactions are not sensuous: her drawing-room is described with a faithful lightness of touch by the author:

> The walls were pink and gold; the pattern on the carpet represented bunches of flowers on a light ground, but it was carefully covered up in the centre by a linen drugget, glazed and colourless. The window-curtains were lace; each chair and sofa had

its own particular veil of netting or knitting. Great alabaster groups occupied every flat surface, safe from dust under their glass shades. In the middle of the room, right under the bagged-up chandelier, was a large circular table, with smartly-bound books arranged at regular intervals round the circumference of its polished surface, like gaily coloured spokes of a wheel. Everything reflected light, nothing absorbed it. The whole room had a painfully spotted, spangled, speckled look about it, which impressed Margaret so unpleasantly that she was hardly conscious of the peculiar cleanliness required to keep everything so white and pure in such an atmosphere, or of the trouble that must be willingly expended to secure that effect of icy, snowy discomfort. (x v)

Thus Milton indoors. Outdoors is equally justly done. The Thorntons' house is next to the mill, across the mill-yard. The detail is realistic, and, equally, signifies that, according to the values of Milton, work is the larger part of life. Elizabeth Gaskell avoids the usual novelist's problem of rendering work as vivid and immediate as personal life by making the two inextricable. The noise and business of the mill pervade the Thornton house, as much as the fluff from the carding-room does Bessy Higgins's lungs.

Against these fixed views of Milton Elizabeth Gaskell charts the gradually changing perspectives of Margaret and Thornton. For both of them Milton is a place of testing, possibly uncongenial, undoubtedly hard, but able to call out and temper the virtue and strength of the individual, and make him face and answer the questions about his or her own nature, and about duties and links with fellow-men. Margaret learns her own courage and power to fight, finds that her simplistic ideas, based on human kindliness and the Bible, will not answer with rugged natures like Higgins's and Thornton's, whose arguments she cannot logically refute. Thornton, in his turn, sure of his place in his society, and of belonging to it by birth, nurture, and personal striving, learns to look upon it differently in the light of Margaret's ideas.

The great strength of Elizabeth Gaskell's rendering of Milton is that while sympathetically recognizing that Milton is socially and economically viable as it stands, she reveals at the same time that it is personally and morally inadequate and imperfect. The single man can work his way up to become master providing he accepts that, if defeated by the powers that gave him the chance to rise, he must take that defeat – as Thornton does. Similarly the workers can break the master's power, if they accept that by so doing they may also break themselves. Each man has the opportunity of Samson to bring down the temple over his own head, leaving others to rebuild in their turn, and have the same choice. Milton is her final word on the city of the industrial revolution. She never returns to it again, having achieved in it a finer and deeper study than any other writer. When the reader thinks back over this novel, he is likely to recall the places – London, Helstone and Milton – and what happens in them which partakes of their nature, quite as vividly as the industrial personalities. Milton is probably the greatest character in *North and South*, more fully revealed and subtler than any single personality – fine though they are – and more memorable.

The characters themselves are by no means insignificant, or subordinated to the pattern, or mechanically arranged. In *North and South* Elizabeth Gaskell continues to extend her range, and show increasing powers. There are more characters than in *Mary Barton* or *Ruth*, of more different types, with more, and more subtle, individual purposes. Whereas in *Mary Barton* they grouped themselves by class, and by families, and in *Ruth* by their contrasting and illuminating relationships with the heroine, here there are different and flexible interconnections which cut across each other. They are grouped in one way by place. Edith Shaw, Margaret's cousin, and her mother, Margaret's aunt, belong to London, along with Captain Lennox and his ambitious lawyer brother Henry; Margaret and her parents and Dixon the maid belong to Helstone; the Thorntons, mother, son and daughter, the Higginses, and the Bouchers belong to Milton; Mr Bell is the sole but potent embodiment of academic Oxford. They are grouped again by class. The Shaws, Captain Lennox and Fanny Thornton are middle-class idlers, living on unearned income (Captain Lennox soon leaves the service); Mr Bell and Mr Hale (who teaches classics in Milton) go together as representatives of the life of the mind and the pursuit of learning; Henry Lennox and Mr Thornton contrast as professional men devoted to their different ideals of making a mark for themselves in the world of action and work. Another grouping links Mr Hale, Thornton, and Higgins as men who rule their actions by hard-thought principles and ideals, which govern themselves and their duties, to God and to their fellow-men. Family ties and affections cut across all these, and create other links, uniting not only the alien and exiled Frederick with Margaret, and Margaret with her London aunt and cousin Edith, but also the former Beresford sisters, Mrs Hale and Mrs Shaw. Mrs Shaw, Mrs Hale and Mrs Thornton are a trio of mutually contrasting and illuminating mothers, devoted in their different ways to their children, but all in some sense failing them. The daughters, Edith, Margaret, Fanny Thornton, and Bessy Higgins explore the relationships between parents and children.

Such elaborate and complex groupings in their changing and merging reveal that Elizabeth Gaskell's art is taking the novel on a last step away from the drama, compared for example with Jane Austen – whom she often much resembles – whose characters pair and group themselves very much as in comedies, with marriageable couples, supported by secondary older characters; or compared with Scott, who has vivid 'type' characters, of heroic or comic mode, all with generally fixed roles in the total action. The effect is quite different from Dickens's also, who, though he often contrives to have all his characters meet all of the other characters, does so for the purposes of his plot, or for the immediate excitement of the telling. Elizabeth Gaskell's need not meet at all: the thematic linking between Mrs Shaw and Mrs Hale is clear, even though within the novel the two never meet. It is socially unthinkable for Fanny Thornton, the artificially fastidious hypochondriac, to meet the poor and dying Bessy Higgins, yet the moral and social contrast between them is clear. This development is one that George Eliot takes up and pushes even further for her own purposes, notably in *Middlemarch*, where all characters at some time or other interact, and all are to some degree seriously treated in the ways generally appropriate to main characters.

Elizabeth Gaskell in this novel continues to treat all characters equally, turning her serious (though far from humourless) regard upon all. But her power to proportion their roles has grown. There are none of the momentary uncertainties of *Mary Barton*, as to whether a character is to assume a major or minor role. The positive, responsive, and active heroine Margaret is much more flexible organizing power than the passive Ruth, and operates along with the author herself to introduce and establish the relative importance of the rest.

This done, Elizabeth Gaskell is free to give deeper and more searching attention to the other characters than has been possible before. Aware as she is of how time and change work on all things within the scheme of her novel, she now extends her powers to suggest how past time also has shaped her characters to what they are. The reader is made to feel how heredity, upbringing and environment have worked upon even the most minor characters, whose consciousness is not only in the present of the novel, but made up of a lifetime of experiences, which lie behind. The details she gives vary from the full to the merest hint; they never hold up the action, are introduced unobtrusively and entirely naturally, whether in her own account, or most commonly, in conversation, or conveyed casually by other characters, who by so doing reveal also themselves. Many of the connections between characters are the result of the past.

Elizabeth Gaskell establishes her method with a simple instance, explaining that Mrs Hale did not go to her niece Edith's fine London wedding, because she had no dress she thought good enough:

> If Mrs Shaw had guessed at the real reason why Mrs Hale did not accompany her husband, she would have showered down gowns upon her; but it was nearly twenty years since Mrs Shaw had been the poor pretty Miss Beresford. (11)

This past of the poor pretty daughters of Sir John Beresford is drawn upon frequently by Dixon (one of Elizabeth Gaskell's most delightful humorous creations) who is always more informative than she knows, filling in the Hale marriage and family life with her tactless, trenchant, and partisan outbursts:

> 'I said to missus "What would poor Sir John have said? he never liked your marrying Mr Hale, but if he could have known it would have come to this, he would have sworn worse oaths than ever, if that was possible!" '

and when Margaret loses her temper at this aspersion on her father, Dixon

> said to herself, 'Miss Margaret has a touch of the old gentleman about her, as well as poor Master Frederick; I wonder where they get it from?' (v)

Futile though it is to conjecture how many children had Lady Mac-

beth, it is new and vivid light on Mrs Thornton when, faced with
the dying Mrs Hale's plea that she will take care of Margaret,

> it was no thought of her son, or of her living daughter, Fanny,
> that stirred her heart at last; but a sudden remembrance *sug-
> gested by something in the arrangement of the room* – of a little
> daughter – dead in infancy – long years ago – that, like a sudden
> sunbeam, melted the icy crust, behind which there was a real
> tender woman. (xxx, my italics)

Such perceptions, and such intuition about the chance working of
the human mind, as rest in the italicized phrase, are the mark of none
but the most sensitive of writers: they are rarely found so unobtrusively and frequently as in Elizabeth Gaskell, to whom they seemed
so natural that it is only too easy for the reader to pass over a sensitivity as vibrant as – and far less subjective than – Virginia Woolf's.
Elizabeth Gaskell rarely asks us to take anything about her characters
for granted. It must have occurred to many a reader to wonder what
parents could have begotten and borne Mr Casaubon, or even Celia
and Dorothea Brooke; to ask themselves under what circumstances
the Bishop of Barchester can have met and wooed Mrs Proudie, or
even what sort of a woman was Mrs Harding, wife of the Warden
and mother of Eleanor and Mrs Archdeacon Grantly. Novelists will
occasionally give us concrete details or facts on such matters; few
can make us feel why and how such things come about. Elizabeth
Gaskell constantly wafts across us the veritable perfume of the past.
Mr and Mrs Hale are rarely together in the novel, divided by mutual
misunderstandings and by the secret of Mrs Hale's illness and Mr
Hale's terror of it when he finds out; yet both of them are vivified
and united by their past youth and glamour, and rendered pitiful by it.
Mr Hale, uncertain and irritable, was once, as Mrs Shaw describes
him,

> the man of her heart, only eight years older than herself, with
> the sweetest temper, and that blue-black hair one so seldom
> sees. (11)

We later look back with the dying Mrs Hale and see them united
and devoted as they once were (and essentially still are), sharing the
misery of their son Frederick's disgrace:

> 'he put my arm in his, and kept stroking my hand, as if he
> wanted to soothe me to be very quiet under some great heavy

blow; and when I trembled so all over that I could not speak, he took me in his arms, and stooped down his head on mine, and began to cry in a strange muffled groaning voice, till I for very fright stood quite still, and only begged him to tell me what he had heard.' (xiv)

We see that what has been is part of what is, and are rendered wiser, as the characters are deepened. Equally true is the account of hard self-contained Mrs Thornton, made so not only by temperament but by those years of her life when she not only kept herself and her two children alive out of her son's earnings of fifteen shillings a week as a draper's assistant, but saved three shillings out of it as well. Having learned this, we feel she has a right to her opinion of the Hales and their sitting-room, even though it is ironically limited:

> Margaret was busy embroidering a small piece of cambric for some article of dress for Edith's expected baby – 'flimsy useless work,' as Mrs Thornton observed to herself. She liked Mrs Hale's double knitting far better; that was sensible of its kind. The room altogether was full of knick-knacks, which must take a long time to dust; and time to people of limited income was money. (xii)

Just as the past enriches and deepens the characters who have little part in the action, so it also operates powerfully on the two major characters. Margaret and Thornton are held apart as much by their different experiences and upbringings as by anything in the conscious present principles which the past has engendered.

Of those who follow Elizabeth Gaskell, Hardy is the most aware of the shaping power of the past over the present, and of the coexistence of the two within the individual nature. Superficially he may seem more mechanical. Henchard for instance is bound upon his wheel of fire by his original act in selling his wife, so that when she returns, he feels bound to take her back, even though he wishes to marry Lucetta. But more fundamentally Hardy is also aware that the fiery resolution of the young Henchard, who could resolve to forswear drink for years, and who was powerful enough to make himself leading man in Casterbridge, is the essence also of the wretched rash intruding fool of the latter part of his history, who, on impulse, admits the furmity woman's charge, who can have the 109th psalm sung in the inn against Lucetta and Farfrae, and who wrecks every chance of redeeming himself as it comes to him. It is this sense of past grandeur that contributes largely to the tragedy of Henchard's end.

This sense of power of the past within the present is naturally not the prerogative of the provincial novelists: it is their use of it that distinguishes them. Thackeray for instance is often poignantly aware of it, as in the noble passage that comes before the concluding episodes of *Pendennis*:

> Are you not awe-stricken, you, friendly reader, who, taking up the page for a moment's light reading, lay it down, perchance, for a graver reflection, – to think how you, who have consummated your success, or your disaster, may be holding marked station, or a hopeless and nameless place, in the crowd, – who have passed through how many struggles of defeat, success, crime, remorse, to yourself only known! – who may have loved and grown cold, wept and laughed again, how often! – to think how you are the same *You*, whom in childhood you remember, before the voyage of life began? (Vol. II, xxi)

But Thackeray does not make the past an element in the actual quality of the response we make to his characters themselves, because he, as a detached narrator, is working within a mode that neither permits nor calls for such depth of characterization.

The future, as well as the past, has its power in Elizabeth Gaskell's characterization. It is when we come to consider the future in *North and South* that a clearly recognizable distinction between kinds of character emerges. There are those in whom she creates a capacity to grow and develop and benefit from experience, and those who in various ways cannot do so. The first group is a small one – Margaret, Thornton, Higgins, Henry Lennox, Mrs Thornton and Frederick. The second includes all the others, subdivided into two groups. Firstly there are those who are in various ways beaten by life, with only death remaining to them, such as Mr Hale, who, his one heroic effort made in resigning from the ministry, has no strength to encounter a new life, or resilience to survive long after his wife's death; or such as Bessy Higgins, who, conquered by her physical working conditions, eagerly looses her hold on life in her thirst for visionary heavenly consolation. Secondly, there are those who opt out, either through weakness, or through not being capable, nor aware of challenge and opportunity. Among these latter are Fanny Thornton, the feeble branch of a powerful stock, whom 'nothing could strengthen to endure hardships patiently, or face difficulties bravely' (xii), and Margaret's cousin Edith, mindless and sybaritic, content to spend her life in dinner-parties and idleness, and her husband, ready to join her and to idle away his days in the gratifications of socializing, and luxuriating in his beautiful wife. The second group accounts for the sadness of the novel; the first renders it an optimistic rather than a depressing work.

Elizabeth Gaskell's original approach to her main characters, and its even more original consequences, are revealed in the first group, the characters with potential. These cut across all age and sex divisions, or concepts of major and minor.

Margaret Hale is Elizabeth Gaskell's third full-length study of the young girl who grows to womanhood. She is a more sensitive portrayal, and one with more duties to perform, than either Mary Barton or Ruth. Being more intelligent and perceptive than either, she grows to greater insight and maturity by the end of the novel. Although she is in the common line of heroines who acquire wisdom and triumph in marriage that reaches back to the eighteenth century of Fanny Burney, Maria Edgeworth and Jane Austen, she has both a more complicated destiny, and more evolved functions than any of their young women. She is, like Jane Austen's Elizabeth Bennet and Emma Woodhouse, clever and attractive, accomplished and self-ignorant. Like them, she is a central consciousness through which her author can explore moral and psychological issues, who, though sometimes deluded and judging wrongly, yet reveals right and truth by her own mis-estimates. She has some affinities also with her precursor by eight years, Jane Eyre, who like her moves through various areas of experience (friendships, deaths, lovers, changes of place and ways of life in which she has no guide but her own sense of right and duty) to her final morally and spiritually right place in life; and she resembles also Helen Huntingdon in *The Tenant of Wildfell Hall* who like her has to learn from her own self-confident (though far more harrowing) mistakes. On this level Margaret is not unsuccessful or at all improbable. She begins as the inexperienced young woman who accepts conventional standards, is happy to be generously kind to the Helstone poor, and can reject 'shoppy' people as possible acquaintances. Elizabeth Gaskell establishes her promptly as a perceptive young woman able to make decisions, who can perceive Henry Lennox's failings and reject his proposal of marriage, and can also deal with the practical problems of moving house at a fortnight's notice. She is thus an admirable medium for presenting Milton, with its ways and standards as alien, possibly, to the reader as to Margaret herself; she permits wryly humorous presentation of incidents like her first meeting with the Higginses, when she asks their names and where they live:

> 'Whatten yo' asking for?'
> Margaret was surprised at this last question, for at Helstone it would have been an understood thing, after the inquiries she had made, that she intended to come and call upon any poor neighbour whose name and habitation she had asked for.
> 'I thought – I meant to come and see you.' She suddenly felt rather shy of offering the visit, without having any reason to give for her wish to make it, beyond a kindly interest in a stranger. It seemed all at once to take the shape of an impertinence on her part; she read this meaning too in the man's eyes.
> 'I'm none so fond of having strange folk in my house. . . . Yo're a foreigner as one may say, and maybe don't know many folk here, and yo've given my wench flowers out of yo'r own hand – yo may come if yo like.'
> Margaret was half amused, half nettled at this answer.
>
> (VIII)

Margaret is often as successful as this, but she is not wholly achieved. Her author occasionally over-emphasizes heroinely attributes in a language that causes momentary uneasiness; at crises such as when Thornton proposes she tends to dwell overmuch upon her regal beauty:

> Her head, for all its drooping eyes, was thrown a little back, in the old proud attitude. Her long arms hung motionless by her sides. Altogether she looked like some prisoner, falsely accused of a crime she loathed and despised, and from which she was too indignant to justify herself. (xxiv)

Margaret is the last appearance in her author's all too brief work of the failure of confidence which makes her fall back on to the traditional matters and manners of the novel, rather than her own abilities. Despite the precedent offered by *Jane Eyre* and *Villette*, Elizabeth Gaskell clings to her beautiful maligned heroine. It is a malady most incident to novelists. Elizabeth Gaskell never suffers another attack, for Sylvia Robson and Molly Gibson are quite different; but others remain prone to it. George Eliot is a compulsive creator of the beautiful and misjudged – in Maggie Tulliver and Dorothea Brook most notably – neither of whom need their extraordinary and idealized beauty to perform their roles. In George Eliot's case the reasons are different (Elizabeth Gaskell has plainly no need of personal emotional release through the perfections of her young women, as George Eliot may well have), but in her convention doggedly survives, as it does even in Hardy, who cannot do without a young lady of unusual charms in his work, and indeed often needs to contrast her with a less flamboyant one, like Eustacia Vye and Thomasin Yeobright in *The Return of the Native*, Lucetta and Elizabeth-Jane in *The Mayor of Casterbridge*, and Sue Bridehead and Arabella Donn in *Jude the Obscure*. One feels that Hardy's women are ideal mistresses, George Eliot's ideal selves, and Mrs Gaskell's ideal daughters. Trollope, though he likes pretty women, resembles the best of Elizabeth Gaskell in his confidence in the power of personality. His most attractive heroine, perhaps, is Mary Thorne in *Doctor Thorne*, whose looks are, rightly, of little moment. By the time Elizabeth Gaskell comes to Mollie Gibson, she knows that a heroine can dispense with extraordinary good looks. Although one might have thought that the unsentimental Elizabeth Gaskell would have appreciated the absence of them in Jane Eyre and Lucy Snowe, one can see also that, having no axe of Charlotte Brontë's sort to grind, which makes plainness essential, she would see no reason deliberately to rob her heroine of what is not outside credibility.

Yet the faults in presenting Margaret Hale are not great, in comparison with the artistic strengths and originality in her other capacities. The conventional elements are superficial. Elizabeth Gaskell is concerned with much more than a love story, and much more than the fortunes and adversities of her heroine, Margaret is the medium for experiencing and judging different societies, and ways of life and standards. Elizabeth Gaskell explores through her more kinds of human relationships than most authors attempt: Margaret is equally convincing with her parents and with those outside her family, whether girls her own age like Bessy or Fanny Thornton, or older men as different as Higgins and the avuncular Mr Bell, or older women like Mrs Thornton. She also explores a wide spectrum of affections, ranging from the love – mixed variously with judgement and imperfect sympathies – between members of the same family, to the unexpected affections growing between new friends, and to the peculiar loyalties to dependents and family servants. Indeed these connections, so common in life and so little explored in the novel, are done with a confidence and conviction more complete than her dealings with Thornton. Margaret is also the means of examining what feels like an almost complete range of human experience: she encounters death, both sudden and delayed, the strains of illness, her own and others' crises both in circumstances of the spirit, as well as moral dilemmas, and all the unexpected and anticipated delights of living, that can fall to a nature that is without evil impulses. She leads forwards in her author's work to *Wives and Daughters*: a novel rendered more sensitive and subtle for having the functions of the heroine performed not only by Mollie Gibson, but shared between her and Cynthia Kirkpatrick. Though *Wives and Daughters* could not have come about without the lessons learned from creating Margaret Hale, yet she herself marks an end in Elizabeth Gaskell's work. She does not create again so independent and powerful a woman, who can so much overcome her circumstances, and exist independently of them. Indeed, her next novel moves into all that Margaret Hale cannot touch: the sufferings of those who are victims of their age and society and, even more, of natures with passions that overrule the will, and can cause tragedy and self-destruction.

Yet Margaret Hale opens the way for others, and George Eliot in particular, with Dorothea Brooke and Romola, who by the time she creates Gwendolen Harleth in *Daniel Deronda*, has explored the avenue to its near-tragic end. Meredith too has his own fine example of the woman of independent spirit pent up by circumstance – Clara Middleton in *The Egoist*. An even later descendant is perhaps E. M. Forster's Margaret Schlegel, who lives like Margaret Hale within a family and social orthodoxy which gradually fails her; who, without being a rebel, faces, explores, and comes to terms with an opposing set of values, embodied in the man she marries.

Margaret Hale is a thinking being. Most of her social relationships, though they engender affection and esteem, are of the mind, and involve talking, thinking, and exchanging ideas about common life, work, money, and religion. Yet Elizabeth Gaskell never turns her into a mere vehicle for debating points, who steps out of character for the sake of the message, or turns into simply a 'wandering voice'. She is always, like the other characters, physically felt, as a sensuous as well as emotional and rational presence. She is made so by her own reactions and those of others; Thornton, on his first visit, his conscious mind arguing on the conditions of factories and labour, yet cannot help noticing Margaret's bracelet:

> It seemed as if it fascinated him to see her push it up impatiently till it tightened her soft flesh; and then to mark the loosening – the fall. He could almost have exclaimed – 'There it goes again!'
>
> (x)

Details of physical movement, hair and dress are of touch and texture as much as sight – when trying on her dinner dress, she makes 'the rich white silk balloon out into a cheese' (xix) – and always simple and unobtrusive.

John Thornton is one of the important ways through which Margaret herself is revealed, and the other main means through which his author can present her material. Throughout his part in the action he parallels and contrasts with Margaret.

Like her he is much more than the conventional lover-hero; indeed he must be one of the least romantic representatives the breed has ever had; he is not even the directly anti-romantic figure, like Charlotte Brontë's Paul Emmanuel in *Villette*, or his pale precursor Crimsworth in *The Professor*. Elizabeth Gaskell establishes him first as a figure of power – the man whose influence in Milton can even get a landlord to redecorate the Hales' rooms:

> There was no particular need to tell them, that what he did not care to do for a Reverend Mr Hale, unknown in Milton, he was only too glad to do at the one short sharp remonstrance of Mr Thornton, the wealthy manufacturer. (vii)

His author establishes his roles and personality by degrees; as a businessman doggedly, even arrogantly, certain of his role and philosophy; as a willing pupil in the classics for Mr Hale, eager to make up the education that his career as a self-made man has left no room for; and as a son whose powerful mother enhances his own power. His first associations with Margaret are in these roles; and not until fifteen chapters from his first appearance does he actually fall in love. He is thus a far more solid and complex entity than most hero-lovers. His love may not be of his life a thing apart, but it is far short of being his whole existence.

He acts as interpreter of Margaret as she is of him, mainly before he has come to love her, during the debates and discussions of their early acquaintance. Afterwards Elizabeth Gaskell shifts her focus to his own thoughts and feelings, and to his relations with other characters. They are mainly sources of conflict, and render him both impressive and moving, whether it is against his mother's proud resentful, and indignant sympathy, or the proud and belligerent Higgins.

In attempting analysis of the thoughts and passions of a man, Elizabeth Gaskell ventures confidently into the regions where most women writers fail as consistently as men fail in their analyses of woman. She does not fail, mainly because she depends as much on charting the results of passion as on analysing passion itself. Rejected by Margaret, Thornton leaves the house

> as dizzy as if Margaret . . . had been a sturdy fish-wife, and given him a sound blow with her fists. He had positive bodily pain – a violent headache, and a throbbing intermittent pulse. He could not bear the noise, the garish light, the continued rumble and movement of the street. He called himself a fool for suffering so; and yet he could not, at the moment recollect the cause of his suffering, and whether it was adequate to the consequences it had produced. . . . He loved her, and would love her; and defy her, and this miserable bodily pain. (xxvi)

Equally true is the way in which, suspecting her of dishonesty and a secret lover,

> He dreamt she came dancing towards him with outstretched arms, and with a lightness and gaiety which made him loathe her, even while it allured him. But the impression of this figure of Margaret, with all Margaret's character taken out of it, as completely as if some evil spirit had got possession of her form – was so deeply stamped upon his imagination, that when he wakened he felt hardly able to separate the Una from the Duessa; and the dislike he had to the latter seemed to envelop and disfigure the former. (xl)

Unfortunately Elizabeth Gaskell is not always so secure as in her understanding of the effects of passion. As with Margaret, she seems occasionally not quite able to depend on her own natural simple literal mode to carry her, and, as with Margaret, she slips uneasily into false rhetoric and over-emphasis:

> He turned away and leaned against the mantelpiece, tears forcing themselves into his *manly* eyes. (xxvi)

We accept the gesture, we reject the fatal adjective.

Like Margaret, he is the last of his line for his author. After him, she has no heroes. She next explores the depths within Philip Hepburn, tragic victim of a passion overruling reason and will. When she returns to the light of common day, it is to Roger and Osborne Hamley, beings of a different, more domestic and more naturalistic order.

Elizabeth Gaskell is well aware of the power of physical attraction. The first meetings of Thornton and Margaret are not those of lovers at all, yet the first links between them are not of the mind, and not recognized by either, such as Thornton's fascinated response to the bracelet slipping on Margaret's arm (already quoted), and her observation of his face and mouth:

> The lines in the face were few but firm . . . and lay principally about the lips, which were slightly compressed over a set of teeth so faultless and beautiful as to give the effect of sudden sunlight when the rare bright smile, coming in an instant and shining out of the eyes, changed the whole look from the severe and resolved expression of a man ready to do and dare everything, to the keen honest enjoyment of the moment, which is seldom shown so fearlessly and instantaneously except by children. (x)

Elizabeth Gaskell is the more assured for being sparing. Utterly confident of her character's physical entity, she never shows uneasiness like George Eliot's who reiterates and over-emphasizes details like the little ripple in Will Ladislaw's nose, Felix Holt's large eyes, and Adam Bede's tall form, repeating and over-emphasizing her character's appearance, to an extent that nullifies the sense of flesh and blood that it is supposed to create.

Thornton as the professional man is even better than Thornton the lover. Few novelists can give us more insight into a man going about the daily business of his life than Elizabeth Gaskell. Her method is the reverse of Dickens's, whose characters are chosen and built up to incorporate certain aspects of society and attitudes towards it. In Thornton, the society, his role and his attitudes work upon each other, change, and conflict to enrich and deepen the personality. Dickens's method tends to the vivid but static and undeveloping caricature, Elizabeth Gaskell's to the psychological study of a nature not simply capable of change, but necessarily changing under outside pressures.

When the novel opens, Thornton is over thirty, no longer a young man, and therefore less malleable or resilient than one at the beginning of his career. He is the first of the novel's explorations of this kind. The mature lover has existed as a comic figure since Shakespeare's Falstaff, with memorable representatives in the novel. As a serious central figure, Thornton has descendants, but no precursor. Margaret gives Thornton the shock to his moral being and way of life that, in a gentler Trollopean way, Eleanor Bold gives Mr Arabin in *Barchester Towers*; that in Hardyesque tragedy, Bathsheba Everdene gives to Boldwood in *Far from the Madding Crowd*, and finally, Margaret Schlegel gives to Herbert Wilcox in E. M. Forster's *Howard's End*.

All of these have their lives changed; all except Arabin are brought to face public ruin. Thornton's is primarily independent of anything Margaret does, but is the more bitter because it makes him unable to try out his new ideas of running a mill in cooperation with his employees. Elizabeth Gaskell reveals his age as a poignant element in his plight:

'I have discovered my new powers in my situation too late – and now all is over, I am too old to begin again with the same heart.' (L)

Thornton is saved, not by his own efforts, but by the natural working-out of his misunderstandings with Margaret. The circle is just which makes him end where he begun, but tempered with a not improbable mercy. Hardy in his turn has his hero who goes from woe to weal and after out of joy, in Henchard, ruined in his prime, with Thornton's self-made, self-justifying qualities, equally prepared to accept the consequences of his own acts. No kind fate saves him; Hardy makes of Henchard's a tragic figure; but the contrast between him and Thornton reveals how little it is really Hardy's purpose to deal through Henchard with the decline of a rural society, eroded and overrun by an urban one. Henchard has no positives ahead, even were he capable of achieving them: Thornton has, and his future is to progress from his past. Henchard's Casterbridge and Wessex are merely a setting for his personal tragedy, whereas busy productive Milton is in Thornton's veins.

When one comes to consider minor characters, one sees how far and how fast the novel has travelled in the thirty years that separate Elizabeth Gaskell from Jane Austen, who are so close in so many ways.

> The indignities of stupidity, and the disappointments of selfish passion, can excite little pity. (*Mansfield Park*, XLVIII)

> A large bulky figure has as good a right to be in deep afflication, as the most graceful set of limbs in the world. But, fair or not fair, there are unbecoming conjunctions, which reason will patronize in vain, – which taste cannot tolerate, – which ridicule will seize. (*Persuasion*, VIII)

Though these two comments of Jane Austen's have mildly startled readers of her novels, they can be eminently justified within the context of her particular art; any such are inconceivable in Elizabeth Gaskell's. From the first she regards characters with a unique and superb balance of sympathy, humour and pathos which springs naturally from their being accurately conceived. Like Hardy after her, she sees (in his own phrase) the sorriness underlying the grandest things, but even more the grandeur underlying the sorriest things;[3] at the same time she registers and conveys the comedy of their incongruity.

It is difficult to choose among the many successes. Any of Elizabeth Gaskell's creations show signs of her great power and insight. However, in *North and South* she continues to extend her range, and is increasingly able to work in and elaborately interlink her characters. No novelist can give greater subtlety to small characters, or is better at being both humorous and sympathetic. She is generous even to the simple-minded, like the younger sister Mary Higgins, who cannot even clean her own house properly, but perhaps at her finest with the middle-aged or elderly, of limited sympathies and perceptions. Her skill with these grows apace and two of the best representatives here are Mrs Hale's maid Dixon, and Mrs Thornton. Both recall earlier, less developed, creations and look forward to subtler insights.

Dixon belongs to the long line of quirky devoted retainers which stretches back through Scott and Fielding and beyond, a line which dies out as the society which needs it dies out. Her closest descendant

[3] Notebook entry, 19 April 1885, in *The Life of Thomas Hardy* by Florence E. Hardy (London, 1962), Chapter XIII.

is George Eliot's Denner, maid to Mrs Transome in *Felix Holt*,
who like Dixon is a survival from a vanished past – Denner's being
even further back, in the Regency, because the 'present' of that
novel is the time of the Reform Act. Denner's portrayal is just as
sensitive, but more serious (since Mrs Transome is a near-tragic
figure, with Denner her only confidante) and less complex because
Denner has less part to play in the main action. Dixon recalls that
other devoted quirky servant, the Benson's Peggy in *Ruth*. Like her
she is useful, devoted, with her own kind of sense, and unconsciously
comic. But she is quite a different personality, and is much more
closely wrought into the fabric of the novel. She is seen much less
for her own sake than Peggy, with her racy speech and interpolated
comic stories (recalling the 'tale within the tale' of Fielding and
early Dickens), but is always subdued and subordinated to the main
purpose. Her great days have been the past, as maid to the unmarried
Miss Beresford, before she became Mrs Hale. As such her reminiscences supply Mrs Hale's past, and fill out the slight and pathetic
figure who appears before the reader, compared with whom, as
Dixon declares (with the wonderful unconsciously nonsensical cliché
at which her author is so adept and will perfect in Mrs Gibson in
Wives and Daughters), 'you'll never be like your mother for beauty –
never; not if you live to be a hundred' (xvi). Since she sees all the
present as a falling-off, she becomes a measure of flux in the social
classes at Milton, where she can no longer be even the personal maid-
cum-housekeeper of the Helstone era, when there is no one to complete the rest of the hierarchy of under-servants. Margaret's adapta-
bility shines by contrast; she can change her role with ease, changing
as she puts it, from 'Peggy the laundry-maid to Margaret Hale the
lady' (ix). So does her increasing maturity, when, in the crisis of her
mother's illness, she fights her way out of being the protected daughter
and claims her right to know as much as Dixon of what is wrong.
Dixon's speech and attitudes could have remained unmixedly
humorous but for these changes in her society. They now become
another trial for Margaret and Mr Hale, recognized by the reader
even while the comedy remains; and become also a trial for Dixon
herself which renders her pitiable:

> Dixon's ideas of helpful girls were founded on the recollection
> of tiny elder scholars at the Helstone school, who were only too
> proud to be allowed to come to the parsonage on a busy day, and

treated Mrs Dixon with all the respect which they paid to Mr and Mrs Hale, and a good deal more of fright. Dixon was not unconscious of this awed reverence which was given to her; nor did she dislike it; it flattered her much as Louis the Fourteenth was flattered by his courtiers shading their eyes from the dazzling light of his presence. But nothing short of her faithful love for Mrs Hale could have made her endure the rough independent way in which all the Milton girls, who made application for the servant's place, replied to her inquiries respecting their qualifications. They even went the length of questioning her back again. (VIII)

She has her uses also to the plot, especially when Frederick is coincidentally recognized by the rogue Leonards. The coincidence is made to seem both probable and palatable when it is Dixon who sees, recognizes and speaks to him first. Her whole wonderful history of the meeting – a comic delight in itself, its tone making it plain that, though the threat is a real one, the peril will not materialize – is above all superbly and naturally worked in the atmosphere of the main action, by dissipating for the reader and Margaret the melancholy of Mrs Hale's death.

Dixon, delightful as she is, is notable even more for what she demonstrates of Elizabeth Gaskell making multifarious yet unobtrusive use of minor characters, whose value increases both thematically and structurally, at every appearance. In *Mary Barton* such characters seemed to have as many relationships with other characters as people in life: now she is less concerned with who knows who, and how they interconnect – Dixon's circle of acquaintance is not much more than the three Hales – but is far more skilful at making such characters illuminate and vary tone, mood, implications of action and themes. As a personality Dixon could appear in *Wives and Daughters*; in the art that presents her, she is closer to the interpenetrating secondary figures of *Sylvia's Lovers*.

Mrs Thornton, on the other hand, is, though splendid, more isolable from the rest of the novel. Formidable, even noble in essence, she is a deep rendering of a new kind of figure in the novel – the person no longer young, the great crises of whose life might be thought to be past, who yet has a full existence and response to life, and the power of suffering. She is original also in having a grip on what are all too often considered masculine affairs. In the past she has built up her son's career, and she has a firm hold on the current business of the mill; one feels that she would have made a good master of men herself. Her closest, and only, immediate precursor of this kind is Charlotte Brontë's Shirley. But what Charlotte Brontë has to claim vociferously – Shirley's power to fill a man's role as landlord – Elizabeth Gaskell takes for granted, and allows to emerge easily in the action and dialogue. Charlotte Brontë eventually destroys her case by letting Shirley, like Millamant, 'dwindle into a wife'. Elizabeth Gaskell's figure embodies authority, and breathes forth a faintly poignant, though unstressed, mood of unfulfilled and unrealizable potential.

Her chief role is in relation to her son. She is the stock from which he has sprung, with the basic qualities of strength, resolution and pride, with high though rigid principles of personal honour and justice to others, untempered by mercy. She provides for the reader the side of Thornton that he cannot himself reveal without seeming boastful or excessively self-analytical. The love between son and mother, wonderfully reticent as it is, reveals the powerful feelings of which the self-restrained man is capable, and convince us that the passion Margaret rouses in him is no way over-indulgent, and is for life. The Thornton family – of parent, son and daughter – balance and contrast with the Hales, and their strengths and failures of sympathy are mutually revealing.

Most economically done, Mrs Thornton has greater depth than Elizabeth Gaskell has yet achieved, and more than many writers after her. She shows her author's power to let slight words and modest acts precipitate events and spiritual turmoil. Mrs Thornton is the first to suggest what will trouble her the most:

'Take care you don't get caught by a penniless girl, John . . . this Miss Hale comes out of the aristocratic counties, where, if all tales be true, rich husbands are reckoned prizes.' (IX)

and seems ironically to bring about what she fears. Faced with the hated Margaret as daughter-in-law, she confronts her doom, and her duty to yield place to her, with a greatness of mind no less because it reveals itself in the homely but symbolic act of unpicking her own and her husband's initials off the household linen. The Biblical and Shakespearean echo in her thoughts is not the least over-grand for her spiritual struggle:

To take Mrs Thornton's place as mistress of the house, was

only one of the rich consequences which decked out the supreme glory; all household plenty and comfort, all purple and fine linen, honour, love, obedience, troops of friends would come as naturally as jewels on a king's robe, and be as little thought of for their separate value. (xxvii)

Mothers and sons, and their relations to each other, have hardly appeared in the novel before *North and South*. As part of the general exploring of personal relationships they do so with increasing frequency. Elizabeth Gaskell's treatment is true, honest, and powerful, and never slips into dishonesty, sentimentality, or falsity of tone, even when at extreme moments feeling breaks through Northern reticence:

'I hate her . . . I tried not to hate her, when she stood between you and me, because – I said to myself – she will make him happy; and I will give my heart's blood to do that. But now, I hate her for your misery's sake.' (xxvi)

The ground once broken is explored again and again; by Trollope in *Orley Farm* (1858); by George Eliot in *Felix Holt* (1865), by Hardy in *The Return of the Native* (1878) and, eventually and most extensively, in the changed climate of Lawrence's *Sons and Lovers* (1913). The mothers of these sons – Lady Mason and Lucius, Mrs Transome and Harold, Mrs Yeobright and Clym, Mrs Morrell and Paul – are not alike – apart from being strong-minded and disappointed because they have no chance to use their faculties to the full – but are part of the novel's extending power to take in the passions of the no longer young, and to utilize such relationships compounded of contradictions, of both love and conflict.

In *North and South* Elizabeth Gaskell, continuing to develop and to explore the virtues of her own methods, has written her first major novel. What few weaknesses it shows come from attempting more than she has previously done: a wider range of action and more conflicting and varied themes, deeper emotions, and more subtle and mature characterization.

She continues to shape the action by cumulation and changes of mood, attitude and perspective, but does better than before at guiding the reader into knowing where he is going, while not letting him lose interest by forseeing how he will get there. Her characterization is still achieved by the giving of full serious attention to all, whether major or minor, but she handles the amount of time and space so that one no longer has any doubt as to the relative importance – structurally – of her personages. Her perfect ear for local speech remains, while the authorial self-consciousness about using it has gone. Though she occasionally slips into false rhetoric with her protagonists, such lapses are no greater than George Eliot's, and insignificant in comparison with Hardy's lifelong grapplings with the recalcitrant idiom of passion. The sensuous response to all the impressions of life as it flows form more and more a part of every scene.

One would have expected her to go on to explore all these found areas and skills more deeply in her next novel, to render the excellent more perfect. Elizabeth Gaskell never does. *Sylvia's Lovers* could never have been predicted from *North and South*, any more than *Ruth* could from *Mary Barton*. She does not resume the subjects, or themes or settings, or kinds of character, or even the language. *Sylvia's Lovers* is a novel of a different age, and almost a different country – north-east Yorkshire instead of south-east Lancashire. What she does take with her from her third novel to her fourth are the powers of her art and her techniques, and the depths of sympathies with the extreme and strange in the human predicament to be found in the most humble and unheroic of humankind.

4

Sylvia's Lovers

'Child, I ha' made thee my idol; and if I could live my life o'er again, I would love my God more, and thee less: and then I shouldn't ha' sinned this sin against thee.' (XLV)

'Thee and me was niver meant to go together. It's not in me to forgive – I sometimes think it's not in me to forget . . .' (XXIX)

'It'd tax a parson t' say a' as a've getten i' my mind. It's like a heap o' woo' just after shearin'-time; it's worth a deal, but it tak's a vast o' combin' an' cardin', an' spinnin', afore it can be made use on. If a were up to t'use o' words, a could say a mighty deal.' (XXX)

'He didn't love yo' as I did. He had loved other women. I, yo' – yo' alone. I – I wish God would free my heart from the pang; but it will go on till I die, whether yo' love me or not. . . . It might be a sin in me, I cannot say; my heart and my sense are gone dead within me. I know this: I've loved yo', as no man but me ever loved before. Have some pity and forgiveness on me, if it's only because I've been so tormented with my love.'
(XXXIII)

On these rocks is built one of the greatest novels in the English tongue; on these rocks founder the lives and destinies of Philip Hepburn and Sylvia Robson, the protagonists of Elizabeth Gaskell's saddest work. Because those who work out their dooms in it have to face the great issues of human destiny, and because they are helplessly in the grip of their own natures and the times that breed them, it must be considered as tragedy. Because all the characters, not just the main ones, are equally caught up in the movement of the whole, the work, where it does not rise to the full grandeur of tragedy, has the power of true pathos.

For comparisons for Philip and Sylvia, and Kinraid, the eternally hopeless triangle, which is the tragedy of Philip and Sylvia, one can only look to the old unhappy far-off things of the ballad and of the Norse heroic edda, where great passions go along, like theirs, with a sparse and simple life. But a novel requires more than heroic simplicity of outline. Its characters cannot be pared down to the elements of a ballad situation, or of a Brynhild and Sigurd, or given the remoteness of Isolde and Tristan. They have to be filled out, given local habitations, society, houses, friends, kin, creeds and history. The English novel has moved towards such tragedy before: in the lives of great men, to reveal their greatness in conflict with their world; in the lives of those in humble circumstances whose natures are so far apart that they become tragic victims; and in the lives of those whose humble natures as well as circumstances render them tragic. But not before this has it revealed the tragic greatness, and the tragic ruin, of those who are humble and obscured, and not in any way above or set apart from their fellow-men and the life around them. Few novelists before Elizabeth Gaskell have ventured upon any of these three kinds. Scott reached his greatest powers with the lives of men of great power or in the grip of a great cause, as in *Waverley*, or *Old Mortality*, or parts of *Redgauntlet*, but he clung to the form which permitted of a nominal happy ending for nominal heroes – his tragic victims like Fergus McIvor, Balfour of Burley, or the Pretender, being only an element in a whole which could not be unreservedly called a tragedy. Richardson in *Clarissa* had explored the second type, with a heroine whose nature was so far refined and superior to her humble context that she became its tragic victim. So, in a quite different way, had Emily Brontë in *Wuthering Heights*, where Catherine and Heathcliff are wholly above and beyond the life in which they find themselves, and almost destroy it while working out their own destinies. The third kind only begins to be discovered in Elizabeth Gaskell's own time, by Hawthorne in *The Scarlet Letter*, by Elizabeth Gaskell herself in ventures in the short story, like 'Lois the Witch' and 'The Crooked Branch', and by George Eliot in her group of early novels *Adam Bede*, *Mill on the Floss* and *Silas Marner*. Of these only George Eliot is in any way attempting similar ends, with similar materials. She consciously and explicitly chooses to explore unheroic tragedy (to use Barbara Hardy's useful term) and pathos without sentimentality, and to urge and reveal 'the human sanctities . . . through pity and terror as well as admiration and delight'.[1] Yet *Adam Bede* (1859), *Mill on the Floss* (1860) and *Silas Marner* (1861), which precede *Sylvia's Lovers*, all in some way evade committing themselves to a totally tragic outcome. None of them moves inflexibly to an inescapable tragic ending like Elizabeth Gaskell's novels, nor does she do so after it. Though *Felix Holt*, *Middlemarch* and *Daniel Deronda* each have a tragic story within them – those of Mrs Transome, Lydgate and Gwendolen Harleth – they are counterbalanced against other stories equally important, of Felix and Esther, Dorothea Brooke, and Daniel Deronda, which reach a moral and spiritual fulfilment. George Eliot's novels preceding *Sylvia's Lovers* (*Adam Bede* and *Silas Marner*) like Scott's novels, leave an escape into some kind of peace and happiness for some of the main characters at the end. In *Adam Bede*, though Arthur and Hetty meet their doom, Adam, chastened and wiser, survives, and the social order of Hayslope, though threatened and torn, can be restored. In *Silas Marner*, though Geoffrey Cass cannot recover what his own sin has caused him to lose, Silas himself is redeemed and the social world of Raveloe which receives him is enriched. Only *Mill on the Floss* ends with the end of its heroine, Maggie, herself, drowned with her brother Tom in the Flood. Yet even this is not a tragically inevitable consequence of all that has gone before, but rather a return to the happy days when the two shined in their angel infancy – poignant, moving, and even emotionally satisfying, but leaving the tragic conflicts of the adult Maggie evaded and unresolved. Only in her very first work 'The Sad History of Amos Barton' – a short story, not a novel – in *Scenes of Clerical Life*, does George Eliot chronicle as her central and whole concern the man who is victim both of his own nature and his environment, who is allowed no escape.

Outside the novel, Elizabeth Gaskell, in her faithful handling and profound, though regulated, compassion closely resembles the poet Crabbe, in his various unhappy stories of *The Borough* and *Tales of the Hall*, one of which, 'Ruth', contains the germ of Sylvia's story.

[1] Barbara Hardy, *The Novels of George Eliot* (London, 1959).

The final greatness of *Sylvia's Lovers* lies in its tragedy and pathos; its originality, importance, and artistic skills lie in many other qualities as well. This is Elizabeth Gaskell's first novel not of her own time or home country, extending her range to a period sixty-seven years earlier, to the wholly new society of North Riding Yorkshire and the whaling community of Whitby, and to characters who belong to it, and to the farming community nearby. The delineation of characters who speak a local language, and who are in no way exceptional within their community, has always been her forte. Here she shows that this power is not tied to Lancashire or to the industrial town-dweller; and shows also that she has no need of central characters who are superior to the life around them.

She apparently sets out to write a quite different kind of work from her previous ones. This is novel for the novel's sake, with no social pretext for the existence of art. A historical novel of the Napoleonic period, set in an isolated and unusual community – the whale-fishers of Whitby, cut off from the life of their own age by their way of life and geographical isolation – where there is no social scale of the traditional kind, since the community is independent of local landed proprietors, gentry and aristocracy; a community with an unusual economy, and of unusual religious beliefs, set in a strange, remote, and hostile landscape; all this setting is unfamiliar both to herself and her readers. The emotional material is equally strange. The main characters embody deep, extreme and enduring passions – the love of Philip for Sylvia, Sylvia for Kinraid and Kinraid's, even, for her, and Sylvia's inflexible nature which cannot forgive a wrong – which in varying measures the minor characters share: Sylvia's father, Daniel Robson, has his fanatical hatred for the press-gangs, and even Hester, gentle and good though she is portrayed, gives no quarter in her standards, remains true for life to her love for Philip, and only with great difficulty extends charity to those like Sylvia whom she considers to have done wrong.

Yet though this is Elizabeth Gaskell's first novel to venture so far from home ground, she has already made several forays in her shorter stories. The chief of these is 'Lois the Witch' (1859), a very painful long-short story of an English girl who, emigrating to New England in 1691 at the time of the Salem witch-hunts, is accused, tried and hanged. The story deals with religious fanaticism, delusion, and deranging passion leading to inescapable disaster and to the painful utterance of the man who loved Lois herself:

> 'All this [repentance] will not bring my Lois to life again, or give me back the hope of my youth.' ('Lois the Witch', III)

She has also in 'The Crooked Branch' (1859) explored the fact of human wickedness and the inescapable pain it must cause to all who are bound by love. Yet this tale is not as painful as Lois's fate, because the kind of evil is less remote. The powers over tone and tragic mood that she learned in these two very successful exploratory worlds come together in the novel.

The story is essentially of the most simple kind. Philip loves his young cousin, Sylvia, who in turn falls in love with the seaman Kinraid and becomes engaged to him. When he disappears and is presumed drowned, Philip conceals the fact that he has actually been snatched by the press-gang. Misfortunes make Sylvia give way and marry Philip out of prudence. Soon after their daughter is born, Kinraid returns. Sylvia sends him away, but takes an oath never to live with or forgive Philip, who leaves and enlists for a soldier, is wounded and disfigured for life, and, when he eventually returns, dies saving his own daughter from drowning, and is at last reconciled with Sylvia. The central emphasis therefore is on nature as doom. The sense of plot as separate from character is reduced to a minimum; personal natures never seem to be manipulated to produce a course of events; the events appear to rise naturally out of personality. This is art superbly concealing art, since it is Elizabeth Gaskell's discretion that selects the material, as well as creating the personalities. An unobtrusive though crucial instance is the existence of Philip and Sylvia's child, Bella. Her birth occurs very shortly before Kinraid's reappearance, the story's great climax. It is so natural and probable that she should be born, that there is no sense of contrivance, or of the shaping author at work. But Bella's birth has many functions: the delight it gives her parents marks the point when Philip 'reached the zenith of his life's happiness' (xxx); this climax itself renders the shock more intense when that happiness is wrecked, when Sylvia discovers that Kinraid still lives, and that Philip has lied to her; Sylvia's great agony at that point is made greater, and her trapped state inescapable, by Bella's existence. Were she childless, she would have only to make the moral and social choice between her marriage vows, and the freedom Kinraid offers. Kinraid begs her to go with him, and set her marriage aside. But the child has a hold on Sylvia's love and duty that is recognizably more imperative than any other; so Sylvia's great oath is the outcome of her predicament, as well as of her nature. The implications behind this situation are the same as George Eliot has explicitly made the basis of *Adam Bede*, that

> there is no inherent poetical justice in hobbles [i.e., wrong actions] and they will sometimes obstinately refuse to inflict their worse consequences on the prime offender, in spite of his loudly-expressed wish. (*Adam Bede*, XII)

and

> 'you can never do what's wrong without breeding sin and trouble more than you can ever see.' (*Adam Bede*, XVI)

But Elizabeth Gaskell chooses her material with such precision that such comments never need be made.

The inevitable rightness of action in terms of character extends to all areas, even the secondary and minor. In terms of action, Philip can only obtain Sylvia when she is cast upon him by necessity, so she must lose the support of both her parents. This she does, when, firstly, her father is hanged for leading the attack on the press-gang; and, secondly, when her mother becomes helpless and childish under the shock. These happenings are precisely right as the consequences of an ageing, impetuous, not very bright, good-natured man with a lifelong hatred of impressment which goes back to his youth (when he cut off his own thumb to avoid impressment himself), and of a devoted wife with already weakened health who has nothing left to live for. That both Bell and Daniel Robson are old to be the parents of Sylvia not only precipitates this disaster, but accounts for many aspects of her own nature. Wherever one looks, the same craft is seen. The chief evidence against Daniel Robson comes from the ne'er-do-well Simpson, to whom Daniel, on hearing his feeble complaints at having lost all in the inn fire, gives 'half-a-crown and tuppence' (XXIII). Had Simpson's character been stronger, there would have been no such incident; had it been weaker, his gratitude would have overborne his resentment, and he would not have given evidence. All the material of the novel is interwoven thus: no event is without its purpose, no character is without some influence on the outcome of the whole. The usual convenient distinctions that novelists make it possible to observe in their work thus become almost impossible in Elizabeth Gaskell's greatest novel. Though there are other stories besides Sylvia's, elaborately and subtly counterpoising it, they cannot be felt as plots or sub-plots, but only as parts of the whole texture of life. Hester Rose has her own sadly hopeless history of her love for Philip, and her changing fortunes as sharer in the drapery business, and dutiful daughter to Alice Rose. The brothers Foster follow their fortunes as drapers and bankers, inwrought with Philip's and his partner Coulson's. No single character could be removed, or altered, without altering the consequences of the whole. Therefore, there are no choric characters whose function is solely to create a sense of society and of the milieu in which the main characters exist. Yet the sense of that society is very powerful, and the choric function of comment and judgement goes on all the time, performed by many in turn.

The novel's materials are thus plainly almost ideally suited to its author's purposes. The only point at which they cause difficulty is when it becomes necessary to tell of Philip's exploits in Palestine and thereafter. These are covered in three interpolated chapters, one (XXXVIII) in which Kinraid, shot down by the French, is rescued by Philip who is himself disfigured and disabled for life by an accidental explosion; and later two others (XLI, XLII) dealing with Philip's slow journey home from Portsmouth. These entail the creation in a very short space of a new world, that of the Mediterranean and of men at war, and involve an enormous coincidence: that Kinraid should be not only involved in the same fight as Philip, but should be saved from death by him. The point at which any novelist's manipulation of action becomes arbitrary and obvious enough to be called coincidence is a difficult one to plot. Elizabeth Gaskell has always tended to accept unlikely coincidence as an element in life – on the irrefutable basis that unlikely things happen very often in real life – which should, to produce the effect of life, be also an element in the novel. She has also genuine thematic and artistic reasons for moving events in the way she does. Here it is morally desirable that Philip should be able to cancel out the wrong he has done Kinraid; it is also desirable to make clear anew that his original wrong arose, not from personal hatred towards Kinraid, but from his obsession with Sylvia, his wish to possess her and his desire to protect her (he thought Kinraid a faithless jilt). It is also useful that Kinraid should recognize Philip, and thus provide a cause for his wife's visit to Sylvia, because that visit in its turn causes Sylvia to contrast the

married Kinraid with the eternally faithful Philip, and soften her
bitterness before Philip returns. Some discrepancy between these
chapters and the rest of the novel is almost unavoidable. It exists, but
it ranks as a flaw only because of the superb quality of the rest, with
which, as will be seen later, it is inwrought by all the artistic means
at its author's command.

The position of the narrator and the personality revealed become
equally absorbed into the texture as a whole. Measured in terms of
proportions, *Sylvia's Lovers* has more of itself covered by the author's
narrative than by dialogue or action, but such a statement is misleading. Elizabeth Gaskell has always avoided as far as possible projecting
her own personality as narrator, still less has she ever had a consciously
adopted authorial tone. Here, even what she has is further reduced,
and, when compelled to use it, she does so most sparingly, and inter-
mingles it with other parts of the novel's technique.

General expectations in the English nineteenth-century novel are
that the writer will find it necessary to render in his own voice
information as to facts about situation and setting, will need at times
to pass judgement on events or character, will have to provide description of character and of setting, make analyses of situations or
thoughts and states of mind, and establish some sort of direct personal
relationship with the reader. At all these points the ultimate consequence will be a distancing of the author from the experience he is
transcribing, and a further distancing, through the author, of the
reader. Such distancing is necessary and valuable to many writers,
since it allows assessment and judgement, and proportioning. Elizabeth Gaskell's purposes, however, are otherwise: concerned though
she is with assessment, judgement and proportion, she always prefers
to allow these to emerge through the closest possible contact between
the reader and the experience, uncoloured by the sense of a narrator
as a medium.

She establishes her position of near-invisibility relative to both the
narrative and the reader as early as possible. Her opening chapter is a
masterpiece of unobtrusive art. It is necessarily wholly expository,
because she cannot begin her story until she has established the sense
of the time and the setting which will enclose it. She thus faces the
problem of virtually all novelists, from Scott onwards, who choose to
write of a time and place that are not the norm for the reader. Anything like Jane Austen's dramatic economical beginnings with the

bare essentials leading instantly into the situation or event are impossible. Most novelists faced with this task follow Scott, by establishing a relationship between the author and the reader which imposes an attitude to the material. Scott frequently devotes a chapter or more to this purpose, giving sources and establishing his own speaking voice, of which the beginning of *Waverley* provides a fairly compact example:

> The title of this work has not been chosen without the grave and solid deliberation which matters of importance demand from the prudent. Even its first or general denomination was the result of no common research or selection, although, according to the example of my predecessors, I had only to seize upon the most sounding and euphonic surname that English history or topography affords, and elect it at once as the title of my work and the name of my hero. But, alas! what could my readers have expected from the chivalrous epithets of Howard, Mordaunt, Mortimer or Stanley, . . . but pages of iniquity similar to those which have been so christened for half a century past? I must modestly admit I am too diffident of my own merit to place it in unnecessary opposition to preconceived associations. I have therefore like a maiden knight with his white shield, assumed for my hero, W A V E R L E Y, an uncontaminated name, bearing with its sound little of good or evil, excepting what the reader shall hereafter be pleased to affix to it.

This (like most of Scott's rather unfairly maligned leisurely openings) is vital to establish a mutual relationship, so that the reader will trust the writer's perspective and judgement on the story proper. The method is a good one, and serves different writers, with different ends. George Eliot follows him, though with greater brevity, in, for example, *Adam Bede:*

> With a single drop of ink for a mirror, the Egyptian sorcerer undertakes to reveal to any chance comer far-reaching visions of the past. This is what I undertake to do for you, reader. With this drop of ink at the end of my pen, I will show you the roomy workshop of Mr Jonathan Burge, carpenter and builder, in the village of Hayslope, as it appeared on the eighteenth of June, in the year of our Lord 1799.

and Trollope, as here, in the opening of *Doctor Thorne*:

> Before the reader is introduced to the modest country medical
> practitioner who is to be the chief personage of the following
> tale, it will be well that he should be made acquainted with some
> particulars as to the locality in which, and the neighbours among
> whom, our doctor followed his profession.

Such examples as these few out of many demonstrate that novelists in
general feel that the need to get into touch with the reader takes
precedence over the statement of facts of time or place, the more
especially when establishing time and place has to be done before
action can begin. Elizabeth Gaskell takes the greater risk, of the
more direct method, depending upon establishing the reader's trust,
not by charming him, by presenting personal credentials, but simply
from the nature of her fact:

> On the north-eastern shore of England there is a town called
> Monkshaven, containing at the present day about fifteen thou-
> sand inhabitants. There were, however, but half the number at
> the end of the last century, and it was at that period that the
> events narrated in the following pages occurred.

She does not hide behind the conscious claim to be inventing, but
determines to convince as fact convinces. It is the most neutral of
methods, in that, though it sets up few expectations, and in isolation
seems even a little bleak, it sets up no false ones, wholly avoiding the
dangers of daunting the reader with the rather ponderous considering
of what it will avoid, like Scott's, or the possible unattractiveness of
too close contact, like George Eliot's, and above all avoids what
amounts to the semi-deceitful self-excusing of George Eliot and
Trollope. There is undoubtedly a sense of duplicity and the inverted
boast about all these three, who are implying with pseudo-modesty
that they are only inventing what is in its nature inferior to fact, to
reality, with the intention of disarming the reader and engaging his
sympathy for what they intend to make, ultimately, in their various
ways, more exciting, or significant, or attractive than 'reality'.
Elizabeth Gaskell has always been as conscious as any of them that
there must be a discernible likeness between the actual and invented
fiction, and just as conscious that the purposes and value of fiction
cannot be judged merely by how far it recreates the actual; but she

F

has never chosen to point out this likeness by using her own personality.

When she moves on to setting her scene, she continues to remain virtually invisible, delineating it, not as she herself responds to it, but by every other method at her disposal, to persuade the reader that what she selects is what any observer would see, so that no sense of a narrative *persona* is perceived. She equally skilfully avoids the feeling that the third participant in this trio of author and material and reader is merely a watcher of print on a page:

> Somehow in this country sea-thoughts followed the thinker far inland; whereas in most other parts of the island, at five miles from the ocean, he has all but forgotten the existence of such an element as salt water. (1)

In such a passage, where the 'thinker' may be a character, or the author, or the reader himself, the separation between them becomes as insignificant as possible. She employs 'you', as the most universal pronoun, equivalent to the impersonal 'one':

> in the moorland hollows, as in these valleys, trees and underwood grew and flourished; so that, while on the bare swells of the high land you shivered at the waste desolation of the scenery, when you dropped into these wooded 'bottoms' you were charmed with the nestling shelter they gave. (1)

She continues to give this feeling of the universal truth of her facts by introducing the responses of those who experience them, as well as of the observer:

> It was also not surprising that the whole town had an amphibious appearance, to a degree unusual even in a sea-port. Every one depended on the whale-fishery, and almost every male inhabitant had been, or hoped to be, a sailor. Down by the river the smell was almost intolerable to any but Monkshaven people during certain seasons of the year; but on these unsavoury 'staithes' the old men and children lounged for hours, almost as if they revelled in the odours of train-oil. (1)

Detachment as well as engagement are thus precisely established and regulated: detachment without any loss of sympathy with Monkshaven and its folk by the comparison with sea-ports in general, and

dy the delicately unobtrusive humour of the single epithet 'amphib-
ious', and the verb 'revelled', which at the same time compel the
reader to participate in the sensuous experience. Thus in regulating
the distance between observer and subject, Elizabeth Gaskell ob-
scures the difference between author and reader, who, almost falling
together into a single identity at such points as this, can separate,
where Elizabeth Gaskell uses the authorial 'I', into entities who,
though separate, think alike. When, a few sentences later, she ob-
serves

> there was also a dread and an irritation in every one's mind, at
> the time of which I write, in connection with the neighbouring
> sea. (1)

the 'I' is an entirely trustworthy medium, scarcely felt as a separate
person.

Since Elizabeth Gaskell is so sparing of authorial comment, the
points at which she intervenes are the more significant and striking.
They are generally of two kinds; moral generalizations which must
be made if the reader is to appreciate the general rather than the particular situation; or breaks at points of crisis, when the reader must
draw back from the minutiae of particular pain to pause for a moment
on the pain in all things. In the earlier part of the tale they are of the
former kind, in the later, the latter. Both kinds are related as closely
as possible to the immediate action and return to it as soon as possible.
The moral generalizations are generally extenuating ones, at points
where the author feels a reader might be inclined to be over-severe
on the characters, as for instance when she explains that the manners
of the day saw no wrong in drunkenness as such, or in smuggling:

> There was no question of the morality of the affair; one of the
> greatest signs of the real progress we have made since those
> times seems to be that our daily concerns of buying and selling,
> eating and drinking, whatsoever we do, are more tested by real,
> practical standards of religion than they were in the days of our
> grandfathers. Neither Sylvia nor her mother was in advance of
> their age. Both listened with admiration to the ingenious devices
> and acted, as well as spoken, lies that were talked about as fine
> spirited things. Yet if Sylvia had attempted one tithe of this
> deceit in her every-day life, it would have half-broken her
> mother's heart. (1x)

Not all the comments are excusing ones; the little aside on Sylvia's first meeting with Hester has the opposite effect:

> Sylvia had leisure in her heart to think 'How good Hester is' . . . without having a pang of self-depreciation in the comparison of her own conduct with that which she was capable of fully appreciating. In this way a modern young lady would have condemned herself, and therefore lost the simple, purifying pleasure of admiration of another. (VII)

The second type, the momentary pauses for the wider view – though, like so many of Elizabeth Gaskell's effects, they lose by being removed from context – fall like flashes of new wisdom when they come in their place, with all the brilliance of truth not merely acknowledged, but 'felt in the mind and felt along with the heart'.

> How easy Hester would have found it to make [Philip] happy! not merely how easy, but what happiness it would have been to her, to merge her every wish into the one great object of fulfilling his will! To her, an onlooker, the course of married life, which should lead to perfect happiness, seemed so plain! *Alas! it is often so! and the resisting forces which make all such delight impossible are not recognized by the bystanders, hardly by the actors.* (XXV, my italics)

A similar point is that at which Philip, hesitating about whether to tell the Robsons in his letter from Newcastle that Kinraid has been seized by the press-gang, waits too long:

> He dressed, wafered his letter, and rushed with it to the neighbouring post office; and without caring to touch the breakfast for which he had paid, he embarked. Once on board, he experienced *the relief which it always is to an undecided man, and generally is, at first, to any one who has been paltering with duty, when circumstances decide for him. In the first case, it is pleasant to be relieved from the burden of decision; in the second, the responsibility seems to be shifted on to impersonal events.* (XIX, my italics)

Perhaps her most outstanding comment is what is almost her last, when Philip, back again in Monkshaven after his long absence, crippled and unrecognizable, sees Sylvia and his daughter again:

> Ay! go in to the warm hearth, mother and child, now the gay

cavalcade has gone out of sight, and the chill of the night has succeeded to the sun's setting! Husband and father, steal out into the cold dark street, and seek some poor cheap lodging where you may rest your weary bones, and cheat your more weary heart into forgetfulness in sleep! The pretty story of Countess Phillis, who mourned for her husband's absence so long, is a fable of old times; or rather say, Earl Guy never wedded his wife, knowing that one she loved better than him was alive all the time she had believed him dead. (XLIII)

Such an apostrophe is very rare in Elizabeth Gaskell, and what looks like a Dickensian echo in isolation here, and an open rhetorical appeal for pity, has an irony that takes it far from sentimentality; Philip has now brutally awakened from his fanciful dream of returning like the heroic Sir Guy of Warwick in the romance, and yet, unknown to him, Sylvia is already on the road to penitence for casting him out, and, like a second Phillis, will indeed be reconciled.

The virtues she shows in exposition and comment remain in the rest of her business. Since her story compels her to make the reader comprehend and feel not only what happens but the causes behind what happens, and since these causes are what goes on in the thoughts and feelings of her characters, she must necessarily render these also in such a way that the reader can participate and respond and share quite as much as he judges. Her methods of doing so are most unobtrusively right, and change and develop with the growing seriousness and complication of passion and motive, as the story progresses. She is adept at revealing complex moods that the character himself does not define, without in any way seeming to place herself in a position of all-knowing superiority. This she does by presenting reaction and passing thought alongside action and speech, not only of single characters who are at the centre, but of all those concerned within the situation, giving intense richness to the simplest of happenings. The method is one that makes the narrator virtually disappear, seeming to be only the medium for conveying the fullest possible knowledge. While the method is still that of her earliest work, and the underlying position is that *tout comprendre, c'est tout pardonner* (even though to forgive is never to excuse), she has advanced immeasurably in *Sylvia's Lovers* in her powers with her authorial method, which is now superbly though most unobtrusively controlled. She gives thoughts and reactions, in almost every dialogue and incident, which are indispensable not only for the interpretation of the thinker, but for the understanding of what is said and done by others, not only in the particular instance, but at points far ahead. The complexity grows from the comparatively simple, when characters and situations are less subtle than they later become, to the almost unanalysably dense in the greatest crises. These authorial analyses are always concerned to regulate response, and to prevent the reader from letting involvement with one character precipitate rejection of another. Only fairly extended quotation can reveal the effects: the following slight incident reveals the ramifications even in the early simple situation, when Sylvia, upset by hearing about the press-gang's first attack, has had to be taken into the Fosters' parlour behind the shop to recover:

> Sylvia declined everything, with less courtesy than she ought to have shown to the offers of the hospitable old man. Molly took wine and cake, leaving a good half of both, according to the code of manners in that part of the country; and also because Sylvia was continually urging her to make haste. For the latter disliked the idea of her cousin's esteeming it necessary to accompany them home, and wanted to escape from him by setting off before he returned. But any such plans were frustrated by Philip's coming back into the parlour, full of grave content which brimmed over from his eyes, with the parcel of Sylvia's obnoxious red duffel under his arm; anticipating so keenly the pleasure awaiting him in the walk that he was almost surprised by the gravity of his companions as they prepared for it. Sylvia was a little penitent for her rejection of Mr John's hospitality, now she found out how unavailing for its purpose such rejection had been, and tried to make up by a modest sweetness of farewell, which quite won his heart, and made him praise her up to Hester in a way to which she, observant of all, could not bring herself to respond. What business had the pretty little creature to reject kindly-meant hospitality in the pettish way she did? thought Hester. And, oh! what business had she to be so ungrateful and to try to thwart Philip in his thoughtful wish of escorting them through the streets of the rough riotous town? What did it all mean? (111)

Elizabeth Gaskell's account reveals everyone's responses; Sylvia's version to Philip, Philip's self-absorbed love for her, Hester's puzzled observation, even Molly's preference of wine and cake to obliging her companion. As far as possible emotion is conveyed by the fact which reveals it, as in the detail of Philip's 'grave content, which brimmed over from his eyes' (line 9); where emotion cannot be so conveyed, it is juxtaposed to other thoughts which make for perspective: Sylvia, though she is 'a little penitent for her rejection of Mr John's hospitality', merits Hester's disapproval – 'What business had the pretty little creature to reject kindly-meant hospitality?'; yet Sylvia arouses our sympathy because she has been misunderstood, while Hester's own next sentence reveals that she herself is to be pitied – 'what business had she to be so ungrateful and to try to thwart Philip in his thoughtful wish of escorting them' – for she is no dispassionate arbiter, but suffering vicariously for Philip's pain: yet the exclamatory form allows the author to reveal the love that the character herself does not acknowledge or recognize. The little situation here, full of powerful cross-currents of emotion between the three, foreshadows their future when they will be more deeply and painfully and helplessly at odds. The powerful and significant authorial directive is near-imperceptible, yet governs every word, down to the gently humorous epithet 'obnoxious' of the red duffel under Philip's arm (which reminds us how her mother and Philip preferred the more useful grey duffel), which thus becomes the symbolic foreshadowing of how he will always in much graver situations bear, along with his 'grave content', the burden of what he disapproves.

The impulse to present her material in this way is with her from the first, and excellent though it manifested itself in the climax of *Mary Barton*, it has immeasurably grown. The flow of the narrative and progress of the emotions is now caused, not interrupted, by registering the responses and the inner impulses of every person involved. The positions of each person in relation to all the others are not only caught for the moment, but are profoundly significant, having in them the essence of the whole of the past, and of what is to be the future. The danger of the method – that with the loss of a sense of authorial directive will go a loss for the reader of a sense of proportion, as was occasionally felt in *Mary Barton* – never arises here; selection and juxtaposition themselves provide proportion. The climax of *Sylvia's Lovers*, when Kinraid returns to find Sylvia married, when Philip is faced with the consequences of his lie, and Sylvia with an intolerable decision, shows Elizabeth Gaskell's powers of narrative at their tragic height. No writer who intervened or visibly directed could achieve or sustain such moral and emotional complexity, except with the loss of participation from the reader, and at much greater length. The climax begins when Sylvia, having met Kinraid at her former home at Haytersbank, runs back into the shop house. Elizabeth Gaskell makes the very inadequacy of speakers' powers to define their thoughts work for her, as Shakespeare (almost alone beside her) can do, supplementing them by details of gesture and expression, in a language whose plainness matches that of the speakers. Dialogue springs, not from the previous speaker's meaning, but out of the implications that are present for the answerer:

> 'Where have yo' been?' [Sylvia] asked, in slow, hoarse tones as if her voice were half strangled within her. (xxxiii)

Kinraid's slow-growing response to this is revealed by his twice-repeated echo of the last word 'Been!' and the physical action:

> ... coming a step nearer to her, and taking her hand, not tenderly this time, but with a resolution to be satisfied:
> 'Did not your cousin – Hepburn I mean – did not he tell you? – he saw the press-gang seize me – I gave him a message to you – I bade you keep true to me, as I would be to you.'

The unobtrusive way in which Elizabeth Gaskell reveals Kinraid's relation to the present – Hepburn's name comes out of the past only with an effort of memory – is masterly. The bare physical description that follows compels the reader to create on his own nerves the mental and spiritual turmoil:

> Between every clause of this speech he paused and gasped for her answer; but none came. Her eyes dilated and held his steady gaze prisoner as with a magical charm – neither could look away from the other's wild searching gaze. When he had ended she was silent for a moment; then she cried out, shrill and fierce –
> 'Philip!' No answer.
> Wilder and shriller still, 'Philip!' she cried.
> He was in the distant ware-room, completing the last night's work before the regular shop hours began; before breakfast, also, that his wife might not find him waiting and impatient.

The transition to the third actor comes through Sylvia's single word, whose first utterance can be merely the cry of shocked horror, but whose second is revealed as a direct call to him. The situation from which he comes, homely and trivial, yet turns the reader towards anticipatory pity. The sentence epitomizes all that is best in him, as conscientious worker and considerate husband: Elizabeth Gaskell has with superb economy elected to name, in the last sentence, not 'Sylvia', but 'his wife'. Both his initial shock and the consequences of Sylvia's are revealed in what he sees:

> . . . the back of a naval officer, and his wife on the ground, huddled up in a heap; when she perceived him come in, she dragged herself up by means of a chair, groping like a blind person, and came and stood facing him.

The neutral, simple image 'like a blind person' extends far beyond Sylvia herself, to the lack of vision affecting all three. Kinraid does not yet know how Philip fits in, while Philip cannot recognize Kinraid, being

> So bewildered that even yet he did not understand who the stranger was – did not perceive for an instant that he saw the realization of his greatest dread.

The scene continues, never letting the reader withdraw from any of the three, drawing in past relationships – with the symbolic bit of ribbon, the love-token given by Philip to Sylvia, and by her to Kinraid – and recapitulating the vital details of the past which mean such different things to the three of them. The power of the speaker's language grows with increasing passion and agony, without ever departing from the natural, and the narrative concentrates where the protagonist's attention is concentrated. The author merely points out that which cannot be appreciated through the participants, as when Sylvia, in Kinraid's arms, is unconsciously 'Philip's protection, in that hour of danger, from a blow which might have been his death, if strong will could have aided it to kill'. The near-cliché 'that hour of danger' is a superb instance of Elizabeth Gaskell's self-effacement: no more precise phrase could suggest so briefly and simply that the danger is the nature of the situation, not Philip's physical risk. So is also the use of names:

> Philip came forwards and took hold of her to pull her away; but Charley held her tight.

where at this point, he whom the author habitually calls 'Kinraid' is seen only in his closest union with Sylvia. The power of Elizabeth

Gaskell as a narrator lies in the way she conceals herself; it is constantly felt, but can only be demonstrated by analysis, subjected to which she reveals that her inclusiveness is never diffusion, but the richest of concentration, and that the self-restraint which compels extreme plainness of language is never simplicity.

Unobtrusive though Elizabeth Gaskell is, she is, as always, writing from a committed Christian position. In such a story as this, involving necessarily some of the most fundamental ethical concepts, she lets moral positions, conflicts, and conclusions emerge from the nature and handling of material. In *Sylvia's Lovers* she presents, for her central characters, a more heart-searching moral problem than ever before, and a more widely-varied spectrum of religious and ethical belief and non-belief than she or any other novelist has hitherto attempted in a novel where religious belief is not a prime concern. Yet almost every incident, act, and character is as closely inwrought with the moral problems as with the plot. It is scarcely possible ever to separate moral implication from story, character, or setting; and what religious beliefs are laid down are almost all revealed in terms of action or of character. Beliefs, in this work, are what people live by, not what they profess. The one religious type significantly not represented is the hypocrite; all characters are candid, even if wrong.

The moral norm in the novel is one of unthinking acceptance of eternal truths rendered accessible through the Church: Elizabeth Gaskell establishes it at the same time and equally with Monkshaven itself, and the sea-going life:

> They who went forth upon the great deep might carry solemn thoughts with them of the words they heard there: not conscious thoughts, perhaps, rather a distinct if dim conviction that buying and selling, eating and marrying, even life and death, were not all the realities in existence. Nor were the words that came up to their remembrance words of sermons preached there, however impressive. The sailors mostly slept through the sermons. . . . They did not recognise their daily faults or temptations under the grand aliases befitting their appearance from a preacher's mouth. But they knew the old, oft-repeated words praying for deliverance from the familiar dangers of lightning and tempest, from battle, murder, and sudden death; and nearly every man was aware that he left behind him some one who would watch

for the prayer for the preservation of those who travel by land or by water, and think of him, as God-protected the more for the earnestness of the response then given. (VI)

This deceptively simple analysis of the religious position of the unthinking is dramatically reinforced by its context. Sylvia is representative of the general mass in that she goes to church rarely – two or three times a year – and has gone on this occasion for two very peripheral reasons: first, because she has duffel for a new cloak and they can, as Molly Corney suggests, 'see Measter Fishburn's daughters, as has their things made i' York, and notice a bit how they're made', and second, because

'Besides, there's to be this grand buryin' o' t'man t'press-gang shot, and 't will be like killing two birds at once.' (VI)

But once there, she is moved to forget her cloak, and to share the general sorrow, and the confused doubt answered only by simple and uncertain faith, represented by the thoughts of the dead man's father:

How came God to permit such cruel injustice of man? Permitting it, He could not be good. Then what was life, and what was death, but woe and despair? The beautiful solemn words of the ritual had done him good, and restored much of his faith. Though he could not understand why such sorrow had befallen him any more than before, he had come back to something of his childlike trust; he kept saying to himself in a whisper, as he mounted the weary steps, 'it is the Lord's doing'; and this repetition soothed him unspeakably. (VI)

The faith is part of the whole of life, reinforced in the artistry by being connected to the other great eternal force in the people's lives – the sea, from which, as they stand at the grave-side 'the soft salt air blew on their hot eyes and rigid faces' the silence 'broken by the measured lapping of the tide far beneath' (VI).

Elizabeth Gaskell has no need as narrator to define or expound the inadequacies of such a state of belief for the reader; it has all been done through incident, character and mood. From this norm, once stated, she can move to other characters and their degrees of moral and religious awareness, making them mutually illuminating, and mutually bringing out their power. The achievement is all the greater because there is no single character who is, by any standards, whether of the historical time of the story, or of the author's own time, either educated beyond literacy (such as that enabling Philip to teach Sylvia reading, writing and geography), or even potentially of intelligence above a very moderate average. To depict such characters as wholly absorbing is a great feat; to render them moving, a greater; and to reveal through them all the moral and ethical positions of the central dilemma, is the greatest. Again in this novel, as in *North and South* and elsewhere, she makes clear distinctions between religion and morals, making no automatic correlations between type and intensity of religious creed or practice, and moral perceptiveness. Both are kept distinct from the intrinsic virtue, or 'goodness' of a nature. The religious man need not be morally aware, or capable of fine discriminations; the good man may have almost any kind of faith. Elizabeth Gaskell here reveals a wide range of combinations of creed, moral awareness, and intrinsic virtue. Molly Corney is the character who represents the minimum of all three, not religious, or moral, or virtuous. She is so little affected by the funeral service for Darley that her mind turns instantly from it to chatter about Kinraid, to whether 'William Coulson looks sweet at Hester Rose' (v11), and to cheap vulgar banter about Philip's friendship with the Quakers:

'What a wonder yo' can speak to such sinners as Sylvia and me, after keepin' company with so much goodness!' (v11)

Her later conduct is all of a piece with this. At the other extreme of religious and moral awareness are the Quakers – or Friends, as the author correctly calls them: the Foster brothers, Coulson,[2] and, especially, Hester Rose, who guide all their acts and thoughts on religious principles, on a sense of right and wrong and duty to their fellow-men, and on love. The Fosters' business methods are proof of their principle: they have

a kind of primitive bank in connection with their shop, receiving and taking such money as people did not wish to retain in their houses for fear of burglars. No one asked them for interest on the money thus deposited, nor did they give any; but, on the other hand, if any of their customers, on whose character they could depend, wanted a little advance, the Fosters, after due

2 Although later she says that he is a Methodist (x111).

enquiries made, and in some cases, due security given, were not unwilling to lend a moderate sum without charging a penny for the use of their money. (III)

Their religion is in no way idealized: Elizabeth Gaskell is wholly fair and accurate in defining the principles of such men of their time and place, for utterly honest in their dealings though they are, and

> scrupulous in most things [yet] it did not go against the con-sciences of these good brothers to purchase smuggled articles. There was a little locking of doors, and drawing of the green silk curtain that was supposed to shut out the shop, but really all this was done very much for form's sake. Everybody in Monkshaven smuggled who could, and every one wore smuggled goods who could; and great reliance was placed on the excise officer's neighbourly feelings. (III)

But the Foster brothers are far from muddle-headed in their prin-ciples. Elizabeth Gaskell finely depicts their scrupulous honesty and precision in all their dealings, as well as catching the Quaker idiom with its use of 'thee' and 'thou' and of the rather ponderous diction that accompanies scrupulosity of mind. Jeremiah Foster, in the superb scene in which Sylvia comes to him for help and tells him how and why Philip has gone, thinks of her plight, and his, and the child's in the light of a universal charity which inhibits any prompt judge-ment, or taking of sides, and permits only pity:

> 'Poor little one!' said he, 'thy mother had need love thee, for she's deprived thee of thy father's love. Thou'rt half-way to being an orphan. Yet I cannot call thee one of the fatherless to whom God will be a father. Thou'rt a desolate babe; thou mayst well cry; thine earthly parents have forsaken thee, and I know not if the Lord will take thee up.' (XXXVI)

Hester Rose, though not as a character a complete success, is ethically perfectly consistent, attempting to rule her acts and even her thoughts out of complete charity, even when Philip unconsciously pains her (he has no idea that she loves him) in making her his messenger and proxy with Sylvia, and when she has to struggle with her own dislike of Sylvia for her unkindness to Philip.

In between these extremes of ignorance and awareness range the rest of the characters in whom limited religion, moral sense and virtue are mixed. Daniel Robson for instance embodies a deep and sensitive love for his wife and daughter, and strong sense of justice and injustice to individuals, which makes him rescue the impressed sailors; but he is incapable of conceiving abstract morality or law, or justice on a larger scale:

> 'When did I say a word against King George and the Constitution? I only ax 'em to govern me as I judge best, and that's what I call representation. When I gived my vote to Measter Cholmley to go up to t'Parliament House, I as good as said, "Now yo' go up theer, sir, and tell 'em what I, Daniel Robson, think right, and what I, Daniel Robson, wish to have done." Else I'd be darned if I'd ha' gi'en my vote to him or any other man.' (IV)

Yet though the richly comic expression is that of a drunken Yorkshire speaker, the moral position is one common enough among the sober and articulate. On the other hand, there is Alice Rose, literate only in her deeply-read Bible, as perceptive of her daughter Hester as Robson is of his, and with a wide instinctive charity constantly at odds with her Calvinist religion which teaches that only a few can be of the elect.

Elizabeth Gaskell's discrimination between religious forms and basic morality is much akin to Trollope's. It is often noted of him that while in the Barchester novels the bulk of the characters are in some way linked to the establishment of the Church of England, yet questions of theology or doctrine rarely arise, nor do variations in religion bear any correlation with virtue. It is probably also true that most readers who enjoy Trollope feel no conflict or deficiency in his work on this account. This is because, like Elizabeth Gaskell, he is writing from his own securely-based unsectarian position, which can permit him to observe and explore shades of religious observance, while at the same time permitting his characters to be measured against a scale of moral values operating alongside. Mr Harding's great dilemma and his decision to resign the Wardenship of Hiriam's Hospital is made irrespective of the ecclesiastical politics that confuse Archdeacon Grantly and Mr Bold. Yet Trollope can be as perceptive and just concerning the archdeacon and John Bold as Mr Harding. Trollope is not so fine nor so scrupulous a writer as Elizabeth Gaskell, but the reasons for their equal moral security are the same. Essentially all the characters are based upon the basic Christian faith that love of one's neighbour is the *sine qua non*.

In Elizabeth Gaskell's novels this has been the basic faith by which her characters stand or fall. Here, though, in Sylvia and Philip she grapples with the kinds of passion that are the hardest to govern or control. Her unironic, unjudging attitude is at its most vital. She has no fear of passions, and has no impulse to condemn them as intrinsically evil, or even wrong. She fully recognizes that, like all powerful impulses, they are dangerous ones. In Sylvia she creates a personality of great power, uneducated on either the religious or the moral level, and almost wholly at the mercy of instinctive and basic responses. She does not ever suggest, herself, that Sylvia is wicked, in this her original state, only that she is at the mercy of events in a way that the conscious moral being is not. While those instincts direct towards love for her parents and their one servant, Hester, there is little amiss. But she has no principles to guide her when her father is arrested and hanged, and her pain turns to unforgiving hatred of the chief instrument in his conviction, Simpson, who gives the evidence that hangs him: so she replies desperately to Philip's attempt to soften her:

> 'But, Sylvie, yo' pray to be forgiven your trespasses, as you forgive them that trespass against you.'
> 'Well, if I'm to be taken at my word, I'll noane pray at all; that's all. It's well enough for them as has but little to forgive to use them words.' (xxix)

Elizabeth Gaskell has always understood such characters, and Sylvia's words recall *Mary Barton*, and Carson's cry,

> 'Let my trespasses be unforgiven, so that I may have vengeance for my son's murder.' (*Mary Barton*, xxv)

Spiritually in a state of nature as she is, she is even more helpless when seized by love for Kinraid. She has no antidote for grief at his loss, and lets expediency direct her into marrying Philip. Having done so, she is brought into contact with conflicting ideas of duty and principle. Again the author passes no judgement, but lets morality define itself, in the painful conflict, for instance, between Sylvia's undying love for Kinraid, and Philip's cry,

> 'What kind of a woman are yo', to go on dreaming of another man in this way, and taking on so about him, when yo're a wedded wife, with a child as yo've borne to another man?'
> (xxxi)

Inevitably, when she discovers Philip's betrayal, she reacts even more passionately than she has to Simpson, but with more deliberation, and with more religious significance for having been compelled to think of her moral position.

> 'I'l never forgive yon man, nor live with him as his wife again. All that's done and ended. He's spoilt my life – he's spoilt it for as long as iver I live on this earth; but neither yo' nor him shall spoil my soul. . . . I'm bound and tied, but I've sworn my oath to him as well as yo': there's things I will do, and there's things I won't.' (XXXIII)

In Philip Hepburn, Elizabeth Gaskell delineates a nature far more aware than Sylvia's of religious and moral concepts. Though not himself a Quaker, he lives with them and shares their principles both of work and of worship. Like Sylvia's his love is of his religious and moral nature a thing apart, which in crises comes to be at odds with it. He feels moral guilt at going to the Corney's New Year's party rather than the Watch-night Service with Hester and Alice Rose and Coulson, even before he has the agony of seeing Sylvia's love for Kinraid. Moral principles combine with his jealousy when he sees Kinraid captured by the press-gang 'a promise given is a fetter to the giver. But a promise is not given when it is not received' (XVIII). So because Kinraid did not hear his reply, Philip can thus quibble within himself that he has not effectively promised to deliver Kinraid's message to Sylvia: that he will come back and marry her, and that he deems her 'as much my wife as if we'd gone to church' (XVIII). And he can also justify letting Sylvia think Kinraid is dead, because Kinraid is a philanderer who has deserted other women.

In *Sylvia's Lovers* Elizabeth Gaskell has advanced far beyond her earlier works in her concept of the moral and spiritual forces within her characters. She presents no simple antithesis of higher and base impulses, but a conflict of passions, equally powerful and equally valid, coming from different sources: the moral and the religious on one hand, and alongside them the fundamental and powerful force of the love of one individual for another. They may well conflict, since both are near-overwhelming drives. But she never suggests that overwhelming love is itself wrong; equally, she never suggests that religion is a set of prohibitions, nor a destroyer of a fundamentally base 'human nature'. She sees the conflict not as universally inevitable, but as, in the special and unique plight of her characters in this novel, inevitably tragic.

Elizabeth Gaskell resembles the Brontës not only in recognizing that passion renders the individual at odds with normal moral standards and religious principles, but in accepting the necessities of passion, and examining the conflict without either condemning the passion or rejecting the morals or religion. They find it harder than she to keep their authorial balance between the two, possibly because their Methodist basis provides a less secure, more extreme, position than her generous Unitarianism. Anne Brontë, who seems to question least, yet comes in *The Tenant of Wildfell Hall* to find that deeply and sincerely held principles will not uphold the soul in crisis. Helen Huntingdon, harrowed by her dipsomaniac husband and rendered desperate by the way he begins to corrupt their son, finds that suffering does not ennoble:

> Instead of being humbled and purified by my afflictions, I feel they are turning my nature into gall. (xxxv)

Charlotte Brontë's novels all examine the predicament of the passionate nature in isolation, who at some point finds that conventional standards, whether of general morals or of religion, are incapable of supporting it, still less providing adequate room for spiritual fulfilment. Jane Eyre, Caroline Helstone, and above all Lucy Snowe in *Villette*, all, though they never fully reject moral duties in the way that Sylvia rejects the duty to forgive, reach points where they can find no consolation or strength in obedience. The force of the love and the hate in Sylvia and Hepburn is equal to that in Heathcliff and Catherine in *Wuthering Heights*, yet Elizabeth Gaskell has undertaken with an innocence almost equal to Emily Brontë's a literary task quite as hard. Emily Brontë, aware of conventional religious and moral standards, and the normal imperatives of common life, persuades the reader to feel them irrelevant to her lovers. Elizabeth Gaskell, well aware that such passions do not bow to such imperatives, sets them at all points in juxtaposition, and adds the further, more tragic complication that though Hepburn is bound to Sylvia as Heathcliff to Catherine, Sylvia is not bound to him. This is not to say that there is any literary link between the two writers, but only that both in their ways undertake within the novel the kind of material that has never before been accessible in so sophisticated an art form. Emily Brontë's is the more exotic, and so the more immediately recognizable in its greatness; Elizabeth Gaskell's, more apparently familiar, and less striking, is not the less great.

The developments from Elizabeth Gaskell's examination of the strife between the codes arising from the natural impulses of human emotions and passions and the codes arising from spiritual self-awareness and education – such as organized religion – are the great tragic preoccupation of Thomas Hardy. Sylvia is 'a pure woman' like Tess Durbeyfield; Philip is bound by love for the wrong woman, and tortured by the conflict of ethics with impulse, as is Jude Fawley (and both have their cousin as their idol). The differences in what the two writers see as the 'tragedy', and in the kind of sympathy they accord to their characters, springs from their own very different religious positions. Elizabeth Gaskell's own Unitarian position, firmly founded on personal faith, allows her a far wider and subtler range of imaginative sympathy and understanding of her characters' own spiritual and emotional dilemmas. She enriches her reader's understanding of the workings of individuals' minds, and of the intensity of suffering possible within even meagre and humble natures. Hardy, himself in the grip of the problems that face his characters, accepting no well-based creed or philosophical system, cannot stretch to such imaginative participation with those whose position he cannot share; but he can challenge, as it never occurs to Elizabeth Gaskell to challenge, the validity of the creeds and systems under which they suffer.

Locality has always been an important part of Elizabeth Gaskell's material. Here it becomes more extensive, more varied, and more inwrought. Instead of providing a coherent base, as Manchester does in *Mary Barton*, or registering symbolically changes in the heroine's career, as in *Ruth*, or contrasting oppositions as in *North and South*, it now offers extending perspectives that radiate from the pulsating centre of Monkshaven. In *Sylvia's Lovers* there are more settings, more carefully interrelated, as well as more varied than hitherto: the town itself, the Robsons' and Corney's farms on the hills above it; the cliffs, shore and the sea, and the wildly extending North York moors. Beyond them she looks out to the Greenland Seas where so much of the whale-fishers' year is passed; to North Shields and Newcastle with their larger fishing communities; to York the seat of justice; to London the seat of Government and the mercantile heart; and beyond these to Europe torn by the wars with Napoleon. Some of these are settings for action, others are areas of influence and reference, registered with diminishing degrees of knowledge and awareness. Few novels hold themselves in relation to so much of their world, with so fine a sense of balance; perhaps none do whose most central interest is so far from the cosmopolitan, set for the most part in a single place. The end section of the story, differing in so many ways from the main part, when the action abruptly leaves Monkshaven for Palestine, and then follows Philip on his long sad journey from the war home to Monkshaven, is the only part where this radiating structure of setting changes; yet even this can be seen as a moving back again by way of Portsmouth and Winchester to the heart of things.

This heart is Monkshaven, the whale-fishing town of the northeast Yorkshire coast, whose pseudonym for Whitby, even, shows an advance in felicity over the earlier 'Milton Northern' for Manchester: the neutral *naïveté* of the earlier coinage cannot compare with the rich suggestiveness of Monkshaven, echoing both the lost, distant, ruined past which broods over the town and its inhabitants, and the vigorous present of its sea-going, harbour-based mercantile business. It is a 'haven' too for Sylvia in her troubles (if an enforced and unhappy one) when, almost destitute, descending to it from her parents' windy farm, she marries Philip.

Monkshaven functions within the novel as the norm of a stable society, the one place that is unchanged and unchanging despite the various personal and public disturbances of the action, which offers, nevertheless, progress and opportunity; where the apprentice sailor-boy can 'rise by daring and saving to be a shipowner himself', where the honest tradesman like Philip can become part-owner of a business, where neighbouring farmers must come to sell their produce, as Sylvia and Molly come to sell their butter and eggs at the Butter-cross. It offers a stable social norm for the whole, revealed not only by the precise topographical descriptions, but by the inhabitants who people it. The brothers Foster, Coulson, and Hester and Alice Rose are the chief of these, supported by other more briefly-appearing characters; all embody the quality that creates stability, of making their inclinations accord with their circumstances. The Fosters have succeeded in their banking and drapery, and are at the top of this scale of social adjustment. The others fit in and avoid disaster. Coulson resigns himself both to becoming the second force to the more dominating Philip in what begins as an equal business partnership,

and to giving up his hopes of marrying Hester, contenting himself
with another less deeply-felt union. Though he fails in his desires
where Philip succeeds in getting his, he succeeds in that he survives
in moderate contentment, and escapes the disaster of those who resist.
Hester and her mother also embody this resignation of the individual
will to social necessity. Yet Monkshaven is not by any means a
destructive symbol of the frustration of the individual will in the face
of social pressure: it embodies a moral positive norm, of the kind that
alien forces for evil, or tragic extremes of personal passion may disrupt,
but cannot destroy. The activities of the press-gang are the greatest
single external force. Though impressment as such is legal, yet lands-
men and some serving sailors, like Kinraid himself, are protected by
law from impressment. Thus the raid made by the press-gang, when
they round up all the townsmen who rush out to answer the town
fire-bell's false alarm, becomes a moral wrong against the town, and
the law of impressment and those who administer it are condemned
accordingly. Yet Daniel Robson's desperate act in rescuing them is
itself a wrong, on the moral and artistic levels, as well as the legal
historical one. He is legally hanged for being present, aiding and
abetting, in the resistance to the press-gang. But such a fate on its own
would make him merely a painfully arbitrary victim of a harsh and
unjust law. He becomes a pathetic near-tragic victim of a moral
power above him by the way his act turns out in relation to Monkshaven. Though the sailors may be rescued, it is only at the price of
social destruction. There is a fight, townspeople are injured and the
Mariners' Arms – the 'Randyvowse' – is broken into, smashed, and
burned down, and the innkeeper Hobbs is ruined. Though Robson
dies, Monkshaven becomes the haven for his destitute family, where
his wife Bell and his daughter Sylvia go when they can no longer run
the farm, and where the near-childish Bell can end her days in peace.
The moral fault in Sylvia's heroic stand when Kinraid returns is
rendered concrete in the way in which it creates pathetic unhappiness
within the household around her, just as Philip's sin, when it is
revealed, results immediately in his becoming an exile from the whole
of life that is symbolized in Monkshaven. All the forces of disaster,
tragic though they may personally and individually be, come from
outside, and disturb, though they cannot destroy, this centre.

For the novel Monkshaven itself has two centres: the Fosters'
house behind the shop, and the 'staithes' or quayside. The former of
these is the still heart of all storms, a centre of refuge, not of strife.

Elizabeth Gaskell's first presentation of it is as shelter for Sylvia when, over-excited by the prospect of the return of the first whaling ship of the season, and by its actual return, with its crew all arrested by the warrant of the press-gang, she collapses into hysteria, and is comforted and revived in the parlour – 'a low, comfortable, room, with great beams running across the ceiling' (111) – where she can rest on a broad old-fashioned sofa. This is where she and Bell her mother come when Robson has been arrested; it is her home after marriage; and the place where her gradual redemption, after Philip has gone, comes about.

The staithes are the scene of action and event, looking outwards to all the goings-on of life in the outer world, to which trade comes, and whence vessels depart to the remote Greenland Seas which, as well as being the source and means of life to all its sea-faring population, are a symbol of heroism, fantastic events, and romance, passing strange and wondrous pitiful. Point both of departure and return throughout the action, the area where town meets sea is the setting for the tale's final disaster and triumph, where at 't'edge o' t'cliff, where they's makin' t'new walk reet o'er t'sea' (xlv) Philip leaps in to save his own child from the waves.

The town is recreated with the fidelity which is one of Elizabeth Gaskell's greatest powers, being rendered so solid that its significance can be revealed almost imperceptibly, and rendered palpable to feeling as to sight, whether it is the general prospect of the town as a whole where

> the red and fluted tiles of the gabled houses rose in crowded irregularity on one side of the river, while the newer suburb was built in more orderly and less picturesque fashion on the opposite cliff. The river itself was swelling and chafing with the incoming tide till its vexed waters rushed over the very feet of the watching crowd on the staithes. (11)

or whether it is Alice Rose's minute dwelling, in a confined court on the hilly side of the High Street,

> wedged up into a space which necessitated all sorts of odd projections and irregularities in order to obtain sufficient light for the interior . . . small diamond panes of glass in the casement window were kept so bright and clear that a great sweet-scented-leaved geranium grew and flourished though it did not flower profusely. (vii)

or the Fosters' House in the new town of Monkshaven where

> the very bricks seemed as if they came in for the daily scrubbing
> which brightened handle, knocker, all down to the very
> scraper. (xiv)

and where, within the parlour,

> the same precise order was observed. Every article of furniture
> was free from speck of dirt or particle of dust; and each thing
> was placed either in a parallel line, or at exact right angles with
> every other. Even John and Jeremiah sat in symmetry on oppo-
> site sides of the fireplace; the very smiles on their honest faces
> seemed drawn to a line of exactitude. (xiv)

The last of these settings very plainly reveals its occupants; almost all
of the others do so in less humorously direct ways, like Alice's small
cramped corner of the world quoted above, so closely parallel to her
own life, lived out in the light of a narrow religion, widowed by an
unkind husband, with the daughter Hester who herself fails of the
desire of her heart – a life like the geranium, sweet-scented but
hardly able to flower.

The other main setting for the action is the Robson's farm of
Haytersbank, set above and apart from the sheltered town, on the
cliff over which rush the 'piping winds' from the North Sea. So it
stands in the same relation to the sea, which prevents plants from
growing in its garden, as does it owner Daniel Robson, who has been
'sailor, smuggler, horse-dealer and farmer in turns' (iv), but whose
heart was in his sailing whale-hunting days, and who thrives as
uneasily as does his own farm, made bleak and intractable by the salt-
laden storms off the ocean. Isolated Haytersbank, cut off even from
the road by a long bleak lane full of round rough stones, and a little,
dry, hard footpath across a field, is a natural dwelling-place for Sylvia,
who grows up with all the charm, and none of the self control, of one
far apart from all but natural impulses. The farm is the affirmation o
and setting for her time of wholeness and health, of her childhood and
her love for Kinraid. Monkshaven changes her, and the qualities that
belonged to her youth, now past and irrecoverable, find their parallel
and expression when, married and a mother, she returns to the sold
and derelict farm to pick herbs to make her mother balm-tea:

> The house was shut up, awaiting the entry of some new tenant.
> There were no shutters to shut; the long low window was

blinking in the rays of the morning sun; the house and cow-house doors were closed, and no poultry wandered about the field in search of stray grains of corn, or early worms. . . . Sylvia went slowly past the house, and down the path leading to the wild, deserted bit of garden. She saw that the last tenants had had a pump sunk for them, and resented the innovation, as though the well she was passing could feel the insult. Over it grew two hawthorn-trees; on the bent trunk of one of them she used to sit long ago: the charm of the position being enhanced by the possible danger of falling into the well and being drowned. The rusty unused chain was wound round the windlass; the bucket was falling to pieces from dryness. . . . Primroses grew in the sheltered places, just as they formerly did, and made the un-cultivated ground seem less deserted than the garden, where last year's weeds were rotting away, and cumbering the ground.

(XXXIII)

Such description not only symbolizes the vanished and lost past of the whole family, but does so at the critical time when the past reasserts itself: immediately she has left the farm, Sylvia meets Kinraid again, whom 'she had last seen in Haytersbank Gully three long years ago, and had never thought to see in life again' (XXXIII). The descriptive passage thus creates the state of nostalgic, heightened sensibility in which Sylvia receives the shock of seeing Kinraid and reaffirms in its images that it is impossible to have 'the old Sylvia back again; captious, capricious, wilful, haughty, merry, charming. Alas! that Sylvia was gone for ever' (XXIX).

Contrasting with the Robsons' farm is the Corneys', Moss Brow, a place of disorderly, slatternly fecundity and easy-going family life. The differences between the two emphasize that Robson, though his heart is not in his farming, is a capable farmer, and Bell Robson a superb housekeeper; they emphasize even more that Sylvia, as a petted only child, has no experience of coping with even minor frus-trations and adversities, and no training in making the sort of com-promises with circumstances of which the Corneys make far too many, whether of leaving the washing and housework for a gossip, or leaving the ripe apples ungathered on the trees, till they become windfalls which 'lay rotting on the ground until the "lads" wanted a supply of pies for supper' (VI). One of the novel's finest scenes, the New Year's Eve party, takes place there when the love between

Sylvia and Kinraid becomes plain to them, and Philip's sufferings begin. The easy breakdown of decorum induced by the Corney's casual manners – 'we're a' on us friends, and some on us mayhap sweethearts; so no need to be particular about [sharing] plates' (xii) – and traditional amusement – like the game of forfeits in which Sylvia has to 'blow out t'candle and kiss t'candlestick' (the 'stick' being Kinraid) – all conduce to a rapid growth of intimacy; while the atmosphere of warmth and overflowing plenty – whether of design on a patchwork quilt or of 'half a hundred-weight o' butcher's meat, besides pies and custards' (xii) – enriches Kinraid, the cousin of the house, and rounds out the pale, remote, wounded hero of his first appearance, at the same time as it excludes Philip, the pale and withdrawn visitor from quite another kind of life.

Outside these main areas radiate the larger areas of the outer world, of two kinds, those felt precisely – if with humorous inaccuracy – for their local relevance, and those whose influence is unconscious yet deeper. Of the first kind are towns. 'Newcassel' is a place of ploughs and horse-purchases for Robson; London is an unvisited mystery, the seat of government where Robson's instructions go to King George (conveyed by proxy of the member he has elected), which Alice Rose sees as 'a sore place o' temptation [where] there's pitfalls for men, and traps for money at ivery turn, as I've heard say' (xvii); York is the seat of a strange and remote justice which can reach out and seize Robson and hang him at the assizes. Presenting them as Elizabeth Gaskell invariably does, as they are felt by the characters themselves, they further make Monkshaven the central focus, and remove any feeling in the reader of standing apart from the action in a position of superior knowledge.

Surrounding all these, with a sense of greater distance and more enveloping space, are the land and the sea, both of them mysterious and partly unknown, as well as local and familiar. The feeling of the high, bare, North York Moors is of what shuts off the outer world from Monkshaven; Philip crosses them, to his desperate despairing exile, over

the high green pastures, the short upland turf, above which the larks hung poised 'at heaven's gate'. He has passed all enclosures and stone fences now, and was fairly on the desolate brown moors. . . . through the withered last year's ling and fern, through prickly gorse he tramped, crushing down the tender shoots of this year's growth, heedless of the startled plover's cry. (xxxiv)

The sea on the other hand is more known, in many aspects. At its farthest it is the Greenland Seas, place of heroism and daring and improbable adventures, remote and familiar, humorous as well as strange, in the reports of whalers, for which Sylvia is willing to learn geography from Philip, although she knows it in the homely idiom of her father:

> 'There's three things to be afeared on, . . . there's t'ice, that's bad; there's dirty weather, that's worse; and there's whales theirselves, as is t'worst of all.' (ix)

and has heard his richly idiomatic tales of icebergs, and grapplings with whales, and near-drownings. But the sea is also a daily part of the life of the port, the Monkshaven world's link with elsewhere, for, when Philip goes to London, he does so by sea, from Newcastle. The shore and the cliffs which come so close to Haytersbank, and the sea which washes them, are a powerful force in the novel's crucial relationships between Philip, Kinraid and Sylvia. Philip, walking on the shore towards Hartlepool in the moments before Kinraid is seized and borne off by the press-gang, seeing

> the crisp curling waves rushing almost up to his feet, on his right hand, and then swishing back over the small fine pebbles into the great swelling sea

feels a delight that 'the cares of land were shut out by the glorious barriers of rocks before him.' (xviii). The vivid accuracy of the sense-impressions here intensifies the bitter irony – that Philip's greatest 'care' is to come upon him in a few moments, in temptation from the sea, and that, as has been already established, the sea's natural affinity is to Kinraid, not himself. It functions as such, again, later, when Sylvia, married to Philip, feels imprisoned in the house, and escapes 'to mount the cliffs and sit on the turf, gazing abroad over the wide still expanse of the open sea' (xxx) and later still, with her child

> would sit on a broken piece of rock, and fall to gazing on the advancing waves catching the sunlight on their crests, advancing, receding, for ever and ever, as they had done all her life long – as they did when she had walked on them that once by the side of Kinraid. (xxxi)

Elizabeth Gaskell represents in the sea both the freedom Sylvia has lost, and the spiritual Unity with Kinraid, the man of the sea.

The settings and description of scene of all kinds are now so closely inwrought with action and character, and above all so essential as one of the chief creators of mood that it becomes difficult to isolate them, and almost impossible to illustrate their power by short quotation, even though Elizabeth Gaskell achieves a masterly economy by their use. One of the many paradoxes of *Sylvia's Lovers* is that a tale of such pain often has large stretches and innumerable moments of poetic enchantment, in all of which the setting is an indispensable part. The impression and the components recall that earlier, equally homely, equally unhappy tale of rural tragedy, Wordsworth's *Michael*, where the relationship between the human feelings of intuitive beings make their progress amidst and by means of a hard and remote landscape and the forces of nature; and where also it is difficult to isolate the components of the creation. Elizabeth Gaskell's power in her settings, like Wordsworth's, seems to rest not in any qualities of a consciously plain style, but in the selection and the awareness simply of the things themselves and their intrinsic power to draw upon universal and deep-seated response.

Even her one flaw here, if flaw it can be called, when she goes right outside the sphere of Monkshaven, to tell of the battle at Joppa and of Philip's weary journey home, is presented by the same means, and is at one with the rest in its sensuous fidelity. For the battle she makes the sea her link with home, and makes a virtue of necessity by stressing the intense contrast. The formidable and cold North Sea has been a source of comfort, strength and life; the Mediterranean, called up in a few phrases, accords with the alien and hostile action, both hostile and terribly beautiful:

> The Mediterranean came up with a long roar, on a beach glittering white with snowy sand, and the fragments of innumerable sea-shells, delicate and shining as porcelain. (XXXVIII)

The startlingly precise adjective 'snowy' throws the reader back with shock to the literally snowy seas of the earlier part, as does the very ambiguous adjective in her allusion (a few lines later) to 'the hot sparkle of the *everlasting* sea' where the quality that had formerly given reassurance now evokes only weariness.

Skilful in handling of setting and background Elizabeth Gaskell has always been; *Sylvia's Lovers* represents her highest point, and,

like the highest points of great writers in general, what has been
done here is done once for all. It may be imitated only with difficulty,
and cannot be surpassed in its own kind.

The setting of *Sylvia's Lovers* is strange to Elizabeth Gaskell, not
only geographically, but historically, being set back in time very little
more than the 'sixty years since' of Scott's *Waverley*, to the wars with
Napoleon. However, her purpose in doing so is quite different from
Scott's. The great events of the world do not concern her, and she
has no wish to recreate them. Her great achievement is to deal with
the consequences of them upon those who could hardly be further
from the political events themselves, and to recreate their reactions
to events they hardly know and cannot understand – an achievement
so successful that the reader scarcely realizes that it is the result not of
choice but compulsion. No other age can provide Elizabeth Gaskell
with the central situations: one of Kinraid's being seized and taken
off by the press-gang, and the other of her father's being hanged for
resisting the authorities by rescuing the impressed sailors. The tragedy
depends on the circumstances; the circumstances cannot be other
than at this particular date. However, though Elizabeth Gaskell has
thus an unavoidable task, it is no uncongenial one. She has always
liked working with imposed material, not creating her plots and situations, but taking what she feels to be in some way the actual, which
it is her power and delight as a novelist to explore, shape and interpret.
Many of her short stories are such excursions into past times, where
great events bring grief and tragedy to those who are innocently
caught up in them. The wars between Britain and France are
material which she explores several times in short stories such as 'My
French Master' (published in *Household Words* in 1853), or the
long recollection in 'My Lady Ludlow' (also in *Household Words*,
June–September 1858) of the romantic story of Pierre de Créquy,
the aristocrat whose vain attempt to rescue his cousin Virginie from
the Terror ends in the guillotine for both of them. Here, in *Sylvia's
Lovers*, she deliberately uses actual historical fact even more detailed; the whole account of the attack on the press-gang, the burning
down of the 'Randyvowse' and the subsequent hanging of the gang's
leader at York, comes from an actual event of 1793.[3]

Her recreation of time past is of the most tactful and least mechanical kind, achieved mostly by mental attitudes and ways of regarding

[3] The details are given by A. W. Ward in his introduction to the novel, Vol. VI
of the Knutsford Edition.

the world, and hardly at all by the kinds of detail of way of life, buildings, manners, language, clothes, and incidental appurtenances of living which can all too often be both tedious and unconvincing. Where such details are given, they serve purposes to the action and to the characters, as in the delightful building-up of the feeling of the Fosters' shop:

> People remembered it as an old-fashioned dwelling-house, with a sort of supplementary shop with unglazed windows projecting from the lower story. These openings had long been filled with panes of glass that at the present day would be accounted very small, but which seventy years ago were much admired for their size. I can best make you understand the appearance of the place by bidding you think of the long openings in a butcher's shop, and then fill them up in your imagination with panes about eight inches by six, in a heavy wooden frame. There was one of these windows on each side of the door-place, which was kept partially closed through the day by a low gate about a yard high. Half the shop was appropriated to grocery; the other half to drapery, and a little mercery. (III)

It is often difficult to say, a hundred years after writing, whether the details Elizabeth Gaskell gives are of history or of the present of her day, when for instance Philip 'seating himself on the counter, swung himself over after the fashion of shopmen' or a moment later Hester 'returned, with a shop-boy helping her to drag along the great rolls of scarlet and grey cloth' (III); thus the excellence of her method is proved, in that there is no perceptible difference for the reader between the creating of historical setting, and the filling in of detail in general. The most powerful and entertaining uses of the period, however, are a matter of characterization, done very largely through that splendid character Daniel Robson, the least educated man, least affected by the movements of time and change.

> 'And when did I say a word again King George and the Constitution? I only ax 'em to govern me as I judge best, and that's what I call representation.' (IV)

This, one of his earliest comments, with its naïve but eternal logic, is the type of all. Where Elizabeth Gaskell finds it necessary to fill in facts herself, as on attitudes to smuggling, they are harmoniously simple, relevant to moral issues, and to character:

When the duty on salt was strictly and cruelly enforced, making it penal to pick up rough dirty lumps containing small quantities, that might be thrown out with the ashes of the brine-houses on the high-roads; when the price of this necessary was so increased by the tax upon it as to make it an expensive, sometimes an unattainable, luxury to the working man, Government did more to demoralize the popular sense of rectitude and uprightness than heaps of sermons could undo. And the same, though in smaller measure, was the consequence of other taxes. It may seem curious to trace up the popular standard of truth to taxation; but I do not think the idea would be so very far-fetched.

(ix)

Such interpolations are always brief and unobtrusive, and merely supplement what is borne out in action and psychology, as in the way the Quaker view of life is touched on, in relation to Philip's emotions and his profession:

He had been brought up among the Quakers, and shared in their austere distrust of a self-seeking spirit; yet what else but self-seeking was his passionate prayer, 'Give me Sylvia, or else I die?' (xi)

and a few lines later, the reasons why neither Philip nor Coulson anticipate or discuss their coming partnership as owners of the shop:

The whole atmosphere of life among the Friends at this date partook of this character of self-repression, and both Coulson and Hepburn shared in it. (xi)

Such unobtrusively assured use of fairly recent history – so strikingly different from the extensive and thorough-going recreation of a vanished century, such as George Eliot undertakes in *Romola*, or such as is the field of secondary writers like Bulwer Lytton and Harrison Ainsworth – is a special power of the provincial novel, differing from Dickens's and Thackeray's own individual handlings of time past. Her method looks directly forward to Hardy's, which, similarly, creates an age by drawing upon what it has in common with the present and all other ages, explaining only those differences which have an essential bearing on the immediate themes and actions, avoiding all 'local colour' or strangeness for its own sake. In the use of history Hardy's *The Trumpet Major* is closer to *Sylvia's Lovers* than is any of his more heavy-weight works, sharing the handling of people on the periphery of similar great events (there is even a press-gang, though it humorously fails to seize Bob Loveday), sparing of contemporary detail, putting poignant personal feelings against the exigencies of the outer world, and ending, like *Sylvia's Lovers*, with a plangent falling away of the present of the story into the past: 'But the memory of man fades away', says Elizabeth Gaskell,

> A few old people can still tell you the tradition of the man who died in a cottage somewhere about this spot – died of starvation while his wife lived in hard-hearted plenty not two good stone-throws away. This is the form into which popular feeling, and ignorance of the real facts, have moulded the story. (XLV)

Hardy's tone too, is regretful, accepting, and elegiac:

> The candle held by his father shed its waving light upon John's face and uniform as with a farewell smile he turned on the door-stone, backed by the black night; and in another moment he had plunged into the darkness, the ring of his smart step dying away upon the bridge as he joined his companions-in-arms, and went off to blow his trumpet till silenced for ever upon one of the bloody battle-fields of Spain. (*The Trumpet Major*, XLI)

Character, always a central part of the novel as understood by nine-teenth-century writers, comes to be almost all-pervasive in *Sylvia's Lovers*, where the nature of the story makes the personal sufferings of the characters the central subject, and where the method employs the sense of character to serve so many purposes. Here she moves towards concentration on a fairly small, closely-connected group, in contrast to her other novels where her great powers have been in comprehend-ing and working into a whole different and disparate personalities, and powerfully-contrasting groups. Such restriction is partly inherent in a story in which a few people are inextricably involved; partly necessary for the depth of understanding of feeling and motive. Yet her original power to give as full a revelation of secondary as of main characters remains, and is here deepened and intensified. In her first three novels, she worked by contrasts, devoting herself to the differ-ences and discrepancies of her characters' reactions to their own different situations. Here, the essential differences in individual human nature are made even keener, yet their social levels, though distinct, are at no great extremes, their culture and understanding, through precisely revealed, are modest, and their individual predicaments are brought much closer together. All, indeed, are humbly placed, not wealthy, uncultured, and unfortunate. All are in the hands of a fate which offers them few real happinesses, great and increasing misfortune, disappointment, and disillusion, and all live out their lives on an inexorable progress to old age and death, in which the increase of wisdom and resignation is the only strength and compensation to which they can aspire, and peace rather than fulfilment is all they can achieve. Elizabeth Gaskell's own great achievement in this novel where no one has a 'happy ending' is to make wisdom, resignation and peace into comfort enough.

Sylvia's Lovers, in its choice and handling of characters as in other matters, is partly different and wholly more profound than the three previous novels. Here for the first time Elizabeth Gaskell casts aside any social theme, to study the personal progress of her two main figures, Philip and Sylvia; as a result all the other characters bear upon them, and offer different degrees of influence, sympathy and understanding. In *Ruth* she had been moving towards such a method, yet even there she had an abstract theme, which demanded the study of characters who, while exploring that theme, did not directly affect Ruth herself.

The main characters, of whom there are comparatively few, group themselves about either Philip or Sylvia. At the beginning of the novel the two groups are almost separate: Philip and those with whom he associates in Monkshaven, and Sylvia and her family, household and friends on the hills above. In Monkshaven the group is a coherent one connected by the shop, trade, and kinship: it comprises John and Jeremiah Foster, the proprietors of the draper's shop; Philip himself, Coulson, and his cousin Hester Rose – the three sharers in the running of the shop – and Hester's mother Alice Rose. At Haytersbank Farm are the Robson family – Sylvia's parents, Daniel and Bell, and Sylvia herself – and their one man, Kester; as associates of Sylvia they are supported by the neighbouring family of the Corneys, a large family of uncertain size, whose most important member is Molly, who marries a Newcastle man and becomes Mrs Bruton. Even the single and notable outsider Charley Kinraid the specksioneer is connected with the Brutons, whose cousin he is. The only characters who can be seen as unconnected with this close grouping are few and minor, and bear upon it indirectly, either as briefly-appearing denizens of Monkshaven, or else involved in that small section of the story which leaves Monkshaven when Philip enlists:

all of them are used only for their bearing on the themes and emotional dilemmas of the main story.

The thematic movement of the novel is the movement of these main groups. Sylvia's world of Haytersbank falls apart when, with her father's death and her mother's illness, she is unable to keep the farm, and is driven into marriage and Monkshaven. Thereafter she becomes more closely integrated with the Monkshaven characters, retaining only the faithful Kester as the link with the early days – the always mindless Molly Bruton having developed in her marriage into crude, unthinking prosperity and vulgar insensitivity. Against Sylvia's gradual absorption into the world of the Fosters and the Roses, which goes on the full length of the novel, is contrasted Philip's sudden and cruel separation from it, when his deceit is discovered, and, three-quarters of the way through the story, he is cut off abruptly and for ever.

Social distinctions between the two groups or those within them are negligible. The broad difference between the farmers and the town dwellers is between the life of impulse and the life of conscious order. This is not to say that the town dwellers are more intelligent, but merely that they attempt to rule their lives and emotions by felt and accepted codes of conduct, as a result of their consciously-felt religion, of their way of life which makes them part of a community and of their generally higher level of education. None of them is learned, but all can read and write, and the men, being shopkeepers, can handle accounts. By contrast Daniel Robson can barely cope with reading, and not with writing: they are not condemned, and Elizabeth Gaskell holds the balance:

> In the agricultural counties . . . there is little analysis of motive or comparison of characters and actions, even at this present day of enlightenment. Sixty or seventy years ago there was still less . . . taken as a general rule, it may be said that few knew what manner of men they were, compared to the numbers now who are fully conscious of their virtues, qualities, failings, and weaknesses, and who go about comparing others with themselves – not in a spirit of Pharisaism and arrogance, but with a vivid self-consciousness that more than anything else deprives characters of freshness and originality. (VII)

As is usual with Elizabeth Gaskell, there is no difference in handling between major and minor characters; all take a full part in the incidents and actions where they are involved, with their reactions, impulses, motives, and influences revealed by her flexible, subtle and superb intermingling of speech, reactions, thoughts, and conduct, revealing equally of themselves and of others. No scene ever concentrates on one alone: almost all scenes refer to and illuminate areas apparently very far from the immediate event. As instance of a very slight occasion, there is the preliminary exchange in the milking-shed, between Kester and Sylvia (only two days after the Corneys' New Year's party) before Charley Kinraid arrives and makes his first declaration of love.

As Charley came to the door, Kester was saying, 'Quiet wi' thee, wench! Theere now, she's a beauty, if she'll stand still. There's niver sich a cow i' t' Riding, if she'll only behave hersel'. She's a bonny lass, she is; let down her milk, theere's a pretty!'

'Why, Kester,' laughed Sylvia, 'thou't asking her for her milk wi' as many pretty speeches as if thou wert wooing a wife!'

'Hey, lass!' said Kester, turning a bit towards her, and shutting one eye to cock the other the better upon her; an operation which puckered up his already wrinkled face with a thousand new lines and folds. 'An' how does thee know how a man woos a wife, that thee talks so knowin' about it? That's tellin'. Some un's been tryin' it on thee.'

'There's never a one been so impudent,' said Sylvia, reddening and tossing her head a little, 'I'd like to see 'em try me!'

'Well, well!' said Kester, wilfully misunderstanding her meaning, 'thou mun be patient, wench; and, if thou's a good lass, maybe thy turn'll come and they'll try it.'

'I wish thou'd talk of what thou's some knowledge on, Kester, i'stead of i' that silly way,' replied Sylvia.

'Then a mun talk no more 'bout women, for they're past knowin', an' druv e'en King Solomon silly.'

At this moment Charley stepped in. (x v)

Charley's impudence and pretty speeches, and Philip's lack of both, Kester's knowledge and Sylvia's complete lack of it (reinforced by his disclaimer), the anticipation that Sylvia is 'past knowing' and will drive at least one man silly, are all prepared in this brief, simple exchange.

The New Year's party, a much more complicated situation,

important for being the only one, apart from Kinraid's return from the
dead, at which Sylvia, Philip and Kinraid are all three present, is far
more subtle, for the author balances the actions, reactions and responses of all the three main characters at every point, making these
most modest of incidents profoundly revealing. The ironic contradiction of appearance and fact runs through the whole, beginning
with the acute comparison between the two men:

> Kinraid was too well seasoned to care what amount of liquor
> he drank; Philip had what was called a weak head, and disliked
> muddling himself with drink because of the immediate con-
> sequence of intense feelings of irritability, and the more distant
> one of a racking headache next day; so both these two preserved
> very much the same demeanour they had held at the beginning
> of the evening. (xii)

The crucial incident of the evening is when Sylvia refuses to redeem
her forfeit, by 'blowing out t'candle and kissing t'candlestick' – that
is, Kinraid:

> Philips's spirits rose, and he yearned to go to her and tell her how
> he approved of her conduct. Alas, Philip! Sylvia, though as
> modest a girl as ever lived, was no prude, and had been brought
> up in simple, straightforward country ways; and with any other
> young man, excepting, perhaps, Philip's self, she would have
> thought no more of making a rapid pretence of kissing the hand
> or cheek of the temporary 'candlestick' than our ancestresses
> did in a much higher rank on similar occasions. Kinraid,
> though mortified by his public rejection, was more conscious of
> this than the inexperienced Philip; he resolved not to be baulked,
> and watched his opportunity. (xii)

Kinraid soon gets his kiss, and the misinterpretations continue, for
Philip is pleased by Sylvia's retiring gentleness (until an overheard
remark destroys his peace), his jealousy is allayed by Kinraid's
behaviour when

> Satisfied with the past, and pleasantly hopeful about the future,
> [Kinraid] found it easy to turn his attention to the next
> prettiest girl in the room, and make the whole gathering bright
> with his ready good temper and buoyant spirits. (xii)

Characters, actions, motives, and responses are interwoven thus
throughout the novel, making it difficult to separate the delineation

of individuals, or to discuss separately the various means used by the author. Elizabeth Gaskell, perhaps the least obtrusive of artists, and most subtle capturer of the impulses of the human mind in action, is at her least obtrusive and most subtle here.

Sylvia Robson is Elizabeth Gaskell's last and finest central heroine, for after her, in *Wives and Daughters*, the role is shared, so that there is no single central girl whose fortunes are followed beyond all others. Sylvia is that most difficult of beings to depict without, for the reader, apparent inconsistency in the analysis, and without, in the writer, either the over-engagement which leads to sentimentality or idealization, or the reserve which leads to ironic or satiric superiority. She is a girl who grows from childishness to tragic maturity. Though Elizabeth Gaskell's young girls are all among her unfailing successes, and though no two are alike, Sylvia, different from them all, shares qualities with Mary Barton and Ruth, as distinct from Margaret Hale. Like Mary, she is both competent and capable within the life she leads, able to run the farm and keep house, even after her mother becomes an invalid; yet, like Ruth, she is emotionally and spiritually undeveloped and uneducated. Where Ruth's innocence leads simply to her seduction, Sylvia's has far graver consequences to others besides herself from which there is no redemption. Sylvia's impulse to love Kinraid, like Ruth's to love Bellingham, is good in its essence; but Sylvia's much more active nature has impulses which Ruth's conspicuously lacks; she resents wrong and injustice, and has the true spirit of her Yorkshire blood. Elizabeth Gaskell cites, at the very beginning of her story, a remark that was actually made to her:[4]

A Yorkshireman once said to me, 'My county folk are all alike. Their first thought is how to resist. Why! I myself, if I hear a man say it is a fine day, catch myself trying to find out that it is no such thing. It is so in thought; it is so in word; it is so in deed.'

(1)

Sylvia's character and her fate are marked by this spirit of opposition to circumstances which compels her to her greatest assertion of her will when Kinraid returns. Trapped by the marriage into which she has been deceived, she makes her great assertion of herself and her rules of life:

'I'll make my vow now, lest I lose mysel' again. I'll never forgive

[4] The remark is authenticated by its appearance, with only slight verbal differences, in *The Life of Charlotte Brontë*, six years earlier, in 1857.

yon man, nor live with him as his wife again. All that's done and ended. He's spoilt my life – he's spoilt it for as long as iver I live on this earth; but neither yo' nor him shall spoil my soul.'

(XXXIII)

Even though with later experience comes greater understanding, and a final reconciliation with Philip, the stand of the individual against fate and circumstance is akin to Jane Eyre's:

'I care for myself. The more solitary, the more friendless, the more unsustained I am, the more I will respect myself.'
(*Jane Eyre*, XXVII)

and akin also to the stand against life itself when it bars the way to the union of Catherine and Heathcliff in *Wuthering Heights*. Like Jane Eyre, Sylvia casts aside not only the practical considerations of safety and the means of living, but the loved one Kinraid as well – just as Jane rejects Mr Rochester – when the essential self is at stake.

Elizabeth Gaskell prepares the way for this tragic extremity in the career of the youthful Sylvia. Though her love for Kinraid is vital to her, it is not the ruling passion of her nature in the way that love for Sylvia herself is Philip's: where his nature is laid bare in his cry of 'Give me Sylvia or else I die', hers is in her words, 'It's not in me to forgive – I sometimes think it's not in me to forget' (XXIX). Such intransigence is rendered credible by being inherited from her impulsive father, who as a young man defied the press-gang by cutting off his own thumb, and whose reaction to threatened arrest is to say 'A'm noane sorry for what a did, an' a'd do it again to-neet, if need were. So theere's for thee' (XXIV). Elizabeth Gaskell provides two occasions when Sylvia herself proves it: when she refuses to go to the dying Simpson, who betrayed her father; and when Kester taxes her with having speedily forgotten Kinraid to take up with Philip: 'If thou wasn't Kester, I'd niver forgive thee' (XXVII). Her ultimate reconciliation with Philip is also prepared at this point, as the simple words 'If thou wasn't Kester' reveal. She can eventually soften, as she almost softens towards Simpson, not from outside persuasion or pressure, but only from the working-out of the impulses within her. Sylvia is made emotionally ready to forgive Philip, not by the mere incident which brings about their meeting, when he saves their child from drowning, but by the long spiritual education when he is away, by her gradual understanding of Hester's creed of resignation, and by the effect of realizing that Kinraid, despite his real love for her, has compromised with life as she has not, and married another. Even so, at the end of her story she has not in any sense been beaten by life; she has emerged to a wisdom that can only come after tragic struggle and resolution.

Elizabeth Gaskell renders Sylvia noble and tragic largely through her thoughts and reactions; she renders her at the same time a girl of her time and environment through her behaviour, the reactions of other characters, and by presenting her as a physical being. All the other characters react to her in variously contrasting ways, but all in some degree respond to her, whatever their moral judgements, as a creature who charms the senses by her words, appearance, and acts. Hester and her mother Alice Rose are the hardest of her judges, yet even Hester, who on their first meeting blames her for rudeness – 'What business had the pretty little creature to reject kindly-meant hospitality in the pettish way she did?' (111), has, in the first instance, 'thought her customer the prettiest creature ever seen' (111). The first view the reader has is the idyllic and delightful one of her on her way to market with butter and eggs, washing her feet in the stream, sitting 'tucked up on a stone, as if it had been a cushion, and she a little sultana' (11). The pleasant homely details of her dress which occur at intervals never let us forget her physical existence, while the tangible accessories of her appearance reveal her nature. Philip's first gift to her is a hair-ribbon,

> with a little briar-rose pattern running upon it . . . the briar-rose (sweetness and thorns) seemed to be the very flower for her; the soft green ground on which the pink and brown pattern ran, was just the colour to show off her complexion. (xii)

It is right that Philip should choose the symbol for her – which plays so large a part in her fate when it is forfeit to Kinraid at the party, becomes the love-token Sylvia gives away to him, and is later found in his hat and taken as proof of his drowning – for Philip is the one who responds most to her. His passion and the revelation of it transfigure Sylvia for the reader from the beginning, for, fanatical though it may be, it is never deluded, and is for the actual, not for an image: when she has agreed to become engaged to him, her gentle submissiveness even distresses him:

> once or twice, he found that she was doing what he desired out of a spirit of obedience which, as her mother's daughter, she believed to be her duty towards her affianced husband. And this

last motive for action depressed her lover more than anything. He wanted the old Sylvia back again; captious, capricious, wilful, haughty, merry, charming. Alas! that Sylvia was gone for ever. (XXIX)

'Philip's idol' was a possible suggested title for the novel. Uneuphonious, ambiguous and misleading as it may be, it is very right in that Philip is as much at the tragic heart of things as Sylvia. He is indubitably a greater achievement even than Sylvia: sensitive studies of women are not uncommon in the novel; studies of such power and conviction as this of Philip are rare; as a study of a passion amounting almost to monomania, in one who is honest, sensitive and high-principled, yet never rises above the limitations of his era and his own limited physical and mental capacities, who is intensely to be pitied and much to be admired, yet with whom the reader never identifies himself, Elizabeth Gaskell's achievement is without peer. Philip's story is one of only faintly-relieved pain in itself, charted in a way that produces intense pain to the reader. Only the justice and the moral balance of the rendering prevent it from being unendurable.

Like Sylvia, Philip is the victim of his nature, which compels him to the devotion which is his disaster. Like her, he is a follower where events lead, with a single disastrous exception. His fatal choice is offered him when he sees Kinraid seized by the press-gang, and does not pass on Kinraid's message:

'Tell her I'll come back to her. Bid her not forget the great oath we took together this morning; she's as much my wife as if we'd gone to church.' (XVIII)

But the causes that lead him to lie by silence, and let Kinraid be thought dead, are far more involved and conflicting than those that direct Sylvia. His act is not merely anticipated and explained, as hers is, but actually brought about by all the mental and emotional circumstances, and the course of events that precede and lead up to it. The reader feels the force of his guilt, but is more aware of what extenuates it than the limited mental capacities of the character himself permit. Elizabeth Gaskell emphasizes from the beginning that Philip's role towards Sylvia is a protective one: he is her superior in knowledge who can teach her to read, favoured by her mother as a possible husband, and committed by her to give Sylvia the protection and guidance of a male relative which her father fails to provide. He knows, as Sylvia does not, that Kinraid has had successes with women in the past, and has deserted at least one of them – Coulson's cousin – before. So, in breaking a not-uttered promise to Kinraid, he has the sense of acting in the best interest, irrespective of any possible advantage to himself. These facts all regulate the reader's response to Philip's painfully over-imaginative reactions to his own act, which spring from a nature incapable of separating reason from passion:

> It was by no fault of Hepburn's that the boat sped well away; ... No fault of his! and yet it took him some time before he could reason himself into the belief that his mad, feverish wishes not an hour before – his wild prayer to be rid of his rival ... had not compelled the event. (XVIII)

> 'Anyhow,' he thought, as he rose up, 'my prayer is granted. God be thanked.' (XIX)

His prayer is indeed, with terrifying irony, granted, and events continue to bestow Sylvia upon him. The tremendous power of Philip comes from Elizabeth Gaskell's imaginative power to reveal the workings of, to use Tennyson's bitter phrase, 'a second-rate sensitive mind not in union with itself'. She makes him as poignant in his very qualified joy as in its hopeless love, in the subtle mixture of honesty and guilt in his mind. He perpetrates only the one lie; when later Sylvia faces him suddenly with the statement and question

> '[Kester] thinks as Charley Kinraid may ha' been took by t'press-gang. . . . Oh! Philip, think yo' there's just that one chance?'

he replies with desperate truth, with only the slightest distortion:

> 'Ay, there's a chance, sure enough. . . . There's a chance I suppose for iverything i' life as we have not seen with our own eyes, as it may not ha' happened. Kester may say next as there's a chance as your father is not dead, because we none on us saw him' –
>
> 'Hung,' he was going to have said; but a touch of humanity came back into his stony heart. Sylvia sent up a little sharp cry at his words. He longed at the sound to take her in his arms and hush her up, as a mother hushes her weeping child. But the very longing, having to be repressed, only made him the more beside himself with guilt, anxiety, and rage. (XXIX)

The conflict within him is followed, detail by detail, between his moral being and his passion, so that his anguished nightmare dreams of Kinraid's return after he is married are no more or less essentially himself than is his bitter rebuke when Sylvia, delirious after childbirth, calls 'Oh! Charley! come to me – come to me':

> 'What kind of a woman are yo' to go dreaming of another man i' this way, and taking on so about him, when yo're a wedded wife, with a child as yo've borne to another man?' (xxxi)

Elizabeth Gaskell, in her unobtrusive direction of her reader's responses, never requires him to take anything on trust. The honest, scrupulous workman is as vital a part of Philip's whole being as the passionate lover. A large part of the first third of the book concerns Philip's dealings with his employers in business as subordinate and proprietor, and with his relations with his friends and associates outside the Robson family. The strife between his nature and his passion is recreated in the narrative pattern when his visit on business to London coincides with his witnessing Kinraid's disaster. Philip is in a turmoil of passionate temptation to conceal the truth about him, at the same time as he faithfully and efficiently carries out his business for the Fosters in London, and investigates the various merits of new ploughs for Daniel Robson. Hypersensitive though he is, he is unanalytical of his own discrepancies, and can implore Hester, without hypocrisy, calling on her own principles of benevolence and unselfishness, to help Sylvia and her mother in their distress, ask her advice about furniture for the house, and even want her to be bridesmaid. Elizabeth Gaskell ensures that the irony of his self-ignorance emerges when, unaware of Hester's love for him, he does not realize the pain he causes; and even more that he is unaware that he is asking for Hester's unselfishness for his own selfish ends.

Her hold is no less sure in the brief episodes in the last quarter of the novel, after he has left Monkshaven, where, though new states of mind appear, there is no lack of consistency. Hope against hope was the driving force behind his long devotion: a similar hope, now feeding on fantasy, drives him to try to re-enact the tale of Guy of Warwick, a fable apt in that it is one of the least triumphant of romances, in which the hero is reunited with his wife only at the moment of death.

His end can hardly be called emotional indulgence, despite its verging on the sensational. Were it not for this, and the brief interval of rest at the hospital at Winchester, Philip's fate would verge upon

the intolerably cruel, not only for his brutally final and wholly dis-
figuring injuries, but much more for the sudden and direct retribution of Kinraid's abrupt return. Elizabeth Gaskell, in her single truly
tragic unheroic hero, while never violating probability, is never
gratuitously or casually brutal – any more than she rigs events to
bring about desired results.

Philip has no precursors in her work, or in the novel, his nearest of
kin being Thornton in *North and South* – as a man in whom the
lover never overwhelms the man of business and of work – and, at a
further distance, John Barton – a man who commits a crime from
noble motives. After Philip, men helplessly ruined by the combination
of events and the foibles – not venal in themselves – of their own
natures become, in the twentieth century, almost a commonplace.
His immediate successors are George Eliot's Lydgate in *Middlemarch*
and Hardy's Jude Fawley. Lydgate also fails tragically in life, not
like Philip from the grip of great passion, but because of what George
Eliot diagnoses as the 'spots of commonness' in his nature, which
make him fall victim to Rosamund Vincy. Jude, vastly more complex, is also a man in the grip of unavailing passion but one who is
also in an adverse world which inhibits his advancement: Jude Fawley's fate, though crueller, is not more tragic, not least because his
whole universe is against him; whereas Philip, but for Sylvia, is in
harmony with his world, where, limited and modest as he and it both
are, he succeeds. Closer perhaps, as a man in the grip of his own
nature and the aspirations which cause him to fail, is E. M. Forster's
Rickie Elliot in *The Longest Journey*, whose author, like Elizabeth
Gaskell, treats the creation with a mature balance of compassion and
dispassion, yet who, unlike her and like Hardy, is deeply concerned
to expose the false values and structure of the society. Elizabeth
Gaskell's concern with the total man, which charts all the impulses of
a human entity with a singular reserve from moral judgement, is
what looks forward to the next century; what divides her from it, and
is one of her great sources of strength, is her lack of criticism of the
universe as she finds it, based not on any naïve faith that all is for the
best in the best of all possible worlds, but on a faith in a benevolent
God and (to put it as little dogmatically as she herself does) a faith
in the power of faith for itself, for man in his task of living.

This faith runs as an undercurrent and counterpoise in *Sylvia's
Lovers*, embodied in Hester, her mother Alice Rose, and the
Fosters. Though for them happiness is a term barely applicable, and

contentment, even, difficult of achievement, they attain a balance and resignation that are far from trivial. Hester is that most difficult of characters for an author to convey, the personality whose role is one almost wholly of inaction. She does little that is not at the prompting or for the benefit of another: even her personal decisions are negative ones concerning the things she cannot do, as when she refuses to marry Coulson, or to be bridesmaid to Sylvia. Elizabeth Gaskell handles her unhoping love for Philip with fidelity, and her piety with a total absence of priggishness. The very few points at which Hester may jar upon the modern reader are inconsiderable beside, for instance, George Eliot's failures with the comparable Dinah Morris in *Adam Bede*. Hester's cry of despair is an instance, when Sylvia and Philip meet at last, just after she has painstakingly established his identity:

> 'Oh, Lord God Almighty! was I not even worthy to bring them together at last?' (x l v)

The attitude and sentiment, though they may jar, are wholly consistent with the self-abnegating principles which her author has embodied in her throughout, and her helplessness in this as in all her other trials is, if rather bitter and slightly self-regarding, ironically apt.

Alice Rose, like her daughter, suffers what cannot be changed, but is treated with an entirely fair and delicate humour. While Calvinist-Methodist resignation is her creed, complaint if not rebellion is her nature, and Elizabeth Gaskell uses both, along with her mixture of sound sense and limited information, to lighten many situations, such as that startling one in which Kinraid's wife appears to provide news of Philip:

> 'Nay,' said Alice a little scornfully. 'I can forgive Sylvia for not being over-keen to credit thy news. Her man of peace becoming a man of war; and suffered to enter Jerusalem; which is a heavenly and typical city at this time; while we, as is one of the elect, is obliged to go dwelling in Monkshaven, just like any other body!' (x l)

Delicately inwrought and interacting as all the characters are, by past as well as present, with the interconnections all indicated in small events and speeches whose main import is on quite other, more central topics, one stands out as of almost equal interest with

Sylvia and Philip, in having his own hard, ironic, near-tragic fate. This is Daniel Robson, Sylvia's father, a unique extension of his author's power of flexible use of character. Beginning as a comic yet sympathetic rendering of the farmer who is humorous for his lack of awareness of his own mental deficiencies, he becomes the helpless and pathetic victim of forces he cannot even understand. The substance of his comedy establishes the elements of his tragedy. At his first appearance he is seen as quite ignorant, both of how his mind works, and of how it compares even with his wife's:

'Tak' off thy pan o' milk, missus, and set on t'kettle. Milk may do for wenches, but Philip and me is for a drop o' good Hollands and water this cold night. I'm a'most chilled to t'marrow wi' looking out for thee, lass; for t'mother was in a peck o' troubles about thy noane coming home i' t'dayleet, and I'd to keep hearkening out on t'browhead.'

This was entirely untrue, and Bell knew it to be so; but her husband did not. He had persuaded himself now, as he had often done before, that what he had in reality done for his own pleasure or satisfaction, he had done in order to gratify someone else.

(IV)

The mixture here, of masculine superiority, love of drink, fundamentally right and very powerful sympathies, with no sense of consequences or others' point of view, lead him to his attack on the 'Randyvowse', rescue of the sailors, arrest, imprisonment, and hanging. The comic Robson who supplies some of the novel's richest scenes – laid up with rheumatism and laying down the law to the tailor, or recalling his rumbustious days as a whaler to the congenial Kinraid – is composed of the same elements as the victim of the law, both comic and pathetic, who cannot flee from arrest because he is too stiff in the joints, and whose rheumatic legs figure in his last comic-heroic appearance, coming out from his hiding-place under the bed:

'Here he be, here he be,' called out the other man, dragging Daniel out by the legs; 'We've getten him.'

Daniel kicked violently, and came out from his hiding-place in a less ignominious way than being pulled out by his heels.

He shook himself, and then turned, facing his captors.

'A wish a'd niver hidden mysel'; it were his doing,' jerking his thumb towards Philip: 'a'm ready to stand by what a've done.

> Yo've gotten a warrant, a'll be bound; for them justices is grand
> at writing, when t'fight's over.'
>   He was trying to carry it off with bravado; but Philip saw that
> he had received a shock, from his sudden look of withered
> colour and shrunken feature. (xxv)

Elizabeth Gaskell makes no change in method or material: Robson
has no more and no less dignity in adversity, no firmer hold on fact,
no change of language or idiom, revealed still through act, words,
and the minimum of commentary. Situation, mood, and (what cannot be demonstrated in quotation) gradual cumulative preparation,
account for the change of response.

  The characterization in *Sylvia's Lovers* differs from that elsewhere
only in being more detailed, more the result of minute but significant
interrelation and noting of mutual responses and reaction. All characters, while individual and independent, are inwrought with far more
than their immediate act, even down to the watchmaker in whose
shop Hester sees the first clue to Philip's return:

> This William Darley was the brother of the gardener at the
> rectory; the uncle to the sailor who had been shot by the press-
> gang years before, and to his bed-ridden sister. (xliv)

Such accuracy is as far as possible from Dickensian coincidence;
it is fidelity to verisimilitudinous detail, which wholly allays any
sense of the coincidental, or any sense of precipitate haste in the
tale's conclusion, and, in its minuscule way, charts the passing of
time, and brings the sense of the wheel coming full circle, by recalling
the event that, in the third chapter, brought about Sylvia's earliest
meeting with Kinraid.

Sylvia's Lovers, more than any other novel of its author's, is about
what happens within people's minds and souls, rather than about
actions. Very little in fact happens in the way of actual events; the
action is a mixture of a few incidents of intrinsic importance – like
the opening attack on the whaling-boat or Darley's funeral, Kinraid's
seizure, and the assault on the 'Randyvowse' – and many others of
no importance at all, which are the homely happenings of common
life, rendered important only by their significance to those taking
part. Elizabeth Gaskell has always felt the need to base her story on
both kinds of action, has always been very good at the latter, while
having occasional difficulties with the former. In *Sylvia's Lovers*

her difficulties are over. She has learned that though she can if need be use startling events, she has no need to do so to supply climaxes, or incidental excitement. Instead of drawing in or writing up exciting happenings like the fire at the mill (in *Mary Barton*), Margaret's heroism in protecting Thornton from the rioters, or Frederick's peril from arrest (both in *North and South*), here in *Sylvia's Lovers*, where she has a tale which offers sensational events, she actually avoids or subordinates them in the interests of her main themes, achieving a movement and proportion of the whole which her early work sometimes lacked. *Sylvia's Lovers* never moves at the wrong pace, or changes its direction. This direction and control is plain from the opening in the first startling happening when the press-gang seize the sailors on the first returning whale-ship of the season, killing one and wounding another. This incident comes to the reader as it comes to the characters, in spurts and bit-by-bit reports at second-hand, all that is actually presented being the sailors, ashore and under arrest, taken to the 'Randyvowse', with the grief-stricken and enraged crowd of kinsfolk and townspeople around them, as seen by Sylvia, Philip and Hester. The incident's importance is not for its intrinsic excitement, but for its effects and what it reveals of the mood of those who are affected by it – the townsfolk and kin of the sailors in their rage and despair, Sylvia in her hysterical, over-emotional sympathy. The most impressive example of the author eschewing the sensational occurs when Daniel is arrested. Bell, his wife, visits him under arrest before he is taken to York, and when he has been condemned, she and Sylvia go to see him. Chapter xxvii ends thus:

'Lass, bear up! We mun bear up, and be a-gait on our way to him: he'll be needing us now. Bear up, my lass! the Lord will give us strength. We mun go to him; ay, time's precious; thou mun cry thy cry at after.'
Sylvia opened her dim eyes, and heard her mother's voice; the ideas came slowly into her mind, and slowly she rose up, standing still, like one who has been stunned, to regain her strength; and then, taking hold of her mother's arm, she said, in a soft, strange voice – 'Let's go. I'm ready.' (xxvii)

But the next chapter opens a month later, when all is over, with

the afternoon of an April day, in that same year; and the sky was blue above, with little sailing white clouds catching the pleasant sunlight. (xxviii)

No one who has read *Mary Barton* or *Ruth* can doubt Mrs Gaskell's power to have dealt with such incidents as she here omits; one must the more admire her discretion in omitting them. She achieves a perfect proportioning of pace and mood over the whole structure of the work.

She also avoids the unnecessarily harrowing. While she never shirks unpleasantness or what is dreadful, she equally never underestimates the consolations of common life. Grim as the happenings are in *Sylvia's Lovers*, and harrowing as are the emotions, she ensures that the reader never loses touch with the common and consoling minutiae of everyday life. These not only provide for the reader the delight of the felt and observed, they emphasize the moral strength that is to be drawn from them, and wholly prevent any over-simplification of response. Such details never diffuse or distract, but intensify and subtilize. They are the stuff of everyday living, domestic, or sublime or eternal, and get their effect both from contrast and from harmony. They are part of the mood and of the structure. A fine instance out of countless others of the homely, contrasting, and structural comes immediately after the assault on the inn and Daniel's rescue of the sailors. The following chapter prepares for his return home, where Bell and Sylvia are waiting, wondering why he is so late, Bell dozing, and Sylvia brooding on her misery for Kinraid:

> . . . Never again would she forget that dear face, if but once more she might set her eyes upon it!
>
> Her mother's head fell with a sudden jerk, and she roused herself up; and Sylvia put by her thought of the dead, and her craving after his presence, into that receptacle of the heart where all such are kept closed and sacred from the light of common day.
>
> 'Feyther's late,' said Bell.
>
> 'It's gone eight,' replied Sylvia.
>
> 'But our clock is better nor an hour forrard,' answered Bell.
>
> 'Ay, but t'wind brings Monkshaven bells clear tonight. I heerd t'eight o'clock bell ringing, not five minutes ago.'
>
> It was the fire-bell; but she had not distinguished the sound. There was another long silence, both wide awake this time.
>
> 'He'll have his rhematics again,' said Bell.
>
> 'It's cold, for sartin,' said Sylvia. 'March weather come afore its time. But I'll make him a treacle-posset; it's a famous thing for keeping off hoasts.'

The treacle-posset was entertainment enough for both, while it was being made. But, once placed in a little basin in the oven, there was again time for wonder and anxiety.

'He said nought about having a bout, did he, mother?' asked Sylvia at length.

'No,' said Bell, her face a little contracting. After a while she added, 'There's many a one as has husbands that goes off drinking, without iver saying a word to their wives. My master is none o' that mak'.'

'Mother,' broke in Sylvia again, 'I'll just go and get t'lantern out of t'shippon, and go up t'brow, and mebbe to t'ash-field end.'

'Do, lass,' said her mother. 'I'll get my wraps and go with thee.'

'Thou shall do niver such a thing,' said Sylvia. 'Thou's too frail to go out i' t'night air, such a night as this.'

'Then call Kester up.'

'Not I. I'm noane afraid o' t'dark.'

'But of what thou mayst meet i' t'dark, lass?'

Sylvia shivered all over at the sudden thought, suggested by this speech of her mother's, that the idea that had flashed into her own mind, of going to look for her father, might be an answer to the invocation to the Powers which she had made not long ago, that she might indeed meet her dead lover at the ash-field stile; but, though she shivered as this superstitious fancy came into her head, her heart beat firm and regular; not from darkness nor from spirits of the dead was she going to shrink; her great sorrow had taken away all her girlish nervous fear. (XXIV)

Structurally this gathers together the time-scale at Haytersbank to connect with the events in Monkshaven, with the allusion to the fire-bell. It is also a fine contrast in its handling of the sense of time, which having rushed past in the turmoil of the previous chapter, is here charted in its apparent slowness by the details of their every act and word, the making of treacle-posset, 'placed in a little basin in the oven', and of Sylvia's going with 't'lantern out of t'shippon . . . up t'brow, and mebbe to t'ash-field end'; it also builds up, with a certain amount of dramatic irony, the suspense before Daniel's return, preparing the way for the downward change of mood from the triumphant heroic Daniel to the stiff, sore old man soon to be arrested for a capital crime: the two women's conjectures of his rheumatism and drinking are accurate, though they fall far short of what awaits them. Sylvia's day-dreaming and her sudden supernatural fear connect the immediate context with the wider, and introduce an element of terror into the safe, homely present, and the routine of the farm life which is so soon to be destroyed.

Homely though the life and action of the novel is, it can yet reach out to the sublime and eternal in the complex, difficult, and intangible way of the Wordsworth of the *Lyrical Ballads*, not only by Elizabeth Gaskell's powers of poetic description, but by the essential nature of what she chooses to describe, seen from a new, strange, or intensely personal angle. The angle is very literally odd at the brief moments when Philip flees from Monkshaven, from Kinraid's return and Sylvia's curse:

> He plunged and panted up this rough ascent. From the top he could look down on the whole town lying below, severed by the bright shining river into two parts. To the right lay the sea, shimmering and heaving: there were the cluster of masts rising out of the little port; the irregular roofs of the houses; which of them, thought he, as he carried his eye along the quay-side to the market-place, which of them was his? and he singled it out in its unfamiliar aspect, and saw the thin blue smoke rising from the kitchen chimney, where even now Phoebe was cooking the household-meal that he never more must share.
>
> Up at that thought and away, he knew not nor cared not whither. He went through the ploughed fields where the corn was newly springing; he came down upon the vast sunny sea, and turned his back on it with loathing, he made his way inland, to the high green pastures, the short upland turf, above which the larks hung poised 'at heaven's gate'. He strode along, so straight and heedless of briar and bush, that the wild black cattle ceased from grazing, and looked after him with their great blank eyes.
>
> (xxxiv)

The accurate and sensitive eye here – for the 'thin blue smoke' and the 'great blank eyes' of momentarily pausing cattle – the rendering of Philip's almost unconscious perception of detail, the symbolic force of his recoil from the sea – emblematic of Kinraid, and vastly and sunnily alien to his agony – all create a poetic quality that is intensified by the extreme plainness of the language which, while descriptive, is a mass of words of motion whereby all nature seems to partake of Philip's compulsion to flight. Such writing, intensifying without impeding, rarely even of this modest length, pervades the fabric of the novel.

Elizabeth Gaskell's own simple language, always so wholly adequate to what is required of it, working without rhetoric, or mannerism, is even more vital to this novel in which she undertakes, without any apparent sense of difficulty or of originality, the remarkable feat of writing characters whose speech is always dialect – and moreover, a dialect which is not her own. Possibly only a Lancashire-bred Cheshire woman could have such an ear for the precise qualities of North Riding Yorkshire, a language close to but different from what she knew. She steers a perfect course between phonetic accuracy and acceptable readability, yet produces a wide variety between the broadest and the more refined speakers, and the degrees of idiom used by individuals depending on the company and degree of formality. Kester, the broadest speaker, infects Sylvia, when she is with him, to idiomatic phraseology; the pronouns 'thee' and 'thou', reflecting their long intimacy and deep affection, are their norm:

> 'Now, Kester, thou mun just be off, and find Harry Donkin th' tailor, and bring him here; it's gettin' on for Martinmas, an' he'll be coming his rounds, and he may as well come here first as last, and feyther's clothes want a deal o' mending up, and Harry's always full of his news, and anyhow he'll do for feyther to scold, an' be a new person too, and that's somewhat for all on us. Now go, like a good old Kester as yo' are.'
>
> Kester looked at her with loving, faithful admiration. He had set himself his day's work in his master's absence, and was very desirous of finishing it; but, somehow, he never dreamed of resisting Sylvia; so he only stated the case.
>
> 'T' 'ool's a vast o' muck in 't, an' a thowt as a'd fettle it, an' do it up; but a reckon a mun do yo're biddin'.' (v)

By significant contrast, though Philip uses 'thee' and 'thou' to Sylvia, she very rarely addresses him other than as 'yo'' even after they are married, and her speech to him is always more regular, less idiomatic, in sympathy with, though not equalling, his own relatively more articulate and literate tongue. Here, in perhaps their most intimate scene of all, choosing a name for the newborn child, when 'perhaps ...

Philip reached the zenith of his life's happiness' the differences
between them are plainly differentiated:

'Anything thou likes, sweetheart. Shall we call her Rose, after
Hester Rose?'

'No, no!' said Sylvia; 'she mun be called after my mother, or
thine, or both. I should like her to be called Bella, after mother,
because she's so fond of baby.'

'Anything to please thee, darling.'

'Don't say that as if it didn't signify; there's a deal in having a
pretty name,' said Sylvia, a little annoyed. 'I ha' allays hated
being called Sylvia. It were after father's mother, Sylvia Steele.'

'I niver thought any name in a' the world so sweet and pretty
as Sylvia,' said Philip fondly; but she was too much absorbed in
her own thoughts to notice either his manner or his words.

'There, yo'll not mind if it is Bella; because, yo' see, my
mother is alive to be pleased by its being named after her; and
Hester may be godmother; and I'll ha' t'dove-coloured silk as
yo' gave me afore we were married made up into a cloak for it
to go to church in.'

'I got it for thee,' said Philip, a little disappointed. 'It'll be too
good for the baby.'

'Eh! but I'm so careless, I should be spilling something on it!
But, if thou got it for me, I cannot find i' my heart for t'wear it
on baby; and I'll have it made into a christening gown for mysel'.
But I'll niver feel at any ease in it, for fear of spoiling it.'

'Well, an' if thou does spoil it, love, I'll get thee another. I
make account of riches only for thee; that I may be able to get
thee whativer thou's a fancy for, for either thysel', or thy
mother.'

She lifted her pale face from her pillow, and put up her lips to
kiss him for these words.

Perhaps, on that day, Philip reached the zenith of his life's
happiness. (xxx)

Many as are the connections that could be made between *Sylvia's
Lovers* and its writer's three earlier novels, and the links that could
be pointed out with other later novels by other writers, to do so is to
suggest that its value is for what it draws upon, and what it yields,
rather than what it is. Any such suggestion is a disservice. Had its
writer lived longer, she might have returned to tragedy; one can be

sure that she, who never repeats herself, would never have created another work like it. Her next and last novel, *Wives and Daughters*, perhaps equally fine, is almost its antithesis. *Sylvia's Lovers* stands alone and apart, in the solitude of greatness.

5

Wives and Daughters

There is no need to declare a case for *Wives and Daughters*: where *Cranford* is the most widely read of her works, *Wives and Daughters* is that most generally praised and admitted to the ranks of excellence. Yet it is easy to over-simplify its place there, its affinities, and its achievement. True as it is to link *Wives and Daughters* with *Cranford* and with *Cousin Phillis* and thus to set it apart from the novels of social concern, *Mary Barton* and *North and South*, and from the tragedy of *Sylvia's Lovers*; right as it may possibly be to delight in it as her last and crowning achievement; and accurate though it is to regard it as the nineteenth-century heir to the riches of Jane Austen, these truths, separately or together, do not do it full justice, and are inaccurate through being only part of the truth. *Wives and Daughters* does resemble *Cranford* in that both are based upon Elizabeth Gaskell's childhood home, Knutsford in Cheshire, and treat the lives and doings of small-town people with sympathy and humour. It resembles *Cousin Phillis* in conveying emotions deep and poignant even though their causes are modest and homely, which are interpenetrated by the movement of the seasons and day-to-day living. Yet it does far more than either, and, though not written with a clear social aim, reaches out to social considerations untouched in *Mary Barton* and *North and South*. Her last novel it certainly is, cut short just before its end by her sudden and early death at fifty-six years old, yet one must feel that Elizabeth Gaskell, like Jane Austen at her, even earlier, death, was far from the end of her career, and that *Wives and Daughters*, like *Persuasion*, shows a reaching-out to new and greater things. *Wives and Daughters* resembles Jane Austen's novels in its materials, part of its form, and some of its techniques, but the likenesses account for little of its greatness, leaving one tempted to say that, like Fielding's giants, it is 'like nothing but itself'. Such generalizations about resemblances can mislead the reader, blinkering him into seeing only what he expects to see, and leading him to minimize or ignore what is new in itself, or presented in ways quite new to the novel form.

Wives and Daughters is almost without flaw, and is done with such apparent ease and simplicity that its power is easy to overlook. Elizabeth Gaskell has always been so good at human character that there has seemed to be little in her work that has not sprung from human motive of a kind that can be verified by reference to 'real life'. She has always also excelled at humour without ridicule or condemnation, combining it with serious understanding and judgement. Both are at their finest in *Wives and Daughters*. However, though they cannot be underestimated, the ease with which she handles them conceals her powers here in other directions on which she has not always been so assured: melodrama, which has tempted her in *Mary Barton*, is wholly absent; a slightly over-perfect heroine, like Ruth or Margaret Hale, is inconceivable against Molly Gibson or Cynthia Kirkpatrick; an absence of plot or a minimal plot, such as she has hitherto employed, gives place here to plotting so skilful, so unobtrusive, that though its presence is almost unnoticed, the shape and form of this – the longest of its author's novels – depends upon it to prevent its numerous characters and areas of concern from being as disparate and episodic as *Cranford's* indubitably are.

This plot, involving the skilful interweaving of several almost equal and mutually enriching stories, is one great advance and difference in technique of *Wives and Daughters* above and beyond the other four full-length novels. The story of Molly Gibson, the surgeon's daughter who grows from child to woman, and in so doing learns of life and suffering and adds to the wisdom of innocence the wisdom of experience, is the chief one that runs the full length of the novel; the other story that runs alongside, that of 'Clare' the former governess, who as Mrs Kirkpatrick, schoolteacher widow of a curate, becomes Molly's stepmother Mrs Gibson, is of concern rather as commentary and giver of perspective than as plot. Molly is the only person who is involved in all the various actions which take place, though the plots are linked quite elaborately by concerning at some point or other almost all the characters who appear. Yet the story of Molly, the uniting thread of the whole, is not contained and complete as are the true 'plots' of the structure. The most striking of these is undoubtedly Cynthia Kirkpatrick's, who, by being secretly engaged against her will to the land-agent Mr Preston, when she promises herself to Roger Hamley, and by breaking away from both contracts to marry eventually an unexpected London barrister, provides most of the intrigue and mystery. She involves Molly both by using her as the instrument for retrieving her compromising letters to Preston, and paying off her debt to him, and by unconsciously causing Molly to suffer for her unacknowledged love for Roger. Yet this plot, even if we count its beginning as Cynthia's arrival in Hollingford, takes place only in the last two-thirds of the novel, and even there it runs alongside the other plot, of greater importance to theme as well as structure. This other plot concerns the Hamleys of Hamley, the squire and his two sons Osborne and Roger. The mystery here, paralleling Cynthia's, is Osborne's secret marriage to a French nursery-maid, concealed from his French-hating father who plans a noble marriage for him, until after Osborne's own death. Roger is privy to this secret as Molly is to Cynthia's, and is also an ignorant participant in Cynthia's story, as her fiancé; but only Molly knows both secrets, and shares in all the plots. In various ways all the characters and all the incidents advance, illuminate, and set in proportion one or other of these two main plots, while at the same time forming smaller plotlets in themselves. The tale for example takes its first decided impulse from Molly's father, the doctor Mr Gibson, his dilemmas as the widowed father of a growing-up daughter, and his decision to solve them by taking a second wife. This serio-comic episode of misjudgement is both complete in itself and of foreground interest for the first fourteen chapters, and is vital to the rest as the means of creating the situation of the confused loyalties and standards in the Gibson household, with its father and daughter, and stepmother and her daughter – Mr Gibson and Molly, Mrs Gibson and Cynthia Kirkpatrick – on which depends so much of the rest of the novel.

The general shape of the action is far more traditional than any of Elizabeth Gaskell's previous works. It resembles Jane Austen, in that, like *Mansfield Park*, it follows the course of its heroine through childhood and young womanhood to marriage, Molly Gibson being similar to Fanny Price in age and development when the story begins.

When she is older Molly's career balances and contrasts Cynthia Kirkpatrick's, as Fanny's does Mary Crawford's. There are also the contrasting young men, Roger and Osborne Hamley, and Mr Preston, who interact with each other as do Edmund Bertram, Tom Bertram and Henry Crawford, in their degrees of excellence and moral responsibility. However, Jane Austen's novel has nothing corresponding to Elizabeth Gaskell's other main action, the tale of the Osborne father and his sons, and Osborne's secret marriage. The career of a young woman up to her marriage, which provides Jane Austen with all the scope she requires, will not suffice, even in this most Austenian of novels, for Mrs Gaskell. Between the two writers, many others have drawn upon this fairly common and convenient basic pattern, adapting it to their own uses. Among them three of the most important and influential came from provincial novelists in the twenty years of Elizabeth Gaskell's writing career – Anne Brontë's *Agnes Grey* (1847), Charlotte Brontë's *Jane Eyre* (1848) and George Eliot's *The Mill on the Floss* (1860); *Agnes Grey* has a heroine who like Molly is both a main figure and also a means of uniting and interpreting the more exciting and significant material contained in the careers of other characters, the various members of the families to whom she goes as governess, in particular the neglected and morally warped Rosalie Murray who, like Cynthia, attracts several lovers, including the heroine's, and finally does not marry the best of them. Though *Agnes Grey* is a slighter whole than *Wives and Daughters*, with a very simple plot and far fewer characters, the resemblances extend to the author's relationship with her heroine, which, though feeling and sympathetic, is also detached. Although Anne Brontë, a lesser author than Elizabeth Gaskell, who uses the first-person autobiographical method, makes this less plain, both of them thus differ from Charlotte Brontë or George Eliot, who in their different ways are passionately and personally involved with their heroines Jane Eyre and Maggie Tulliver.

The resemblances between *Jane Eyre* and *Wives and Daughters* are less close in the handling of the main plot and the heroine, but are rather in the way both writers set their heroines in a variety of contexts, which they help to interpret, and which advance them in experience and moral growth. Jane Eyre like Molly encounters a high society which repels her – though, admittedly, Mr Rochester's house-party visitors at Thornfield Hall are of a different species from the Cumnors of Cumnor Park; while Jane Eyre's welcome and acceptance by the Rivers family to some extent parallels Molly's by the Hamleys.

The Mill on the Floss is, where materials are concerned, the closest, with a family of divided sympathies, in a close modest rural community where everyone knows each other, where Maggie, the subdued heroine, contrasts with her brilliant and beloved cousin Lucy, as Molly does with her brilliant step-sister, though their roles are reversed in that Stephen Guest, Lucy's lover, defects to Maggie, while Roger Hamley only comes to Molly after Cynthia has cast him off.

The examples give no suggestion of imitation or borrowing, but only of the ways in which basic plots and patterns are developed to quite different emotional and thematic ends by writers with different purposes, who, as the age progresses, can use these basic patterns to explore different and more extensive areas of experience. Although the novel of the later nineteenth century takes many new directions, the pattern of the contrasting main characters and contrasting family and social groups within a small provincial community continues to be fruitful, serving D. H. Lawrence well, in *Sons and Lovers*, *The Rainbow*, and *Women in Love*. It can also be traced with adaptation in E. M. Forster, who bases *Howard's End* on the contrasting and conflicting Schlegel and Wilcox families, whose final balance of their opposed systems of values is achieved through the influence of the place, Howard's End, itself.

Although *Wives and Daughters* bears witness to Jane Austen's comment that 'three or four Families in a Country Village are the very thing to work on',[1] and although the central figures in the action are, as Scott said of Jane Austen's, 'from the middling classes of society', the range of the whole is far wider than Jane Austen's, or than Elizabeth Gaskell's own has been hitherto. At the top, socially speaking, are the family of Cumnor Park, the Earl and Countess, their son Lord Hollingford, and their unmarried daughter, Lady Harriet. With all the attributes of wealth and power, they embody a higher society than Elizabeth Gaskell has hitherto dealt with, done without any feeling of uneasiness or uncertainty. Next to them come the Hamleys – the two sons Osborne and Roger, the invalid wife and the squire himself – impoverished and untitled, yet with a pride and status above the Cumnors', arising from their ancient stock,

[1] Letter to her niece Anna, 9 September 1814.

going back far beyond the Queen Anne who established the Cumnors, if not far enough to substantiate Mrs Goodenough's splendid claim that 'there was Hamleys of Hamley afore the time of the pagans' (IV). Though socially impoverished gentility has been Elizabeth Gaskell's subject more than once before – most conspicuously in the 'elegantly economical' ladies of *Cranford* and in the benevolent despotism of the autocratic Lady Ludlow – and though she has shown on a smaller scale how competently she can depict the country landlord's pride, pretensions, and family and business relationships, in the Buxtons of *The Moorland Cottage* and in Lady Ludlow, this is the first time she has taken upon herself to reach so high, or analyse so deeply.

Mr Gibson the surgeon and his family occupy a middling position in this society, able to associate with the upper levels by virtue of his professional position, but also at home with the ordinary inhabitants of Hollingford, represented by the Miss Brownings and Mrs Goodenough, whose way of life and income resembles that of the single ladies and widows of Cranford, but who are below them in pretensions to gentility. Servants also are given due attention when their part in the action warrants. A new area is indicated by Lord Cumnor's land-agent Mr Preston, who, though he attends to confidential business affairs, and is a man of intelligence, is yet in a socially anomalous position, somewhat on a level with the rector, and not out of place at the Miss Brownings' evening card-parties. Were this Elizabeth Gaskell's only novel, the casual twentieth-century reader might as easily slip into considering her a social snob – not recognizing the documentary sensitiveness of the way she notes social demarcations – as happens to Jane Austen. However, although the whole class of what Elizabeth Gaskell calls, without patronage or superiority, 'the poor', form no part of *Wives and Daughters*, the witness of all her previous novels proves that the exclusion is a mark not of ignorance or neglect, but of artistic discretion.

This extension of Elizabeth Gaskell's social range is not only of the areas she chooses to use in isolation, but of their interaction; not only the central Molly meets with all, but all meet with all in this closely-linked society: school visiting brings the modest Miss Brownings face to face with the Countess of Cumnor and Lady Harriet; a dance brings Molly into conversation with Lord Hollingford and Mr Preston, and Cynthia with the local bookseller; Mr Gibson dines with the Cumnors; and the Hamley sons visit his wife and daughters.

Such social meetings, which cross the class boundaries, are new to her. In her earlier novels, class boundaries have often been broken down, as when, in *Mary Barton*, Carson has dealings with the strikers and John Barton, or in *North and South*, Thornton communicates with the mill-worker Higgins. But such meetings have arisen out of crises, and have been conscious breakings through the barriers of class and culture, with the purpose of allowing man to understand man in the times of greatest need and most painful stress. In depicting them Elizabeth Gaskell had technically an easier task, for she lays aside the observance of social decorum and etiquette. Among the characters and their predicaments in *Wives and Daughters* social decorum prevails, even when prejudices and snobberies are laid aside. The unmarried Lady Harriet Cumnor is old enough and sure enough of herself to lay aside her rank and befriend Molly, to accept Molly's rebuke for her ridicule of the Miss Brownings as 'Pecksy and Flapsy', and also, conversely, deliberately to exploit her social position to redress injustice, when Hollingford gossip ostracizes Molly for her supposed secret liaison with Mr Preston. Elizabeth Gaskell's hold on social interrelations and discriminations is at its most assured and most subtle. This far from rigid system permits her to chart the fluctuations brought about by circumstance and individual merit. Mr Gibson for instance by virtue of his position may dine, on special occasions, at the Hall, as his predecessor the doctor Mr Hall has done, but his knowledge of and interest in scientific research which he shares with Lord Hollingford bring him into a different and closer connection with the whole family, in the same way as later on, Roger Hamley as scientist and explorer does also.

How elaborate, subtle and flexible is this system of social inter-connections emerges gradually during the action, and is defined with humour, point, and economy by those who cannot acknowledge it, most notably Mrs Gibson, who, almost farcically clinging to her own views of her privileged intimacy with the Cumnors, looks down on the Miss Brownings, misinterprets every action of Lady Harriet, and is one of the last to admit that Preston is a social climber, or that Roger Hamley has a position based not on his rank, but on his achievement.

It is not only in her social range that Elizabeth Gaskell has extended her powers in *Wives and Daughters*. Her other extensions are thematic, emotional, and technical, and bring out the paradox of the whole work, that an apparently modest story – 'an everyday story' as it is subtitled – can comprehend almost all the areas of human experience with which she has already dealt; can go deeper into some of the most central areas of human experience than was done with the more apparently important subjects of her earlier novels; and can, by being so inclusive, give a full and more maturely interpreted vision of human existence. The three main purposes as a novelist, which she has always had, of concern for society at large, for individuals' relationships with each other in social, local and family groups, and the single soul's duties to and struggles with itself, are all present in *Wives and Daughters*. But she has now balanced their priorities within herself, in a way that has released her full powers to reveal all three. In her early novels she felt the need to have a specific social or moral 'question' to grapple with, to justify her writing, though in presenting any such question she depended with more and more assured success upon the progress of the single souls whose predicaments embodied the problem. Thus, while she has always used human relationships as her means of presenting social or moral issues, to balance the two impulses which drive her to write has been the problem which has directed her course as a novelist. Her maturing is her growth of power to make them work together. In *Wives and Daughters*, the cooperation is perfect. The human relationships are both the subject in themselves, and the method of revealing the wider more abstract issues. There are two common ways of reading *Wives and Daughters* in the light of her earlier work; yet neither recognizes its true power. The most obvious and most frequent is as the successor to *Cranford* and *Cousin Phillis*, as a story of private and personal progresses, where the wonderfully felicitous understanding and analysis of human nature, of what goes on within individuals, and how they affect each other's lives in the ordinary course of human events, is the chief purpose and great success achieved. In carrying out this purpose and achieving this success, Elizabeth Gaskell uses for all three works the material of her life before marriage, of Knutsford, the country town unaffected by the fast-changing industrial and scientific advance of the nineteenth century. The other way of reading *Wives and Daughters* is by the light of *Mary Barton, North and South* and *Ruth*, and to see in it the author charting the changing shape of society, the gradual breaking-down of the class system as the old order changes, and the gradual infiltration of the squirearchical structure by the new men of science, learning, and the professions, as the younger generation reshapes itself amid the older one. For these novels she does not keep exclusively to one kind of material, but draws upon a wide area, of which the most powerful and new is the Manchester of the greater part of her married life. Only by acknowledging both of these concerns, and perceiving a third can one fully respond to the excellence of the work. The third is the impulse Elizabeth Gaskell has frequently shown to write on historical subjects, of which her two most famous and achieved are *Sylvia's Lovers* and 'Lois the Witch', in which she ventures far from what she herself has lived and experienced – to Yorkshire and New England in these two, and in other minor short tales to London, the France of the Revolution, and even to India.

It is not possible to point out a main theme in *Wives and Daughters*, whether a personal psychological one, or a large social abstract one, any more than it is possible to do so in *Middlemarch*, or, to go abroad to greater things, *War and Peace*; yet within it Elizabeth Gaskell integrates most of what have been her big themes in her earlier work. Some of these themes reappear in a similar form, many of them with a new and more original guise, some potentially more subtle, and along with them, other quite new issues. They are all subdued to quiet pleasant Hollingford, present without the intensity or large destructive force of their earlier forms, but no less significant or penetrating or true for being less stridently presented and less dangerous. One of her earliest themes of all was the predicament of masters and men, and their mutual duties in a changing world, seen in *Mary Barton* and *North and South*. What led to disaster and death there is here, in *Wives and Daughters*, one of the many predicaments facing Squire Hamley in his near-hopeless struggles against the changing times, his own character, and the blows of fate. His dying wife persuades him to undertake the drainage and reclamation of part of his land, with a government loan. Grief at her death and disappointment in Osborne, the son who is to inherit, make him neglect it. In his lament for what he has done he raises all the points that are at the heart of the employer's dilemma:

'I know I turned them off – what could I do? I'd no more money for their weekly wages; it's a loss to me, as you know. He doesn't know, no one knows, but I think your mother would, how it cut me to turn 'em off just before winter set in. I lay awake at night thinking of it, and I gave 'em what I had –

I did, indeed. I hadn't got money to pay 'em, but I had three barren cows fattened, and gave every scrap of meat to the men, and I let 'em go into the woods and gather what was fallen, and I winked at their breaking off old branches.' (xxx)

Along with this theme in *North and South* and *Mary Barton* she grappled also with the conflicts of class with class, with groups who viewed and judged the world they shared from different sets of values. In *Mary Barton* these were essentially those of rich and poor; in *North and South* they were rather of different cultures, social and professional, rural and industrial, academic and mercantile, in London, Helstone and Milton. Here in *Wives and Daughters* the groups are much nearer on the social scale, and the discriminations therefore more subtle. The main ones are the Hamleys and the Cumnors, both landowning, old-established, families, taking pride both in their positions and their responsibilities. The differences are far from simply that the Cumnors are wealthy and the Hamleys relatively impoverished, or that the former are Whig and the latter Tory. There are no key scenes, or single speeches, or summaries from the author such as stood out in *North and South* (like the distinction made there between the 'gentleman' and the 'man'). The effect is built up from a great number of individually slight, precisely observed, and cumulatively overwhelmingly convincing details. Both the Earl of Cumnor and Squire Hamley take an interest in their land and tenants, while juxtaposition points the difference between the Earl's easy, forgetful chat, and the Squire's genuine sense of duty, at the same time as it emphasizes that the Earl is efficient by proxy through his agent Mr Preston, while the Squire is ineffectual by nature and ignorance. As in *North and South*, Elizabeth Gaskell does not permit the reader to decide easily that one is more right than the other. The Cumnors are patronizing and insensitive, and spend much of their time away from their estates, in London or abroad, yet are probably, economically judged, much better for their tenants and dependants than the Hamleys. Popular opinion, represented by the chat of Hollingford, is as enthusiastic for the Earl and for the 'dear Countess' as for the man and his ancestors who 'had been called squire as long back as local tradition extended . . . ever since the Heptarchy' (iv); Molly gains equal status in Hollingford eyes from her visits to both families. Both families have their intellectual members: Lord Hollingford has scientific interests which enable him to be both Roger Hamley's *confrère* and patron, and Osborne represents the older-established academic values of classical studies and literature.

The question of what constituted personal success in a man, and how it was achieved, was also central to *North and South*, embodied in Thornton, rising to wealth and power by his own exertions and talents. Here the figure reappears as Roger Hamley, the younger son of whom nothing brilliant is expected, who, by a similar kind of dogged strength of character and intellect, becomes Senior Wrangler, fellow of his college, traveller and man of science. But whereas Thornton's career is thematically central to *North and South*, and emblematic also of the oppositions of class and society, Roger's is only one element among many, no more important to the whole than Osborne's contrasting career as the victim of his nature and up-bringing, which cause his potential artistic brilliance to come to nothing, and render him helpless to make his way in the world when his hereditary role as wealthy heir is taken from him.

The subtle intermingling continues both to recall and contrast with the earlier novels in the sense of place, particularly the relation of the provincial world to the distant London. In *Mary Barton*, the strikers' petition to Parliament takes them to an alien and almost unintelligible city, where their wrongs are equally alien and un-intelligible, and ignored. In *North and South* social London contrasts, to its disadvantage, with serious purposeful Manchester, but is also the place whose society is wide enough to permit the final coming together of Margaret and Thornton. London in *Wives and Daughters* partakes of all these views. It is the place which recognizes Roger's worth amongst its learned societies, has the money to finance his expeditions, and eventually begins to 'lionize' him in his success. It is also the place where the intelligent professional man Mr Gibson may meet congenial minds, among the barrister relatives of his wife, and where Cynthia can blossom in a society which, while not exacting too high a moral standard from her, allows her genuine social talents to flower. Yet London can still be felt as somewhere alien and foreign – as it was in *Mary Barton* and, very differently, in *Sylvia's Lovers* – when old Mrs Goodenough can 'remember its being a three-days journey' and 'hope it won't turn Cynthia's head' (XXXVIII). France, even more remote, familiar though it is to Cynthia who was at school there, recalls the fabulous country of ineffectual and feeble Frenchmen existing in the imagination of Sylvia Robson's father (who could seriously debate whether it took three or four Frenchmen to beat an English soldier) when Mrs Good-enough declares, apropos of Mr Gibson, Molly and Cynthia

'I shouldn't like having my daughter, if I was him, so cheek-by-jowl with a girl as was brought up in the country where Robespierre and Bonyparte was born.' (XXXVIII)

The effect of combining these serious and far-reaching themes, and putting them with others touching more closely upon personal qualities and predicaments, by no means renders them trivial. They are as significant as their more momentous counterparts elsewhere, in the same way as Jane Austen's moral touchstones: found in the course of common life are far-reaching and immutable truths about human life.

Personal and individual concerns also, which figured in different places in her earlier novels, here form parts of the thematic pattern. Though *Wives and Daughters* is essentially in the tradition of the novel of manners, and uses the comic mode, yet it takes into itself the elements of tragedy that formed *Sylvia's Lovers*, without in any way reducing their intrinsic seriousness. There the tragic dilemma was made to spring from the unchangeable essence of personality, the characters being driven along their inescapable course by both their own essential personalities and by the passions that ruled and over-ruled their essence. Here, though no series of events reaches a tragic end, the tragic elements of *Sylvia's Lovers* are present again in the story of Squire Hamley's long estrangement from his son Osborne. Osborne's secret marriage is the contingency, paralleling Philip concealing Kinraid's seizure by the press-gang. What led in *Sylvia's Lovers* to a tragic catastrophe, here leads to the long, sad, and pain-fully deteriorating situation, of misunderstanding between father and son, with the father just as unable to escape from his prejudices as Sylvia from her unforgiving nature. This is by no means a mere re-use or repetition of the earlier material: apportionments of guilt and blame do not parallel those in *Sylvia's Lovers*, for the elements are wholly transmuted in this dilemma, not of lovers, but of a father and son. The passion and love which enslaved Philip to Sylvia makes a surprising and wholly original reappearance elsewhere in *Wives and Daughters*, in a minor character, the uncongenial agent Mr Preston, who, totally unlike Philip in his vain, self-seeking, ambitious nature, is as helpless in his passion for Cynthia as Philip for Sylvia. Thus Elizabeth Gaskell's habitual view which admits the capacity for full human feeling to all her characters finds in *Wives and Daughters* perhaps its most congenial vehicle, which permits her to spread the components of her themes more widely than ever before over her characters and materials.

The most striking instance of this power concerns her female characters. All her novels in some degree show her concern with the individual woman's growth of wisdom and maturity, whether it is the comparatively simple Mary Barton, or Ruth, or the more complex Margaret Hale, or the poignant Sylvia. Here there is no single heroine acquiring wisdom and self-knowledge in the old tradition that reaches back beyond Jane Austen to Maria Edgworth and Fanny Burney. Yet the theme itself is in the forefront. The rich traditional combination in a heroine of faults or illusions with the potential for good, whose greatest example is probably Jane Austen's Emma, is here refined and subtilized by division. In Molly Gibson Elizabeth Gaskell charts the growth of wisdom and maturity, without any attending faults or follies. In Cynthia Kirkpatrick she-reveals the growth of self-knowledge, yet it is accompanied by no easy or automatic increase in virtue, but rather a sadly inevitable recognition that the twig once bent by careless upbringing and an ineradicable heredity can never grow into the straight tree. A third sharer is Lady Harriet who, with wit, intelligence and maturity (she is in her late twenties when the action begins) can yet allow experience to correct some of her prejudices. Finally, there is Mrs Gibson, neither young nor wise, whose history as it is revealed at intervals throughout the novel, emphasizes that the experience that should produce wisdom and reform may yet merely intensify folly.

Even though *Wives and Daughters* amalgamates so much of her previous work, it contains over and above things that are quite new. These can be roughly divided into matters concerning individuals, and the connections between individuals and their society. In *Wives and Daughters* Elizabeth Gaskell creates and examines personalities who are quite new to the novel, both in themselves and their situations. These mainly radiate from the remarkable Cynthia, who will be examined in more detail later. Her essential nature has already been mentioned, with its mixture of self-awareness with hopelessness of improvement which leads to the remarkable event of her refusal to marry Roger, even though she recognizes his excellence and his devotion. As usual Elizabeth Gaskell makes it impossible for the reader to separate necessities of plot from essentials of personality.

It is only by a great effort of detachment that the reader can perceive the mechanical necessity for her refusal, which is to leave Roger free to marry Molly. As an instance of Elizabeth Gaskell's unfailing eye for the unconventional unexpected probability, Cynthia's choice recalls Ruth's refusal to marry Mr Bellingham, when all the laws both of moral propriety and of the expectations of fiction invite her acceptance of him.

Cynthia also exemplifies the pressures and powers of society. She has been formed by the company she has been forced to keep, having to fend for herself at an early age, deprived not only of the love of her dead father and neglectful mother, but even of association with that mother, however inadequate. Such a set of causes and effects, obvious enough to the twentieth-century reader, is considerably less so to the writer or reader of the 1860s. Osborne Hamley, another instance of the effects of upbringing and environment, is even more psychologically subtle. His two very different parents, an ill-educated, farming, solitary father, who avoids the society of equals for himself and his sons, and a gentle, ailing, cultured mother, both of whom take his exceptional brilliance and outstanding potential for granted, cause him to align himself with his mother, never realize that talents must be developed by practice and education; and so to be unable to face the challenges of a university, or to fulfil the responsibilities and duties of an adult life.

Such a complication of themes and materials and such a variety of new and original combinations arises from a different attitude on the author's part, and produces a different mood. Elizabeth Gaskell has always had two areas of great assurance: her own beliefs about man's nature and his purposes in life – which may be broadly summarized as religion and morality – and her understanding and portrayal of the way individual natures react and respond to what happens to them in the course of time and life. She has never expressed any sense of difficulty with either, nor has her technique ever shown signs of insecurity. With regard to the novelist's other great problem, his relations with his reader, she was conscious of being less comfortable,[2] and

[2] She once wrote: 'I can not (it is not will not) write at all if I ever think of my readers, and what impression I am making on them "If they don't like me, they must lump me" to use a Lancashire proverb. It is from no despising of my readers. I am sure I don't do that, but if I ever let the thought or consciousness of them come between me and my subject I could not write at all.' (letter to Charles Eliot Norton, 10 May 1858).

H

varied both in her methods and her success, even though in her full-length novels – as contrasted with some of her shorter stories – she never sank into awkwardness. In *Wives and Daughters* her attitudes show interesting signs of change, a greater breadth of understanding, and, where her relations with her readers are concerned, total assurance.

Elizabeth Gaskell has always had a secure and generous religious faith, and has written with a moral purpose. Her development has shown that as her artistic power increased the faith became less explicit, and the moral and social purpose more organic, and less of a pretext or prop for the artistic impulse. In *Wives and Daughters* religion in any obvious form virtually disappears. While in her previous work one recognized that churchgoing was no part of the life of *Mary Barton*'s mill-workers, nor of the isolated farm-dwellers Sylvia Robson and her family, it is astonishing, in a novel like *Wives and Daughters*, wholly working through day-to-day activities and unsensational events, that the organized religion which necessarily formed a regular, even routine, part of them is given only the slightest mention – no more than noticing that Molly, suspected of a clandestine association with Mr Preston, is not spoken to after church, and that Mr Gibson's mischievous wit can reduce to confusion the vicar Mr Ashton, 'a thoroughly good and kind-hearted man, but one without an original thought in him' whom Mr Gibson

> had once or twice amused himself by leading on in his agreeable admissions of arguments 'as perfectly convincing', and of statements as 'curious but undoubted', till he had planted the poor clergyman in a bog of heretical bewilderment. (IV)

Undogmatic as she has always been, nevertheless she has always made the Bible a precept and a comfort for her characters, whose phrases rose easily to the lips of those in distress in *Mary Barton*, of the Bensons and the Bradshaws in *Ruth*, and of almost all the characters in *Sylvia's Lovers* in moments of great crisis. The refined society of *Wives and Daughters* is less likely to do so, but the comfort and strength that it represents is never explicit even in the author's own voice, in comment or reflection (as it was in *Sylvia's Lovers*), or even at points when it would be appropriate, in connection with Molly's despair at Mr Gibson's re-marriage or with the gentle and dying Mrs Hamley. Though God is unself-consciously mentioned by the candid Squire Hamley in his grief, Molly's threnody for his wife is not from scripture, but from James Shirley:

> Only the actions of the just
> Smell sweet and blossom in the dust. (XIX)

Elizabeth Gaskell's reticence is evidence both of how confident she now is that the fabric of the novel itself will carry the necessary doctrine, and of how she no longer feels the pressure on her to show she is aware of her reader by addressing him. Her moralizings stand out, not by being expressed obtrusively or didactically, but by being penetratingly, even painfully, true.

> Molly sate in the dining room, making tea for the gentlemen as they came down. She could not help hoping that the Squire and Osborne might come to a better understanding before she left; for after all, *in the dissension between father and son lay a bitterer sting than in the illness sent by God*. (XVIII, my italics)

Here, as often throughout, she lets a character, without the author intervening, take the weight of making the moral statement, secure in characterization which leaves the reader in no doubt that such reflection, while in keeping with the personality, is a general statement of truth borne out by action and events. Molly is her primary means of making such statements, but not her only one; many of her others can do so, the chief among them being Mr Gibson and Roger, especially in the earlier stages, when Molly is still very young. The moral considerations which in *Sylvia's Lovers* were subtle, painful, and perplexing from the unique predicament, are equally so here, in much less momentous situations, because of the greater intelligence, sensibility and self-awareness of the characters, and the clear-cut moral rules which their society upholds, which, when stated, seem so naïve as to preclude subtlety in realization. Molly is compelled by accident to keep two secrets, the knowledge of Osborne's marriage, and the details of Mr Preston's power over Cynthia, which rests on a debt of £25, and a promise to marry him given when she was sixteen years old. As Molly has no doubts that she is morally obliged to keep the secrets, the ethical dilemmas result from contingencies and consequences of silence. In the workings-out of Molly's dilemmas here, and in the other crises and problems of the novel, Elizabeth Gaskell is further than she has ever been from demonstrating poetic justice, or even the kind of fair dealing that a novelist so often presents. The novel's first real event, the entertainment of the school-visitors at the Towers, contains the first instance, both comic and pathetic. Molly, who falls asleep lost and exhausted in the grounds, is found by Lady Cuxhaven and 'Clare' (the future Mrs Gibson) and brought food. As she is too ill to eat it, Clare does so; as they return to the house, Lady Cuxhaven meets them:

> 'How is she now?' she asked; then glancing at the plates and glasses she added, 'Come, I think there can't be much amiss.'
>
> (11)

Molly is never cleared of the imputation of greed and good health, left upon her by Clare's sly silence, and the pain and embarrassment caused by it render the incident both comic and poignant, like the more important later events, when Molly is generally misunderstood for being loyal to Cynthia, keeping her secret, and helping her break Mr Preston's hold over her. She is never publicly cleared in this case, either, of being thought to have a clandestine relationship with him; even though the truth eventually comes out to her father and to the family at the Towers, her own prognostication of consequences is the true one, that

> 'when nothing more happens, and nothing comes of what has happened, the wonder and the gossip must die away.' (XLVIII)

Mrs Gaskell quite consciously and deliberately eschews regarding Molly's modestly heroic act as heroic in its outcome: she gives her neither a hero's public exoneration, nor the complete heroic secrecy of the event known only to author and reader. As so frequently happens, Elizabeth Gaskell works in terms of what she feels to be probable in terms of common life and observable human nature, wryly setting Molly up again in the eyes of Hollingford gossip by calling upon Hollingford snobbery, when Lady Harriet deliberately and publicly walks round the town with her, paying formal calls and leaving visiting cards. Such a handling of moral questions and the material of common life has always been one of her methods, but with central action she has hitherto preferred to produce both the effect of complete probability and also of full justice. Such was the outcome of misunderstanding in *North and South*, with Margaret, and in *Sylvia's Lovers*, where the tragic consequences of the tragic passions of Sylvia and Hepburn were of the same nature and fabric as the acts which caused them. *Wives and Daughters* is true comedy because of this

essential difference of attitude in the author to the materials which are
operated upon by her moral position, rather than because of the
subjects and events themselves, which are often neither humorous
nor comic.

Though one never doubts the faith in a divine purpose that lies
behind all Elizabeth Gaskell's work, yet *Wives and Daughters* comes
near to questioning it, by posing problems, and offering speculations,
to which she provides no answer. Parts of the action, and parts of
characters' responses to events, suggest a newer and deeper perception
of the nature of life, and the hopelessness of perfection in human
relations. The most striking are among Molly's reactions to her
father's re-marriage. Roger Hamley's advice to her is wise, penetrating and sympathetic, based on the fact that Mr Gibson is acting for
Molly's sake, and that Molly's right course is 'to think more of
others', as she naïvely summarizes it. Her response is daunting to a
simple moralist:

> 'It is difficult' he went on, 'but by and by you will be so much
> happier for it.'
> 'No, I shan't,' said Molly, shaking her head. 'It will be very
> dull when I shall have killed myself, as it were, and live only in
> trying to do, and to be, as other people like. I don't see any end
> to it. I might as well never have lived.'
> There was an unconscious depth in what she said, that Roger
> did not know how to answer at the moment. (xi)

Neither does the author. Molly's perception is not a momentary
flash, for Elizabeth Gaskell offers its proof in what follows. Mrs
Gibson, selfish and unresponsive, separating Molly and her father
and changing their lives, brings Molly, cast down by sorrow at Mrs
Hamley's death, to look again at herself:

> She thought of the day her father brought her the news of his
> second marriage. Could she ever be so passionately unhappy
> again? Was it goodness, or was it numbness, that made her feel
> as though life was too short to be troubled much about any-
> thing? Death seemed the only reality. (xviii)

Though Molly receives compensations and comforts – in Cynthia's
friendship, and in a few happy escapes alone with her father – her
questions are never answered. Roger is only comparatively right that
she will be 'so much happier' if she is unselfish and submissive. No

effort of anyone's can make a happy situation out of the Gibson marriage; she has been right both in diagnosis and prognosis, and a year later

> she was gradually falling into low health, rather than bad health. Her heart beat more feebly and slower; the vivifying stimulant of hope – even unacknowledged hope – had gone out of her life. It seemed as if there was not, and never could be in this world, any help for the dumb discordancy between her father and his wife. Day after day, month after month, year after year, would Molly have to sympathise with her father, and pity her step-mother, feeling acutely for both. (XXXVII)

And Molly herself becomes happy at last only by escape. Her situation and conclusions recall Caroline Helstone's in Charlotte Brontë's *Shirley*, when, faced with the fact that she will not marry, and is likely to be for the rest of her life unmarried, she rejects as unsatisfying and unfulfilling the conventional solution of devoting her life to good works. Both authors recognize that to deny oneself wholly, even for the good of others, can be spiritual death. The need for personal fulfilment becomes the great and growing concern of the novel throughout the century and beyond, examined, not as Elizabeth Gaskell examines it, in respect to both religion and society, but to social and psychological pressure. In both *The Mill on the Floss* and *Middlemarch* George Eliot explores the kind of compulsion and conflicts society and their own natures lay upon her heroines Maggie Tulliver and Dorothea, and they are followed by Hardy's Tess Durbeyfield and Jude Fawley; but with all of these the Christian moral solution, of selfless self-denial, is questioned and rejected, or ignored. Trollope also, in his less intellectual, yet soundly intuitive way can explore the same areas, with a power easy to underestimate. *The Small House at Allington*, rightly admired as one of the best of the Barchester novels, concerns itself with the career of Lily Dale, whose prospect of fulfilment lay in the fiancé who jilted her. The analysis of her sufferings and spiritual recovery is original and perceptive, and, like Elizabeth Gaskell's analysis of Molly, never suggests that resignation and recovery can lead to more than qualified happiness or fulfilment. Trollope's handling needs to be followed into his concluding work *The Last Chronicle of Barset*, which finally scotches the expectation left at the end of *The Small House at Allington* that Lily may find a second spring in marriage with the devoted John Eames, and contains the even more original portrait of the mature Lily who, no longer in love even with the memory of Adolphus Crosbie, has lost the resilience and power to live again to the full, and thus determines not only her own fate but that of Eames as well.

The blow struck in Molly at Elizabeth Gaskell's early faith that situations may be cured by men of goodwill – the solution offered in *Mary Barton* and *North and South* – is repeated in the story of the Hamleys, which combines Elizabeth Gaskell's concern with death with the dilemmas of human nature. Here also she suggests how inadequate are goodwill and good intentions to bring together the squire and Osborne, whose estrangement not only continues but deepens as long as Osborne lives, despite their mutual love and concern, and despite Roger's active understanding of both. All three feel that Mrs Hamley, had she lived, could have brought them together; it is only another death, Osborne's own, that in a paradoxical sense does so. Thus it is in a novel neither tragic, nor filled with urgent social matters of the day, that Elizabeth Gaskell presents her most serious questionings of accepted moral tenets, and easily-held views of human nature and interaction in society. The comedy rests in the modest scale: the seriousness in the wide implications. She offers no answers to what is in its nature unanswerable, but only proposes maxims for comfort and palliation, not for cure, like Roger's simple advice to the young Molly, or Molly's own opinion, when she sees the unhappiness of the Hamleys, that openness and candour in even the worst circumstances are preferable to secrecy and deceit:

> ... she found it very uncomfortable; there was a sense of concealment and uncertainty about it all; and her honest, straightforward father, her quiet life at Hollingford, which, even with all its drawbacks, was above-board, and where everybody knew what everybody was doing, seemed secure and pleasant in comparison. (XVIII)

Wives and Daughters makes clearer than any of her novels what has always been her moral concern; how wrong is caused, how the good can cause it and incur suffering, and how and in what ways redress is possible. She is thus sharply separated from George Eliot in her moral attitudes, and aligned with Charlotte and Anne Brontë. The difference is most clearly seen in the handling of secondary characters. If one can generalize and simplify about such complex novelists, George Eliot's concern is in the first place with retribution; the others' is with reconciliation; compassion is common to all three. George Eliot the non-Christian is the harshest moralist. Before reconciliation or comfort is offered to her characters, the consequences of wrongdoing have to be experienced; in *Adam Bede* Arthur Donnithorne loses what is most precious to him, his way of life and future as a good, benevolent and well-loved squire, as penalty for his seduction of Hetty; in *Silas Marner*, Godfrey Cass loses the one child he has by his secret, unhappy marriage, as the consequence of deserting that child for the chance of the happy marriage and family he desires; in *Felix Holt*, Mrs Transome loses the love and esteem of the son whom she committed adultery to conceive; and in *Middlemarch*, Bulstrode's schemings and deceptions finally cause the loss of the public esteem and advancement for which they have been undertaken. Though George Eliot's sense of probability is not in her early works as great as Elizabeth Gaskell's, her moral sensibility is as acute, and her power to make moral consequences spring from essentials of character is, in her best work, as great. Yet over her work as a whole it is plain that she is very much concerned with the evil consequences of human failure, and more aware of retribution for faults that are not even crimes than she is of the pathos of the consequences of character traits which are hardly even faults. Where George Eliot is most compassionate is with characters who are at odds not with moral laws but with society. These are her main characters like Maggie Tulliver and Dorothea Brooke, whose problems can hardly be expressed in terms of morality at all, but only in terms of the characters' emotional and aesthetic needs and their conflict with the world and conventional standards surrounding them.

By contrast Elizabeth Gaskell and Anne and Charlotte Brontë rarely concern themselves primarily with retribution, but rather with how essential goodness and worth may struggle through despite the troubles brought upon them by circumstances, whether those occasioned by society, or the make-up of their own natures, or of the natures of others, or of real wrongdoing. In *Jane Eyre*, a powerful figure in Jane's life is Mrs Reed, who neglects and grossly ill-treats her as a child. Yet the whole movement of the novel and the measure of Jane's increasing maturity is towards compassion, not retribution. Mrs Reed dies suffering, partly for her ill-treatment of Jane, but much more for her failures in bringing up her drunkard suicide son: Jane's valediction emphasizes the pity, not the justice, of her end:

'Love me then, or hate me, as you will,' I said at last, 'you have my free and full forgiveness: ask now for God's; and be at peace.'

Poor, suffering woman! it was too late for her now to make the effort to change her habitual frame of mind: living, she had ever hated me – dying she must hate me still. (*Jane Eyre*, xxi)

In Charlotte Brontë's last novel, *Villette*, Mme Beck, who does all she can to thwart Lucy Snowe's happiness, is treated with complete, even humorous, fairness, and is not only not condemned by the narrator, but suffers no consequences of her acts, almost the last sentence of the novel telling us that she 'prospered all the days of her life'.

Anne Brontë's natural attitudes and bent as a writer are explicitly, even naïvely, moral, yet she too is concerned with compassion rather than retribution. *Agnes Grey* charts the career of the spoilt, worldly beauty, Rosalie Murray, who ends her career as the neglected wife of a brutal husband, with a daughter she cannot love. Cruelly fitting though this is, the attitude of the narrator Agnes emphasizes the pity of it rather than the justice; while even in *The Tenant of Wildfell Hall* she emphasizes, as far as her subject will let her, the pathetic rather than the retributory aspects of her tale. Her heroine Helen Huntingdon suffers far more than a just punishment for being a young and foolish girl who thought her love could reform a feckless reprobate; and throughout she stresses the elements for good that allow the various drunken libertines and their wives to struggle free into moderate order and comparative felicity.

Elizabeth Gaskell is the least ready of them all to give even the suggestion of fate meting out punishment. In *Wives and Daughters* the only character qualifying as a genuine malefactor is Mr Preston, whose foibles lead him to social climbing and dallying with women. He has made advances to Mrs Gibson as well as her daughter Cynthia, and even tried to do so with Lady Harriet. Yet, despite his grim hold on Cynthia, Elizabeth Gaskell neither allows him to be condemned for a passion beyond his control, nor to suffer any retributive consequence comparable to the suffering he has caused, but merely the shame of having his doings known to his employer the Earl of Cumnor and his family.

Significantly the Brontës and Mrs Gaskell are perhaps the last who write from a Christian position, which frees them from George

Eliot's, and all later writers', responsibility to detect or reject a cosmic order which has to be expounded along with their ethical ones. Like Jane Austen, who speaks with an ironical voice that should not obscure her literal seriousness, they can say honestly, and without violating their art as novelists or their standards as moralists;

> Let other pens dwell on guilt and misery. I quit such odious subjects as soon as I can, impatient to restore every body, not greatly in fault themselves, to tolerable comfort. (*Mansfield Park*, XLVIII)

Elizabeth Gaskell's one limitation that remains – if it is a limitation – is to ignore the possibility of innate evil or deliberate wickedness of intention. Evil consequences and acts she has always admitted. Though the worst character here is Preston, who acts out of an ungenerous but uncontrollable love for Cynthia, the suffering he inflicts is not the worst that happens, most of which comes from the unavoidable event, like Mrs Hamley's death, from insensitivity and selfishness, like Mrs Gibson's, or from good intentions and faulty judgement, like Lady Cumnor's various interventions, or Mr Gibson's choice of a wife.

With so serious and confident a basis of principle and belief Elizabeth Gaskell now has an almost complete assurance in her position as narrator in relation to her reader, the only aspect of her art that has ever caused her much uneasiness. The moral weight, as has been shown, can be borne by the action, the characters' responses, and the judgements they themselves can form and express. In this novel she is at her most self-effacing. She avoids almost entirely any explanation to the reader, or sense of addressing him person-to-person, letting the weight of interpretation fall upon dialogue and analysis of character, on the mutual interpretative power of scene with scene, on description, and on variations of tone and mood. She is thus showing herself to be gradually moving away from the norm of the nineteenth-century novel, which depends so largely on the narrative voice and personality, and on the personal relationship set up between author and reader. It has never been her aim to create an impression of herself in her writing, as it is the aim of Thackeray – who above all others, uses the authorial personality as a way of doing his job – or of Dickens, or of George Eliot, who is consistently the guide, philosopher, and friend of her reader, or of Trollope, who talks as man-to-man, or even Charlotte Brontë, who, writing through a character's first-person narrative, frequently uses direct personal address to her reader. *Wives and Daughters* gives the impression that the author explains nothing to the reader, because there is nothing that needs explaining. Even admitting that in so domestic a tale this may be truer than of an industrial one like *Mary Barton*, or one with an unusual setting like *Sylvia's Lovers*, yet much of the art is concealed. The material of *Wives and Daughters* is not the wholly familiar. It is set back to the times and customs of a generation past – beginning 'five-and-forty years ago' (1) – whose atmosphere is created by carefully selected detail and allusion, rather than by detailed exposition. From her opening page, with Molly's bonnet of 'solid straw'

covered over from any chance of dust, with a large pocket-handkerchief, of so heavy and serviceable a texture that, if the thing underneath it had been a flimsy fabric of gauze and lace and flowers, it would have been altogether 'scomfished' (again to quote from Betty's vocabulary) (1)

the reader is made aware of a former age and remoter scene. Wider historical reference is made equally unobtrusively, through the groups of characters as they are introduced:

it was well for a place where the powerful family, who thus overshadowed it, were of so respectable a character as the Cumnors. They expected to be submitted to, and obeyed; the simple worship of the townspeople was accepted by the earl and countess as a right; and they would have stood still in amazement, and with a horrid memory of the French *sansculottes* who were the bugbears of their youth, had any inhabitant of Hollingford ventured to set his will or opinions in opposition to those of the earl. (1)

Such references appear throughout as they are necessary, in careful notice of incidental details of reading-matter, social manners or the general conduct of events. Such details all seem to be serving other more immediate purposes. Details of what people read, such as Molly's enthusiasm when at Hamley she was 'in the middle of the "Bride of Lammermoor" [published 1819], and would gladly have stayed inside to finish it' (vi); or Mrs Gibson's remark that Molly has 'never read Miss Edgeworth's tales . . . just the thing to beguil your solitude – vastly improving and moral, and yet quite sufficiently interesting' (xiv); or Mrs Hamley's enthusiasm for the poems of

Mrs Hemans (at her most popular around 1820); these details –
Molly's omnivorous enthusiasm for the best modern works, Mrs
Gibson's stale and conventional gestures to literature (Maria Edgeworth's prime preceded Jane Austen's), and Mrs Hamley's slightly
sentimental tastes – all occur unobtrusively to throw light on the
characters; yet at the same time they are most precisely chosen in
relation to the time when the action takes place. Equally helpful and
unobtrusive are allusions in the action to social habits, such as Mrs
Gibson's furtive enthusiasm for 'the dirty dog's-eared delightful
novel from the Ashcombe circulating library' (xi); or the card-
games as an evening amusement, when Molly and Squire Hamley
play at cribbage; or the prices of the various teas used by the Miss
Brownings:

> 'I told her we gave only 3s. 4d. a pound for it, at Johnson's –
> sister says I ought to have told her the price of our company tea,
> which is 5s. a pound, only that is not what we were drinking.'
>
> (xiv)

or the delightful reactions to such public affairs as may impinge on
remote Hollingford, such as the arrival of the railways, with producing the brilliant concept of 'sitting on teakettles' (xxxviii); or the
Earl of Cumnor's defending himself for quoting Byron – whom the
Countess rejects as 'a very immoral poet' – 'I saw him take his oath
in the House of Lords' (xii) in 1812. The delicacy and art of this
kind of placing is a very far advance for the writer who came forward
in *Mary Barton* to explain in her own voice about Chartism.

The occasions on which Elizabeth Gaskell speaks with an identifiable authorial voice, though rare, have a new authority, are
occasionally even epigrammatically incisive, and have a tone of firm
generalization such as has been rare before in one whose art is so
much made up of the particular:

> It was a great relief for [Lady Cumnor] to have Mr Gibson to
> decide for her what she was to do; what to eat, drink, avoid.
> *Such decisions ab extra, are sometimes a wonderful relief to those*
> *whose habit has been to decide, not only for themselves, but for*
> *everyone else;* and, occasionally, the relaxation of the strain which
> a character for infallible wisdom brings with it does much to res-
> tore health. (ix, my italics)

> [Roger] felt as if high principle and noble precept ought to

perform an immediate work. But they do not, for there is always the unknown quantity of individual experience and feeling, which offer a tacit resistance, the amount incalculable by another, to all good counsel and high decree. (xi)

No one would know what became of her – and, *with the ingratitude of misery*, she added to herself, no one would care. (x)

But fate is a cunning hussy, and builds up her plans as imperceptibly as a bird builds up her nest; and with much the same kind of unconsidered trifles. (vii)

The first two of these aphorisms might have come from George Eliot, whose habit it is so to generalize from the particular; the third only Elizabeth Gaskell herself could have so unobtrusively and concisely inserted; the last is equally original and personal with its modestly humorous and self-deprecating image, and barely noticeable Shakespearean echo in the last two words.

Such an occasional standing back from the material is revealed also in Elizabeth Gaskell's attitude elsewhere. It is evident in two main areas, both of them concerned with characters. She to some extent abandons here what has been her consistent, powerful and very original method, of presenting all characters with equal candour, and the minimum of detachment, treating all to the same kind of sympathetic explanation and understanding, so that no relevant motives or responses are unknown to the reader. Here she makes gradations between characters, so that about some of them the reader learns very little beyond what emerges from their speech and actions. About others, he learns only what goes on at moments of crisis or reflection. The distinctions are functional, and depend on the shape of events or themes, and not on type of character, or even on the size of the part played. The one whose thoughts, feelings, and motives are least explained is Lady Harriet, whose importance to the plot is considerable, and whose role as critic and commentator is a delight, and supplies all we need to know of her. Close to her come the Hollingford ladies as a group: Miss Browning, Miss Phoebe Browning, and Mrs Goodenough, whose thoughts are not given because Elizabeth Gaskell has created in them beings whose thoughts can all be expressed, and situations that permit them expression. Mrs Gibson is striking among the leading characters in being very rarely revealed in her thoughts and feelings, and again the reason is not so much a conscious exclusion of material on her author's part, but rather that in her Elizabeth Gaskell has created a type who has so little power of connected thought or genuine feeling, who pours out in speech all that is within, that interior study is superfluous. The results, despite the loss of the kind of rich and complete comprehension one felt in *Sylvia's Lovers*, are no disadvantage to the work as a whole; the method is perfectly appropriate to a work with so many areas of interest, with such elaborate action, composed of so many small events.

Three characters in particular – Roger, Molly and Mr Gibson – Elizabeth Gaskell treats generally differently from the rest. They take on many of what are frequently the duties of the narrator, interpreting action, directing response, and providing judgement, and their consciousness and responses are reliable enough to guide the reader, despite their own bias of personality. Mr Gibson performs this function primarily in the earlier part of the novel, in events in which he is the chief initiator, when Molly is too young to act as a dependable or an adequate guide to events in which she is the chief sufferer, and when Roger has not yet appeared. His role continues until after his marriage to Mrs Gibson. Thereafter Molly is at the centre, mature enough to respond and interpret correctly, involved – usually passively rather than actively – in the greater part of what goes on – while Mr Gibson, having made his great blunder of judgement in his choice of wife, withdraws from much active participation. Elizabeth Gaskell has herself used Margaret Hale in *North and South* in this way as a narrative lens which recalled the much stricter use of a central consciousness in Jane Austen. In *Wives and Daughters* she comes closest to writing Jane Austen's kind of novel, a fact which may account for the high esteem it has always enjoyed ever since its first appearance with readers, who have responded to the familiar method and material more easily than to that which is most characteristic and original, in the four earlier works, with their omniscient, yet unjudging and very self-effacing narrator. Even in *Wives and Daughters* Elizabeth Gaskell by no means abandons all the narrative to Molly, where to do so would make it impossible to include much of what is most important. Being no theorist about her art, she is no slave to an over-rigid system when it will not serve her. The story of the Hamleys involves events and scenes which do not directly concern Molly, and at which she cannot be present, especially during the long sad period of Osborne's illness and inertia, and, of Squire Hamley's decline into failure and despair, after Mrs Hamley's death. Here she contrives that many scenes shall involve Mr Gibson, or her third main narrative consciousness Roger Hamley, using them not so much to interpret what happens, as to provide the perspective that a sensible, sympathetic, yet detached mind can give. In the closing stages of the novel, when both Molly and Roger become main actors, caught up by their growing love for each other, Mr Gibson reassumes his position of narrative authority, as understanding interpreter.

In regarding her characters as a whole, however, Elizabeth Gaskell adheres to her well-tried habit, of juxtaposing the reactions of various characters, allowing speech to reveal reaction, and supporting both with her own account of thoughts where these are not conveyed otherwise. Since the characters are generally articulate, she has less need than in earlier novels to account for thoughts, and, thus, fine though *Wives and Daughters* is, it robs her of one of her most original gifts, to convey the complex feelings and ideas of inarticulate people, a gift which was with her in her first novel *Mary Barton* and reached its acme in *Sylvia's Lovers*.

Just as *Wives and Daughters* has a more elaborate and better worked out plot, so it is structurally more complex than her other novels. Her method has always been one of aggregation, juxtaposition and intermingling and merging of events and moods, rather than of separating into large sections or episodes, bringing out dramatically one prevailing mood and contrasting it with what precedes and follows: *Wives and Daughters* is her most agglomerate, least dissectible of novels. It does not fall into neat sections, or move to climaxes of undivided attention. Clear, coherent and perfectly connected as is all the action, structurally it is near-indivisible. Always concerned to produce the movement of life – with its mixture of the portentous with the apparently trivial, the unusual with the routine – even at the expense of obvious form, recognizing that what in the abstract appears momentous may when experienced give way to the more immediate, she succeeds, in *Wives and Daughters*, in preserving a near-perfect balance.

The opening two chapters – Molly's visit to the Towers – establish the structural method of the whole. The prime concern is Molly's responses to her accumulation of distresses, lost in the park, too faint to get back to the house, left to sleep after those who have brought her have gone home, having to face the ordeal of nursery

tea and appearing before the family and visitors after dinner, and
finally rescued by her father. In this literal 'chapter of accidents',
Elizabeth Gaskell recognizes and recreates how dreadful they are to
the child (though in themselves slight), conveys the unexpected
momentary reliefs, and starts on their way a crowd of future events
which, having their beginning here, make this apparently contained
incident a part of what is to follow, as well as establishing the essentials of characters and social attitudes which will recur later at more
important points with a significance that has been foreshadowed here.
Most painful to Molly is 'man's inhumanity to man', the thoughtlessness and lack of sympathy of 'Clare' (the future Mrs Gibson) who,
having forgotten to waken her, gives her the blame and ignores her
trouble:

> 'Well, don't go and make a piece of work about what can't be
> helped now! I'll lend you night-things, and your papa must do
> without your making tea for him tonight. And, another time,
> don't over-sleep yourself in a strange house; you may not always
> find yourself among such hospitable people as they are here.' (11)

Human misunderstanding causes other incidental pain, such as Lord
Cumnor's good-humoured attempts at conversation:

> 'Oh, ho!' said he. 'Are you the little girl who has been sleep-
> ing in my bed?'
> He imitated the voice of the fabulous bear, who asks this
> question of the child in the story; but Molly has never read the
> 'Three Bears', and fancied that his anger was real . . . Lord
> Cumnor was very fond of getting hold of what he fancied was a
> joke, and working his idea threadbare; so, all the time the ladies
> were in the room, he kept on his running fire at Molly, alluding
> to the Sleeping Beauty, the Seven Sleepers, and any other
> sleeper that came into his head. He had no idea of the misery his
> jokes were to the sensitive girl, who already thought herself a
> miserable sinner, for having slept on, when she ought to have
> been awake. (11)

All such details have a momentum of their own, which takes them
beyond their context and immediate effect. Lord Cumnor's blundering tactlessness is a recurrent source of humour and delight throughout, with unexpected uses, as when he unconsciously brings down on
Mr Preston the humiliation he has deserved and so long evaded, by

making public that he has been engaged to and virtually blackmailing Cynthia. 'Clare's' functions and character also are established in this incident: the apparent kindness prompts Mr Gibson to see her as a suitable second wife for himself and second mother for Molly; the real thoughtlessness, self-seeking, and hypocrisy cause her to be a permanent torment to Molly, and influence the wayward Cynthia's hazardous course to marriage. Both establish the reader's attitude towards Molly of mingled sympathy and detachment: Molly recognizes neither 'Clare's' unkindness, nor Lord Cumnor's good nature.

The mingling with pains of consolations, small, unexpected but reliable and real, is equally unobtrusively done: the comfort of sensuous natural things – to a small child with a headache of 'a little white bed in a cool and pretty room' where 'the muslin curtains flapped softly, from time to time, in the scented air that came through the open windows' (11); the pleasant idea of 'Clare's' daughter Cynthia, a girl of her own age; or the unexpected satisfaction of merely being useful:

> so, as long as she was in the nursery, she got on pretty well, being obedient to the wishes of the supreme power, and even very useful to Mrs Dyson, by playing at tricks, and thus keeping a little one quiet, while its brothers and sisters were being arrayed in gay attire. (11)

Such comforts and pleasures, of the physical perceptions and natural surroundings, of human relationships, and a use in life, seen in detail here, pervade the novel as a whole.

Structurally and emotionally the event ends with Mr Gibson's arrival, and Molly's release; but Elizabeth Gaskell will never settle for a climax at the expense of naturalism. The chapter and the action continue with the return home, during which Molly's fancy symbolizes the relationship of father and daughter:

> 'I should like to get a chain like Ponto's, just as long as your longest round, and then I could fasten us two to each end of it, and when I wanted you I could pull; and if you didn't want to come, you could pull back again; but I should know you knew I wanted you, and we could never lose each other.' (11)

Molly makes the most modest personal claim here – her father need not come even though she may want him – but Mrs Gibson will almost prevent even that, until, eventually, Gibson comes to realize his own dependence on Molly, barely before she will leave him to marry Roger. Elizabeth Gaskell retreats gradually from the close-up of small events in this chapter, by telling of Mr Gibson's later visit of apology at the Towers:

> He found them all on the wing; and no one was sufficiently at liberty to listen to his grateful civilities but Mrs Kirkpatrick, who, although she was to accompany Lady Cuxhaven, and pay a visit to her former pupil, made leisure enough to receive Mr Gibson, on behalf of the family, and assured him of her faithful remembrance of his great professional attention to her in former days in the most winning manner. (11)

Thus in this chapter of small happenings all the main areas of concern (except the affairs of the Hamleys), and the tone and manner which will convey them, are laid down. The interweaving of interests so that while the immediate is obviously progressing, other less obtrusive ones are making their own advance; the variety and juxtaposition of tones, so that humour impinges naturally upon the serious, tense, or moving, and relief and comfort on the stressful, and so that a single situation is seen from many points of view, have all been Elizabeth Gaskell's hallmark. *Wives and Daughters*, with an enclosed society where all the characters know one another, and any event is known to and affects all of them, yields her qualities at their richest.

To emphasize that Elizabeth Gaskell will never sacrifice comprehensiveness for the sake of structural climax or emotional concentration is not to deny her power to create climaxes, changes of pace and concentration, or wide varieties of mood. Climaxes come from the needs of theme, not mechanically from magnitude of events; depths of focus from the closely-followed to the general sweep are finely changed and merged; prevailing mood is intensified rather than dissipated by the subtle variations within it. It is these structural qualities that produce the impression, given every time one reads *Wives and Daughters*, of unexpectedness, surprise, and diversity.

In the handling of such climaxes Elizabeth Gaskell shows in one respect a very striking advance over her earlier self. She has never before been able to resist providing a great test for her heroine, such as Margaret Hale's protection of Thornton from the mob of strikers, or her lie to save her brother from arrest, or Ruth's confrontation with Mr Bellingham, or Mary Barton's public confession at Jem's

trial. In *Wives and Daughters* the opportunity is given Molly for
equivalent heroism, in outfacing Mr Preston and getting Cynthia's
letters back. Though she does so, her author subordinates the event
itself to its causes and consequences, to Cynthia's plight, and to the
consequent gossip about Molly. There is no trace of the rather romantic and unreal dwelling upon the confrontation that marred the earlier
ones. The structure reveals that the real heroism lies in what follows,
when Molly, with her eyes open, accepts the subsequent scandal, and
all the consequences of being thought badly of by her friends.

Perhaps the most dramatic and crucial scene of all is that in which
Mr Gibson finally confronts his wife and faces the realization of her
faults, corrupt standards, and duplicity, and of the mistake he has
made in marrying her (xxxv). Even this is not a climax in the conventional way, with the reader aware of events leading upwards
towards it. It is a shock, occurring as it does immediately after another
climax, when Molly learns that Roger has proposed, and become
engaged to Cynthia. The reader has expected this event, but the
shock is greater than Molly has expected, and Elizabeth Gaskell's
rendering of it through the insensitive silly Mrs Gibson recreates the
shock for the reader:

> 'Isn't it charming? Young love, you know, ah, how sweet
> it is! . . . the temptation of seeing her alone had been too great
> for him. It was symptomatic, was it not, my dear? . . . I had
> expected sympathy from you at such an interesting moment.'
>
> (xxxiv)

Molly, escaping to her room,

> felt as if she could not understand it all; but as for that matter,
> what could she understand? Nothing. For a few minutes, her
> brain seemed in too great a whirl to comprehend anything but
> that she was being carried on in earth's diurnal course, with
> rocks and stones and trees, with as little volition on her part as if
> she were dead. (xxxiv)

Words fail to fit Mrs Gibson's thought because she is too woolly-
minded to distinguish her thought – the senseless word 'symptomatic'
is superb; words fail Molly because the turmoil in her is beyond
words; Elizabeth Gaskell's simple echo of Wordsworth is the inspired and perfect rendering of the state in which, in an anti-Words-
worthian fashion, 'the light of sense goes out'. The scene continues

with the further shocks of Roger's farewell, and Cynthia's strange
unreal mood, in which she can say 'Perhaps, after all, we shall never
be married'. All aspects seem to have been covered, and the reader
expects no more from Mr Gibson's learning the news than his first
reaction provides:

> 'I am surprised. He's a very fine young man, and I wish Cynthia
> joy; but do you like it? It will have to be a very long engage-
> ment.' (xxxv)

The perceptive reader will realize that Mr Gibson's surprise and
mixed reaction is because he has assured Squire Hamley that neither
of his sons is likely to become involved with Molly or Cynthia, but
awareness of this embarrassment suppresses the memory of what Mrs
Gibson next, with outrageous triumph, reveals in reply, of what she
has learned by shameless eavesdropping on a professional conversation
between Mr Gibson and Dr Nicholls:

> 'He will have to run many risks [says Mr Gibson], and go into
> many dangers, and will come back no nearer to the power of
> maintaining a wife than when he went out.'
> 'I don't know that,' she replied, still in the arch manner of
> one possessing superior knowledge. 'A little bird did tell me
> that Osborne's life is not so very secure; and then – what will
> Roger be? Heir to the estate.' (xxxv)

and the wrath of Mr Gibson bursts upon her, in a magnificent exchange where his characteristically terse, trenchant questions get a
rich medley of maddeningly oblique answers:

> 'Who told you that Osborne Hamley's life is in more danger
> than mine – or yours?'
> 'Oh, don't speak in that frightening way! My life is not in
> danger, I'm sure; nor yours either, love, I hope' . . .
> 'Who told you anything about Osborne Hamley's state of
> health?'
> 'I am sure I wish no harm to him, and I daresay he is in very
> good health, as you say.' (xxxv)

Equally masterly is the way that, even when truth comes out, no
contact of nature with nature occurs. Mr Gibson characteristically
withdraws into the cryptic review of his whole marriage – 'Well, I

suppose as one brews one must bake' – while Mrs Gibson continues to make bad worse, trying to gain an advantage:

> 'You are vexed now because it is not Molly he's in love with; and I call it very unfair to my poor fatherless girl. I am sure I have always tried to further Molly's interests as if she was my own daughter.'
>
> Mr Gibson was too indifferent to this accusation to take any notice of it. (xxxv)

The movement away from the pitch of tension is equally fine. Mr Gibson worsts his wife by using her own common weapon, the partial truth:

> 'Dr Nicholls would tell you that Osborne is as likely as any man to live and marry and beget children.' . . . she was dismayed, and Mr Gibson enjoyed her dismay; it restored him to something like his usual frame of mind. (xxxv)

and there is equally wry irony in what substitutes for reconciliation:

> 'Well, don't be angry, dear! Do you know I was quite afraid you would lose your temper at one time.'
>
> 'It would have been of no use!' said he gloomily. (xxxv)

Although

> Mr Gibson had been compelled to face and acknowledge the fact, that the wife he had chosen had a very different standard of conduct from that which he had upheld all his life, and had hoped to have seen inculcated in his daughter. (xxxv)

yet the movement and action take no rest: his interview with Cynthia follows, he repeats that despite Cynthia's wish to keep it secret, he must keep his promise and tell Squire Hamley, and events move promptly onwards, within the same chapter, to his doing so.

In contrast to such brilliantly unexpected climaxes are points at which the expected great moment does not occur, of which an instance is Mrs Hamley's death. She dies slowly, and with the gentle, virtuous resignation and sadness of her family that would seem to make it as congenial to Elizabeth Gaskell to record as it would have been irresistible to Dickens or Thackeray. Yet Mrs Hamley's death slips as quietly into three sentences of the narrative, as, one feels, such deaths do into the multifarious goings on of everyday living:

> At length – and yet it was not so long, not a fortnight since Molly had left the Hall – the end came. Mrs Hamley had sunk out of life, as gradually as she had sunk out of consciousness and her place in the world. The quiet waves closed over her, and her place knew her no more. (XIX)

At this point the narrative is busy with Cynthia's entry into the household and the story, and since Molly last saw Mrs Hamley she has encountered the shock of learning that Osborne is secretly married. Elizabeth Gaskell's structure obeys the demands of her themes, to which, even where Mrs Hamley's devoted and despairing husband is concerned, the consequences of her dying are graver than the event itself.

The movement of the whole novel is chronological, with a sense of time passing evenly and inexorably on its way. Elizabeth Gaskell always avoided gaps as far as she could, reproducing the flow of life with precise measurement of days, weeks and years, allowing herself to break the time-flow only with returns by way of reminiscences, or accounts in her own voice, which fill in the past. *Wives and Daughters* adheres most closely to her proven method, with increased skill, filling in the past in delicately-placed, briefly-observed reminiscences where they make the most point, and bridging gaps in time so unobtrusively that her skill can be readily overlooked. There are here more of the intervening conversations which, fine though they were, gave one the sense in *Mary Barton* of losing one's way amid innumerable little events; in *Wives and Daughters*, with its many levels of interest and society, any such intervening event or conversation provides extra commentary, or serves to keep in mind other threads and themes; nor does her perfectly chosen material here ever force her to make a complete break, as *Sylvia's Lovers* did when Philip Hepburn went away, and she had to chronicle his return. All the linkings are relevant and purposeful, as general necessary commentary on what has passed or is to come, or some comment on character, or some detail that gives the 'feel' of change; and, if a clear break does occur, it has been so well prepared that the narrative picks up the thread without a jerk. A representative instance of such skill is Molly's waiting period during Mr and Mrs Gibson's wedding tour, when she stays with the Hamleys. At this point

Elizabeth Gaskell provides the first, unexpected appearance of the much-expected Osborne Hamley, which sows the seeds of the conflicts to come, and then narrates the charming, incidental, Cranford-like visit of Lady Harriet to the Miss Brownings, which proves, equally unexpectedly, not only that Harriet can behave decently and think rightly, here with her mocked-at 'Pecksy and Flapsy', but that they can be informally happy together, talking of old lace, with Miss Phoebe not even wearing her cap. The return itself is prepared even verbally, with Molly telling Roger that she goes home 'next Tuesday, I believe' (xiv); so that Chapter xv begins 'On Tuesday afternoon, Molly returned home' with a smoothness of technique that highlights the jar of mood and expectation when it goes on,

> — to the home which was already strange, and what Warwickshire people would call 'unked' to her. New paint, new paper, new colours; grim servants dressed in their best, and objecting to every change; — from their master's carriage to the new oilcloth in the hall, 'which tripped 'em up, and threw 'em down, and was cold to the feet, and smelt just abominable'. All these complaints Molly had to listen to, and it was not a cheerful preparation for the reception which she already felt to be so formidable. (xv)

In such handling of structure and time Elizabeth Gaskell is alone, learning only from her own practice and experience, though writing as perhaps a last inheritor of the mantle of Jane Austen. Both have the disadvantage, to other novelists after them, that such qualities of their art are too self-effacing and organic for easy imitation or development. Their contribution is rather of producing awareness of success, and a feeling that mechanical juxtapositioning, striking contrast, irregular movement in time, apt though they can well be to novelists of a more dramatic mode like Dickens, for whom to heighten and simplify are among their greatest strengths, cannot sort well with the material of common life. This awareness leads to other individual solutions; for George Eliot, who has been working since 1858 alongside Elizabeth Gaskell, and whose greatest novel *Middlemarch* comes four years after *Wives and Daughters*; and for Hardy, whose first real novel, *Under the Greenwood Tree*, comes six years after it. George Eliot's methods are more simple and more direct, probably appropriately since she has more, and more complex, material to handle, and since her task is already made easier by her being a frankly directive author-narrator. Her custom is to divide her work into clearly defined blocks, not only by chapter-divisions, but by sections and 'books'. She gains in detachment, and a clear sense of the proportions of her multifarious actions, as when for instance, after the small crisis in which Lydgate's casting-vote for Mr Tyke loses Mr Farebrother the chaplaincy of the Infirmary, and ranges Lydgate involuntarily as supporter of Mr Bulstrode, she then turns abruptly to Dorothea, beginning the next chapter thus:

> When George the Fourth was still reigning over the privacies of Windsor, when the Duke of Wellington was Prime Minister, and Mr Vincy was mayor of the old corporation in Middlemarch, Mrs Casaubon, born Dorothea Brooke, had taken her wedding-journey to Rome. (*Middlemarch*, Book II, XV)

She rarely attempts to bridge her gaps between one area of interest and the next like Elizabeth Gaskell, by using the character's own sense of connection, preferring to make the jerk of focus, together with her own detaching irony, into a way of directing the reader's response. The gap is frequently much greater than in the example above: at the end of Chapter XXXIV (Book IV), she abandons Mr Brooke's plans to make Will Ladislaw his secretary (which distress Dorothea and irritate Mr Casaubon, who would be glad to have his nephew Ladislaw far away from Middlemarch) to begin Chapter XXXV, which concerns itself with the miser Peter Featherstone's funeral, with a short wry paragraph:

> When the animals entered the Ark in pairs, one may imagine that allied species made much private remark on each other, and were tempted to think that so many forms feeding on the same store of fodder were eminently superfluous, as tending to diminish the rations (I fear the part played by the vultures on that occasion would be too painful for art to represent, those birds being disadvantageously naked about the gullet, and apparently without rites and ceremonies).
> The same sort of temptation befell the Christian Carnivora who formed Peter Featherstone's funeral procession; most of them having their minds bent on a limited store which each would have liked to get most of. (XXXV)

George Eliot keeps her sense of the whole by detaching the narrator, and through the narrator, the reader. Despite the unfortunate occa-

sional almost arch tone, the reader feels the secure hold on the progress of events and areas of action, yet, aware of the mechanical
complexity, loses much of what Elizabeth Gaskell conveys of
minutely subtle personal interrelations and responses. Among contemporaries Trollope comes nearest to Elizabeth Gaskell in this respect, concerning himself less with making characters' responses cause
exciting action, than with how characters' responses, reactions, and
interrelations make small events very diversely significant. During
the superbly-done episode of the Ullathorne Sports, in *Barchester
Towers*, he narrates the death of the Dean of Barchester, a memorable dispute between the bishop's offensive wife Mrs Proudie, and
an equally memorable interview between Mr Arabin and the
'Signora Neroni' of dubious reputation (daughter of the cathedral's
prebendary, Dr Stanhope), while Eleanor Bold (in love with Arabin
as he with her) receives proposals of marriage from the bishop's
repulsive chaplain Mr Slope, and the Signora's dilettante brother
Bertie Stanhope. Thus Trollope, like Elizabeth Gaskell, works with
all his areas of interest at the same time, for Arabin will (eventually)
be the next dean, the Signora will perform her one good act, and make
things easy for Arabin and Eleanor, Mr Slope will be disgraced,
Bertie Stanhope will have to go back to Italy, and other less immediate consequences will be affected, not so much in their outcome,
but in how they will be judged.

Elizabeth Gaskell's methods lead forward to a writer very unlike
her in aims, Virginia Woolf, who converts Elizabeth Gaskell's
means to her own purpose and conscious intention: the representation of the fluidity and intermixture of the fabric of experience, in
which the present is composed of sense-impression, present emotions,
and all the call up of impressions, thoughts and emotions of the past.

Elizabeth Gaskell is not good at titles. They seem to interest her no
more than do the names she gives to her characters, which are
commonplace, generally neutral, with no significance in themselves,
forming simply convenient labels attaching to personalities.[3] Virtue
though this is with characters, it is less so with titles. *Wives and
Daughters* (settled upon *faute de mieux*)[4] is not an adequate, though it

---

[3] She uses the small group of names over and over again in her novels and stories:
a Molly Gibson, even, plays a minor part in *Mary Barton*.
[4] She wrote to her publisher 'you may find a title for yourself for *I* can not. I
have tried all this time in vain' (letter to George Smith, 3 May 1864).

is an illuminating, title. It points towards various thematic connections between characters that cut across both the way characters are
organized, and the way they are presented. The family relationships
in *Wives and Daughters* are unusual for a novel, which calls itself,
as this does, 'an everyday story', notably because only one family, the
Cumnors, is complete, with the normal component of husband, wife
and children; elsewhere, among the daughters Molly has no mother,
Cynthia has no father, and neither are wives; Mrs Gibson is the wife
of Mr Gibson, who is only stepfather to Cynthia; Squire Hamley's
wife who dies in the first third of the story has no daughters. Yet the
themes are undoubtedly wholly concerned with family relationships,
inviting one to consider 'Fathers and Children' or the repellent term
'Siblings' as alternative summary-titles which would comprehend
the Hamley family, which for most of the story has neither wife nor
daughters. Such incomplete families are not unusual in Elizabeth
Gaskell's work – Mary Barton is motherless, the Thornton family
in *North and South* lacks a father, and even the Robsons in *Sylvia's
Lovers* have only the one daughter – and Elizabeth Gaskell is not at
all unusual herself in choosing such families for her material. The
incomplete family is almost the norm for central characters in the
nineteenth-century novel. It is difficult indeed among the major
writers to think of a complete family one of whose members is the
hero or heroine of a novel. The reasons, though probably not conscious ones on the part of the writers, are various, and the advantages
considerable: happiness has no history, and the complete stable family
is that most likely to cope with the hazards of life; the nature of the
hero is to be set apart, an isolation easier to render in one who has
been set apart by circumstances. Where novelists do provide a protagonist with a family, this setting apart is still contrived by lack of
sympathy and misunderstanding, as for instance in *The Mill on the
Floss*, or *Tess of the D'Urbervilles*, and by the losing of a parent as the
action takes its course.

  Elizabeth Gaskell's title points to the assumption shared by all
her characters, that wifehood is the right and desirable evolution from
daughtership. Even Cynthia, universally attractive and enjoying her
power, wishes for marriage as a haven of safety from the hazards of
her own charms. It points also to the role, rather than the state, of
being either wife or daughter: Molly is spiritually a daughter at
Hamley long before she becomes so 'in law'; Mr Gibson takes
Cynthia as his daughter, and Mrs Gibson is morally as well as legally

his wife. The problems of the daughter-relationship within the family are brought out also by Lady Harriet, who, lively, intelligent and attractive, will not follow the pattern, is unmarried (twenty-eight years old when the story opens) and likely to remain a daughter in perpetuity; the problem recurs in a different form when Osborne's widow, the little French 'bonne', comes to Hamley, and has to struggle to make her place as daughter to anti-catholic, anti-French Squire Hamley, who hoped his son would have married into nobility.

The family groups with their variations on the normal family household all reveal and develop the important concern of the novel with human relationships, a concern which has always been Elizabeth Gaskell's theme, even when, in her two early novels of social reform, it was also her method of tackling other themes. She is as little preoccupied as any nineteenth-century writer with the romances of the young, and much more interested in the affections and ties which link people in general, whatever their age, to their kind. *Wives and Daughters* proportions its time and attention amongst almost all the relationships possible to two generations, outside and inside the family group. The action concentrates necessarily on those capable of change; the handling never ignores those which are more or less static, but uses them to throw light on action, provide comment or proportion.

The most vital relationship in the novel – and, Elizabeth Gaskell implies, in life – is that between parent and child. At the heart of the novel are the father Mr Gibson and his daughter Molly, whose mutual affection and understanding are indestructible. Contrasting with them are Squire Hamley, Roger and Osborne, as a family united in affection, though susceptible to bitter misunderstanding. Elizabeth Gaskell emphasizes that the Squire's deep love is the great cause of his anger and irritation when Osborne fails (because of the secret marriage he will not own to) to do well at Cambridge, and becomes estranged from his father. A third exploration of the relationship of parent and child is Mrs Gibson and Cynthia, between whom there is hardly any bond at all. Elizabeth Gaskell is an acute and sound psychological observer, whose characters reveal a strong sense of cause and effect. She never sentimentally assumes that family affection is axiomatic and automatic, but demonstrates its degree in ways any twentieth-century psychologist will bear out. Molly and her father need the minimum of expression for their affection based on Molly's lifetime of confidence in him, conveyed in conversations that are a delight for their wry understatement and implication. At the other extreme are Cynthia and Mrs Gibson, who are so alien to each other that explanation becomes necessary, given by Cynthia at sparing and relevant points to her partial confidante, Molly. Elizabeth Gaskell rightly and skilfully notes both causes and effects: Cynthia's admission that

'It's not in my nature to go with ecstasies, and I don't suppose I shall ever be what people call "in love".' (xxxvii)

is clearly related to her upbringing:

'Now, don't go and condemn me. I don't think love for one's mother comes quite by nature; and remember how much I have been separated from mine! I loved my father, if you will,' she continued, with the force of truth in her tone, and then she stopped: 'but, he died when I was quite a little thing, and no one believes that I remember him. I heard mamma say to a caller, not a fortnight after the funeral, "Oh, no, Cynthia is too young, she has quite forgotten him" – and I bit my lips to keep from crying out, "Papa, papa, have I?" But it's of no use. Well, then mamma had to go out as a governess; she couldn't help it, poor thing! but she didn't much care for parting with me. I was a trouble, I daresay. So I was sent to school at four years old; first one school, and then another; and, in the holidays, mamma went to stay at grand houses, and I was generally left with the schoolmistresses. Once I went to the Towers; and mamma lectured me continually, and yet I was very naughty, I believe. And so I never went again.' (xix)

The other important relationship at the centre of the novel is that between husband and wife, explored in Mr and Mrs Gibson, Squire Hamley and his wife, and the Cumnors, with their varying degrees of intimacy. Although none of these marriages is perfect, all are workable, and show a deeper insight than most novelists can give to secondary characters or static relationships. The most complete success belongs to the unromantic uncouth Squire Hamley, who expresses his devotion for his delicate high-bred wife in the mundane details of dressing for dinner, and getting whatever she needs for her health, and who rejects love as a motive for younger people's actions:

'Pooh! away with love! Nay, my dear, we loved each other so dearly we should never have been happy with anyone else;

but that's a different thing. People aren't like what they were when we were young. All the love now-a-days is just silly fancy, and sentimental romance, as far as I can see.' (v)

The Cumnors are treated humorously, but nevertheless reveal a mutual confidence that survives the Earl's blundering good-natured thick-headedness and his wife's domineering autocracy. Even the Gibsons' o'erhasty marriage, entered into because Mr Gibson wants a woman to provide him with a stable household, and because Mrs Gibson has, like Jane Austen's Charlotte Lucas, 'a pure and disinterested desire for an establishment', survives, and, in a bitterly limited way, supplies what each required of it. Elizabeth Gaskell stands out among her fellow-novelists for stressing the assets rather than the inadequacies of such marriages. Though these marriages recall Jane Austen's – the Gibsons have reminded most readers of the Bennets in *Pride and Prejudice*, the Cumnors may echo the Middletons in *Sense and Sensibility*, the Hamleys have links possibly with the Crofts (where the wife has more sense and sensibility than the husband) in *Persuasion* – Jane Austen's marriages generally point to what is desirable by demonstrating its lack; Elizabeth Gaskell is always stressing the value of affection and custom, and the existence of sound marriages without the assets of intelligence or sensitivity.

She is equally interested in relationships between people of the same generation, both brothers and sisters, like the three sisters and brother among the Cumnors (who are slightly but clearly indicated) or the brothers Hamley; or between girls, like Molly and Cynthia, or Molly and Lady Harriet; or between the sexes. This last is a most striking element, in that in most of them love is not involved. The genuine friendship between Roger and Osborne and Molly and Cynthia is brought out by all their actions and speech, emphasized rather than obscured by all Mrs Gibson's machinations and speculations about attachments, which bring out, by being totally at odds with the evidence, the friendly unromantic relations between them. Even Molly's devotion to Roger is of a kind that it is easy to misjudge, not recognizing itself, or even existing as the love of woman for man, until (three-quarters of the story over) Cynthia's burst of insight opens Molly's eyes:

Suddenly she started up, stung with a new idea, and looking Molly straight in the face, she said –
'Molly, Roger will marry you! See if it isn't so!' (LI)

I

and the consequences are immediately seen, when Roger returns, in their changed behaviour to each other.

Existing separately from these relationships, and forming only a small proportion of the whole, are the areas of feeling that most novelists find central: the attraction between sexes. They all spring from two people: Mr Preston, who at various times has attracted various unnamed girls, as well as both Cynthia and Mrs Kirkpatrick before her marriage to Mr Gibson; and Cynthia, whose power to charm is clearly not a matter of the intellectual personality. To lament that Elizabeth Gaskell is not interested in passion or able to convey it, is not only untrue – as *Ruth* can witness – but misreads her purposes, and greatly undervalues her penetration in other human affections, which all too often take second place in novels to the romantic love that, powerful as it may be, is only one of the many kinds of attachment that man experiences.

The novelist who most resembles Elizabeth Gaskell in his response to and interest in relationships between people is Anthony Trollope, who, as the Barchester group of novels progresses, builds up his families and establishes subtle and elaborate interconnections between parents and children, husbands and wives, and brothers and sisters. In these areas he is at his most assured, and, like Elizabeth Gaskell, perceptive and sympathetic, even though he lacks her powerful sense of direction and structure. Like her he can convey the bond of custom and affinity that keeps unromantic unions together, like the mutual respect between Archdeacon Grantly and his wife; or (perhaps his finest study) the clergyman Mr Crawley, who, in *The Last Chronicle of Barset*, is accused, and very nearly convicted of, theft, and who, fanatical and obsessive, is for the greater part of the novel on the verge of breakdown, yet retains, and is supported by, the loyalty of his wife and daughters. Like Elizabeth Gaskell in all but *Sylvia's Lovers* and *Ruth*, Trollope in all but *The Small House at Allington*, uses love leading to marriage as a plan and pretext, rather than a chief concern. Even in that novel the interest is as much, and the originality far more, in the jilted Lily's relations with her mother, sister, and uncle than with Adolphus Crosbie who has jilted her, or John Eames who remains devoted. John Eames himself is as absorbing in his dealings with his new-found friend and patron Lord de Guest, as in his unflagging adoration of Lily. Trollope's handling of and delight in family units, such as the heterogeneous Stanhopes, or the brother and sister Thorne of Ullathorne (in *Barchester Towers*), is

close to Elizabeth Gaskell's, though he allows himself more freedom
to ridicule, and feels less duty to assess, than she: Elizabeth Gaskell
could not derive Trollope's delight from the Stanhopes, with its
careless father, its elder sister devoted only to advancing the family's
prosperity and saving its finances, its man-trapping imposter siren of
a second sister, and its good-natured dilettante brother Bertie, who
will live off anyone's money if handy.

Wise and tolerant and realistic as both Trollope and Elizabeth
Gaskell are, they share another quality unexpected in writers who are
often humorous in tone and not given to passing judgement on
human weakness, which, through their characterization, affects the
mood of the work as a whole: few of their characters have their hopes
fulfilled, or reach an approach to complete happiness, a state most
striking in Elizabeth Gaskell's least portentous works, *Wives and
Daughters* and *Cranford*. Both Mr and Mrs Gibson, though they get
what they married for, do not attain what they thought would be the
concomitants; Squire Hamley, all of whose hopes rest in his wife,
sons, and estate, has to lose his wife and son, and nearly lose his estate,
and make a long and painful adjustment of those hopes to his second
son and an unexpected heir; Cynthia's nature, though able to recognize great worth, makes her unable to achieve more than a very
ordinary, second-best fate; Roger loses his first love; even Molly,
who survives by a wise passiveness, and achieves her heart's desire,
suffers much from those she loves, and has to come second, and late,
into Roger's life. Like Thackeray, Elizabeth Gaskell can say 'which
of us in this world has his desire' and, for most of her characters, can
continue as he does '– or, having it, is satisfied?' The mood of sadness,
in an unsensational work with no startling disasters, is a consequence
of the full attention she has always given to even secondary characters: she compels us to feel pity even for Mr Preston as a man at
the mercy of his passion, reprehensible though his manners and deeds
may be. In this she is strikingly different from the Jane Austen she so
often recalls, of *Pride and Prejudice*. The Gibsons may be closely
akin to Mr and Mrs Bennet, and Lady Cumnor to Lady Catherine
de Bourgh, yet Jane Austen requires from her reader only momentary sympathy for Mr Bennet (when he admits he is morally respon-
sible for his daughter Lydia's lack of morals), does not see Mrs
Bennet as worthy of sympathy at all, and presents Lady Catherine
with vigorous satire. But Lady Cumnor has many good qualities
and makes calls on our sympathy, while (as will be discussed later)

even Mrs Gibson is not made the butt for unrelieved satire. Gentler and less dismissive towards characters than most novelists, she is finally one of the least compromising about their natures and their fates. Though the shorn lamb is never deprived of hope of future comfort, Heaven never tempers the wind.

Structurally the characters fall into groups according to family or place, or both: the Cumnors at the Towers, the Hamleys at Hamley, the Gibson household at Hollingford, which also contains the local society of the Miss Brownings, Mrs Goodenough, and their incidental acquaintances; at a further distance is Ashcombe, the scene of a society broken up almost as soon as the novel begins, where Mrs Gibson had her school, and Mr Preston is agent for the Earl's land; furthest of all is the London of Mrs Gibson's relations by her first marriage, the lawyer Kirkpatricks. Such simple clear groupings revealing different aspects of the world are the common method of the social novel, from Jane Austen and Scott onwards, which Elizabeth Gaskell has herself used in *Sylvia's Lovers* and *North and South*. Here in *Wives and Daughters* the handling and presentation of character do not coincide with but cut across the social and topographical groups, showing an extension of her art by the degrees to which she can bring to bear the many skills she has learned in her earlier work.

As a narrator Elizabeth Gaskell has used two main methods in her best work, though effectively only one in her full-length novels. However, *Cranford*, and *Cousin Phillis* – the one not conceived as a novel, the other too short to be so considered – both depend for their success on having a character-narrator, through whose perceptions all the rest are seen and interpreted. The method is combined in *Wives and Daughters* with the near-invisible omniscient narrator, so that some of the characters from time to time become the means of presenting other characters. Molly, Mr Gibson and Roger Hamley share in this function, with the consequence that some characters are revealed predominantly by the Cranfordian method. They are chiefly the Cranfordian ladies of Hollingford, the Miss Brownings and Mrs Goodenough, and the very briefly appearing Mrs Dawes (who spreads the news of Molly's goings-on with Mr Preston), who appear at first through Mr Gibson, then through Molly's dealings with them. Roger is used in the same way to control the amount and kind of what the reader learns about Osborne in his frustration, unhappiness and illness, and Squire Hamley in his grief. These three characters, Molly, Mr Gibson and Roger – are thus themselves set apart from the rest; their major status, and the ties that unite all three of them, become evident and rendered in the functions they share, even though the action requires that both Roger and Mr Gibson shall not play major parts, and that Roger shall for long periods be absent.

Molly Gibson is a most unusual heroine both in Elizabeth Gaskell's own work and in the novel in general. She is endowed with no outstanding qualities of mind or heart; Elizabeth Gaskell emphasizes that Molly's father has deliberately limited her education:

'Don't teach Molly too much [he tells her governess]: she must sew, and read, and write, and do her sums.' (111)

and though Molly succeeds 'by fighting and struggling hard' in getting French and drawing-lessons, and though she makes use of the Hamley library to read Scott's novels, and has native intelligence enough to be fired by Roger's biological enthusiasms, and read his scientific articles, she never becomes erudite or accomplished, never incurring, as her father wryly fears in his educational apprehensions, 'a dilution of mother-wit'. She makes no spiritual and moral progress to wisdom, as do so many heroines, including Elizabeth Gaskell's own Mary Barton, Ruth and Margaret Hale. Nor has she those almost automatic qualities of heroines, outstanding beauty or elegance. On her first visit to the Hamleys

She looked at herself in the glass with some anxiety, for the first time in her life. She saw a slight, lean figure, promising to be tall, a complexion browner than cream-coloured, although in a year or two it might have that tint; plentiful curly black hair, tied up in a bunch behind with a rose-coloured ribbon; long almond-shaped soft grey eyes, shaded both above and below by curling black lashes.

'I don't think I am pretty,' thought Molly, as she looked away from the glass; 'and yet I'm not sure.' (vi)

Though her looks improve, she is always overshadowed by Cynthia, who surpasses her in both beauty and elegance. Molly never reaches far beyond prettiness and neatness, and shows that Elizabeth Gaskell, who has always had little enough impulse to create paragons, has overcome her occasional impulses towards idealizing beauty.

Structurally Molly Gibson is at the heart of the novel. She is the character who enters most closely into the lives and confidences of the greatest number of persons, knowing from childhood the whole of Hollingford, brought into the family at Hamley, connected at crucial moments with the Cumnors of the Towers – making them a disastrous visit as a child, looked after by them at her father's wedding, cared for by Lady Harriet, dancing with Lord Hollingford at the Charity Ball, and finally staying at the Towers, convalescent when Cynthia is married in London – and even coming into painful touch with the shabby past of Ashcombe, through meeting Mr Preston there on her father's wedding, and through helping Cynthia to break herself free from her hateful debts and enforced engagement. Elizabeth Gaskell gives her the sympathy and sensibility that the vehicle for so much of the narrative needs, without making her too wise for her age and role in her own affairs. When for instance she has inadvertently overheard that Osborne is married, her reactions are as naïve in expression as is proper to her nature, while their good sense puts the situation firmly into proportion:

> She would never have guessed the concealed romance which lay *perdu* under that every-day behaviour. She had always wished to come into direct contact with a love-story; here she had, and she only found it very uncomfortable; there was a sense of uncertainty and concealment about it all. (xviii)

From this reaction to her first experience of secrecy and subterfuge she can develop to make the finer discriminations needed in Cynthia's case, so that, by means of Molly's distress, Cynthia's situation – with all the elements of romantic excitement attending two secretly devoted men (Roger and Preston), speedy passion (the foolish young surgeon Coxe), and an off-stage London suitor (the lawyer Henderson) – is stripped of romance, and seen as the cause of everyday discomfort and embarrassment.

Molly is unusually passive for a heroine, acting almost wholly out of response to events, or from sympathy with and direction by others. Since passivity generally means suffering, Molly is one of the main causes for the novel's pervasive sense of muted distress which coexists with its humour, in the constant ironic twists whereby those who are fond of her (most of the characters, in fact) cause her discomfort or pain, whether it is Miss Browning suspecting romance with Roger where none exists, or Lady Harriet chatting away at the Gibson's wedding to cheer her up when Molly wants only silence, or Cynthia being deliberately provocative to her mother, to draw Mrs Gibson's reproaches on herself instead of Molly.

Of previous fictional heroines, Molly most closely parallels Jane Austen's Fanny Price, in *Mansfield Park*, in both her role in the action, and her functions. Both are young and right-thinking, less psychologically interesting than other characters, and in touch with and responsive to all that concerns the main events; both eventually marry the brother-like friend only after he has recovered from an ill-advised passion for another. There is no sense of Elizabeth Gaskell having borrowed either the characters — for Fanny, Edmund Bertram and Mary Crawford are all very unlike Molly, Roger Hamley and Cynthia — or the moral positions, for Cynthia is never condemned as Mary is; nor is Molly, like Fanny, neglected, her worth unacknowledged, helpless and isolated, the person whose sufferings are most immediately felt by the reader.

Elizabeth Gaskell, who has always had the power to make virtue attractive, creates in Molly a charming heroine, passive but far from insipid, with a robust nature, flashes of fun, and a quick response to joy and the pleasures of the senses. She can flash out at Miss Browning for her innuendo about an attachment between Roger and herself:

'Miss Browning, I can't help seeing what you fancy . . . but it is very wrong; it is all a mistake. I won't speak another word about Mr Roger or Hamley at all, if it puts such silly notions in your head.' (XIII)

When Mrs Gibson and Cynthia go to London for a week, she anticipates the freedom to enjoy her father's company in richly incongruous and convincing terms, doing 'every thing that is unrefined and ungenteel':

'We'll have bread and cheese for dinner, and eat it on our knees; we'll make up for having to eat sloppy puddings with a fork instead of a spoon all this time, by putting our knives in our mouths till we cut ourselves.' (XL)

Rejecting all false refinement, she responds fervently to real aesthetic delight, however modest the occasion, as Elizabeth Gaskell's precise observation shows:

First of all, she went to the window to see what was to be seen. A flower-garden right below; a meadow of ripe grass just beyond it, changing colour in long sweeps, as the soft wind blew over it. (VI)

Only Elizabeth Gaskell could have rendered so engaging a character out of functions so demanding, and with attributes which, though valuable, are also, precisely as she intended, 'every-day', like her story.

Close to Molly both in nature, functions, and treatment is the man who partners her, Roger Hamley. Like her he embodies selfless good sense, and is the unromantic unheroic hero, without looks or elegance, whose reactions and understanding are the means of presenting events and characters. While his personal role in advancing the plot is a more active one, his narrative function is much less, as the means of presenting most of Osborne's predicament and conduct, and a considerable part of Squire Hamley's, in both of which he is supplemented by the third narrative medium, Mr Gibson. Though he is Cynthia's most devoted lover, and also the unexpected saviour of his family's fortunes, both of these heroic roles are subdued to the light of common day, for as a romantic figure he is overshadowed by Osborne, while his academic and scientific success, when he becomes Senior Wrangler, fellow of his college, and scientific explorer and traveller *a la* Charles Darwin, are all of a kind that carry little of the prestige and traditional honour of the talents for classics and poetry which Osborne represents (even though he fails). Elizabeth Gaskell invests him with a sympathy and tact to match Molly's, shown first in their first real encounter, when he stumbles upon her despairing over the sudden news of her father's re-marriage. His sympathy expresses itself not only in an awkward though effective homily, but in ways both characteristic and delicate:

> they remained in silence for a little while; he breaking off and examining one or two abnormal leaves of the ash-tree, partly from the custom of his nature, partly to give her time to recover.
>
> (x)

Like her, he is most important in relation to his family, as in the fine scene in which Squire Hamley almost comes to blows with Mr Preston, suspecting that Preston's workmen have been trespassing and pulling up his gorse. Roger, after intervening with cool dignity, manages to get his father to move away:

> Roger took hold of the reins of [his father's] old mare, and led

her over the boggy ground, as if to guide her into a sure footing, but, in reality, because he was determined to prevent a renewal of the quarrel. It was well that the cob knew him, and was, indeed, old enough to prefer quietness to dancing; for Mr Hamley plucked hard at the reins, and at last broke out with an oath – 'Damn it, Roger! I'm not a child; I won't be treated as such! Leave go, I say.'

Roger let go; they were now on firm ground, and he did not wish any watchers to think that he was exercising any constraint over his father; and this quiet obedience to his impatient commands did more to soothe the Squire than anything else could have effected just then. (xxx)

The third character with a narrative function is Mr Gibson, acute, intelligent, ironic, reticent, and with a 'thistly dignity', whose over-impulsive act in proposing to the Cumnor's pretty companion and former governess Mrs Kirkpatrick – solely so as to get a settled household in which Molly will not be at risk from amorous young medical apprentices – sets in train all the predicaments of the action. His position as doctor gives him, like Molly, entrée to all the families and puts him in their confidence. He can therefore hear things Molly cannot, his greater sense and experience give a better judgement, and being a man, he allows conversations between men on subjects not otherwise accessible. Through him the reader comes to know of Osborne's weak heart and uncertain life, and can see more intimately the workings of other men's minds, like Squire Hamley's when he hears Roger is engaged to Cynthia:

'I thought Roger would tell you himself' [says Mr Gibson].
'That shows you've no sons. More than half their life is unknown to their fathers. Why, Osborne there, we live together, we have our meals together, and we sleep under the same roof – and yet – Well! well! life is as God has made it. You say it's not an engagement yet? But I wonder what I'm doing! Hoping for my lad's disappointment in the folly he's set his heart on – and just when he's been helping me!' (xxxv)

The reader is also enabled to appreciate characters whom neither Molly nor Roger can interpret, who are yet necessary, like, notably, Lady Cumnor, whose autocratic and irritable manner is intensified by an illness that she conceals as far as possible, but whose progress is supervised and conveyed by Mr Gibson.

Mr Gibson's wry wit is a spice to many dialogues, rendering solid and credible his endurance of the many irritations of his home life, by being a visible armour; it is a pungent contrast to Mrs Gibson's false and woolly sentiment, expressing by near-contradiction the real love of father and daughter. He is a full working-out of one of the many small *aperçus* in Elizabeth Gaskell's short tales, in one of which, for instance, she speaks of a character who

> could love deeply, but could not talk about it. The perpetual requirement of loving words, looks, and caresses, and miscon-struing their absence into absence of love, had been the great trial of her former married life. ('The Manchester Marriage')

Within *Wives and Daughters* he is one of the explorations of degrees of capacity for feeling, in which Molly rates highest and Mrs Gibson lowest. We learn one of the earliest facts about him in his thoughts about the apprentice Mr Coxe's hot-headed love for Molly:

> 'It's an awful worry – to begin with lovers so early. Why, she's only just seventeen – not seventeen, indeed, till July; not for six weeks yet. Sixteen and three-quarters! Why, she's quite a baby. To be sure – poor Jeanie was not so old, and how I did love her!' (Mrs Gibson's name was Mary; so he must have been referring to someone else.) (v)

Though we are told no more about Jeanie, and why he did not marry her, his actions in general, as well as his speech, convey how, pre-ferring sense and practical considerations to guide him, he deliberately suppresses feeling, and so, as in his unfortunate marriage, does vio-lence to feeling unwittingly.

The other characters are all set apart from these three because, though their reactions and thoughts often throw light on other characters, they are not necessarily dependable witnesses. There are degrees among them of comedy and seriousness, and of how far their author penetrates into their thought-processes and responses.

Probably the most important single individual, and the most com-plex, is Cynthia Kirkpatrick. She represents not only a new kind of character in literature, but also the height of Elizabeth Gaskell's power to render dispassionately, without passing judgement, qualities that any novelist before her would find reprehensible, and to do so with a depth, rather implied than stated, that links her with Philip Hepburn in *Sylvia's Lovers*. She is set apart from the other characters by being treated without humour, revealing herself by her own acts, which give clues to and proof of her nature, and by what she tells of herself in a few enlightening scenes with Molly and Mr Gibson. Her author consistently avoids presenting her thoughts, not because she is unable, but rather because she makes it a part of Cynthia to avoid self-analysing a nature which lacks the moral strength to perform the kind of action that would be the consequence. Cynthia needs to be loved and approved, but is not capable herself of loving; she cannot therefore give up Mr Gibson's good opinion of her by confessing her involvement with Preston. The love she requires, and what she can obtain, are two different qualities whose difference Elizabeth Gaskell makes perfectly clear. Cynthia herself states plainly what her actions bear out, that she has more affection for Molly and for Mr Gibson than for anyone else, and needs them the most, not merely their affection, but their esteem. An enlightening scene occurs when Mr Coxe, the young surgeon, has proposed to her (he came to ask for Molly, but was swept away by Cynthia's charms instead), and Mr Gibson has rebuked her. She says to Molly:

> 'I do believe your father might make a good woman of me yet, if he would only take the pains, and wasn't quite so severe . . . I knew [Coxe] liked me, and I like to be liked; it's born in me to try to make everyone I come near fond of me; but then they shouldn't carry it too far, for it becomes very troublesome if they do.' (xxxvii)

The love she needs is the kind of which her childhood, fatherless and with an unloving mother, robbed her. The love she can so easily obtain is what she can arouse by her femininity and sexual allure. Elizabeth Gaskell makes both qualities quite clear, not only in Cynthia's demonstrated powers to charm, but, when Cynthia first comes on the scene, in one of her own infrequent, but always penetrating, authorial analyses of what she calls 'Cynthia's unconscious power of fascination':

> Some people have this power. Of course, its effects are only manifested in the susceptible. A school-girl may be found in every school who attracts and influences all the others, not by her virtues, nor her beauty, nor her sweetness, nor her cleverness, but by something that can neither be described nor reasoned upon. . . . A woman will have this charm, not only over men but over her own sex; it cannot be defined, or rather it is so delicate

a mixture of many gifts and qualities that it is impossible to decide on the proportions of each. Perhaps it is incompatible with very high principle; as its essence seems to consist in the most exquisite power of adaptation to varying people and still more various moods – 'being all things to all men'. (xix)

Even the apparent contradiction of her charm for other women is simple confirmation (proved by the accurate parallel, in schoolgirls, of the attraction of the same sex) that Cynthia's power has a sexual basis. Elizabeth Gaskell recognizes and reveals also Cynthia's own kind of feeling for men: she is still so drawn to Preston that she hates and fears him, a reaction which tends to confirm Mr Preston's own confidence that he can make Cynthia love him after marriage. Cynthia herself separates her two capabilities of loving, being wholly unwilling to allow Roger to occupy a place even such as she would permit Mr Gibson to (as she says) 'live in the house with any one who may be always casting up in his mind the things he has heard against me' (xliv).

Elizabeth Gaskell's wise charity towards those who are the victims of their own nature and environment is as subtle in Cynthia as it was in Philip Hepburn in *Sylvia's Lovers*, and no less of an achievement for being subdued within the bounds of the untragic and everyday. Cynthia as a personality recalls at some distance Jane Austen's Mary Crawford in *Mansfield Park*, who also charms, and suffers for possessing the charm which is 'incompatible with very high principle'. But Jane Austen renders the faulty morals through spurious charm, and cannot within the ethos of her work extend the same dispassionate charity as Elizabeth Gaskell. After Cynthia, the type recurs again and again in the work of Hardy, who, to judge by the way such women recur, is obsessed by them. His women – Fancy Day, Eustacia Vye, Anne Garland, Lucetta Templeman – are as much at the mercy of their natures as the men they enthrall, and being objects for the heroes, rather than studies in themselves, though they incur much blame, do not receive the dispassionate assessment that Cynthia gets.

Elizabeth Gaskell's handling of secondary characters is a mixture of reaching out to the wholly new, and brilliantly recombining the old. Lady Harriet and Mr Preston stand on either side of Cynthia in sharing some of her originality. Lady Harriet is remarkable and wholly convincing as an independent-minded mature woman with no impulse towards marriage, witty, intelligent, and outspoken, treating all she meets with the same forthrightness, able to see through Mrs Gibson as well as through her own mother and father, and enjoy the good qualities of her brother, the Miss Brownings and Molly with a gusto, which, if not entirely tactful, is entirely free of offence. This accurate judgement and detachment is what she shares with Cynthia. Mr Preston on the other hand is the masculine equivalent of Cynthia's sexual power, which he not only operates more deliberately, but suffers himself intensely. His slightly but powerfully indicated episode of philandering at Ashcombe with both Cynthia and her mother suggests a subject fit for Henry James, untouched with such coolness in the novel before him, even though it made a very uneasy and psychologically chaotic element in Thackeray's *Henry Esmond* (1852).[5] Elizabeth Gaskell treats him with her usual honest fairness, suggesting his suffering under the passion that rules him, and will not let Cynthia go, at the same time as his own words prevent any sentimental pity for him:

'I don't give in to humbug – I don't set myself up as a saint – and in most ways I can look after my position pretty keenly; you know enough of her position as a penniless girl, and at that time with no influential connections to take the place of wealth and help me on in the world. It was as sincere and unworldly a passion as ever man felt; she must say so herself.' (XLIV)

Elizabeth Gaskell's art plainly continues to develop here as it has always done, by trial and practice, not by thought and theory, when such startling originalities as these appear easily and without jar both in the centre and at the peripheries of a work whose form is so evidently richly traditional.

Types and handlings of characters she has used before, who are as frequent as the new ones, are not perceptible from the texture of *Wives and Daughters*, but only by consciously recollecting and referring back to her earlier work. What is striking about them is both that they merge imperceptibly with the rest, and are, though reminiscent, totally distinct from their precursors. The Miss Brownings

[5] There can be no suggestion of borrowing on Elizabeth Gaskell's part. Hers is a cool balanced little chronicle, quite different in narrative attitude and emotional positions from the story of Esmond, whose love for the mother-figure of his childhood finally ends, when he exhausts his passion for her coquette daughter Beatrix, in marriage.

could have inhabited Cranford, yet, dominant and submissive spinster sisters though they are, do not resemble, though they recall in their good sense, innocence and sympathetically humorous rendering, Miss Jenkyns and Miss Matty. Within the novel, they mingle without any jar of tone or presentation with Lady Harriet as well as Mr Gibson.[6] Other characters recall earlier workings of their type in her own short stories, but for any of them it is hard to make connections with those of any other novelists.

A possible exception is Mrs Gibson, formerly Mrs Kirkpatrick, *née* Clare, who has rightly recalled to many readers Jane Austen's Mrs Bennet of *Pride and Prejudice*, with whom she has much in common both in traits and treatment. Elizabeth Gaskell's comic portrayal of a selfish woman, woolly-minded and incapable of logic, based on *idées fixes* of gentility, dress, and snobbery, is as brilliant as Jane Austen's, but is both less concise and more psychologically developed. Even with a woman so morally worthless, her author calls for justice and understanding, through Molly's sympathy and her own brief but telling explanations, of how for instance Mrs Gibson puzzles over her husband's bitter ironies:

> on these occasions [she] would say in a manner more bewildered than hurt –
>
> 'I think dear papa seems a little put out today; we must see that he has a dinner he likes when he comes home. I have often perceived that everything depends on making a man comfortable in his own house.'
>
> And thus she went on, groping about to find the means of reinstating herself in his good graces – really trying according to her lights, till Molly was compelled to pity her in spite of herself, although she saw that her stepmother was the cause of her father's increased astringency of disposition. (XXXVII)

She becomes a richly comic ironic mixture in her self-exposure – though she has in a general sense made her man comfortable, she has also prevented him even in his eating from doing what he likes (from

6 Edgar Wright's objection that they age too rapidly, as Elizabeth Gaskell changed her ideas about them, need not be valid. Phoebe at an age around forty could well fancy herself a possible second mother for Molly in the opening chapters, and still be the old-fashioned figure of the later ones. There is no violence done to probability in her not being as well preserved in mind or body as the actual second Mrs Gibson.

having early dinners, or eating cheese) – and her pathetic inadequacy, most strikingly revealed when Mr Gibson proposes to her:

> She hid her face in her hands.
>
> 'Oh, Mr Gibson,' she said; and then, a little to his surprise, and a great deal to her own, she burst into tears: *it was such a wonderful relief to feel that she need not struggle any more for a livelihood.* (x, my italics)

She also suggests depths of action and motive more disturbing than novelists generally permit to satirically inadequate minor characters; jealousy of her daughter constantly mingles with admiration and ambition for her, and, though virtually incapable of affection at the stage of her life the plot concerns, her author suggests convincingly that she has had passions that prevent her from seeming merely comic, or tiresome, now. She did love her first husband, despite the way she sentimentalizes his memory, and she was a part of the sordid triangular episode at Ashcombe, when Preston philandered with both mother and daughter. At her wedding to Mr Gibson

> A little cloud came over her face at the sight of Mr Preston – the sweet perpetuity of her smile was rather disturbed, as he followed in Mr Gibson's wake. (xiv)

A point which the reader remembers, when he encounters Preston's very casual manners to her later.

Since the novel is not quite complete, one is tempted to wonder whether Mrs Gibson would have lived to the end of it. There are several small remarks about her health in the later chapters, from the point at which in Chapter l she is 'slow in recovering her strength after the influenza' until the last sentence the author wrote, in which Mrs Gibson asks Molly to

> 'cover me up close, and let me go to sleep, and dream about dear Cynthia and my new shawl.' (lx)

Even though Elizabeth Gaskell is not inclined to kill people off for the convenience of others, and certainly not for the sake of an undilutedly happy ending, neither does she, improbably, 'strive Officiously to keep alive'.

In Mrs Gibson there are signs of her author exploring new areas in the novel, and reaching out to situations not interpretable in moral terms, which lead, not to the poignant tragic results of *Sylvia's Lovers*, but to situations without remedy or cure, like Mr Gibson's marriage, in the exploration of characters who are not to be dismissed because they are stupid, or condemned because they cause distress, and whose own distresses cannot be ignored merely because they themselves cannot see what they do wrong. Elizabeth Gaskell sees both the comedy and the pity of the stupid and limited. Mrs Gibson is both dislikeable and laughable; her author permits both the dislike and the amusement, but requires also an understanding that makes the reader uneasy, and contributes to the total response to *Wives and Daughters* which makes it a far from happy work.

Elizabeth Gaskell has always been aware that in the midst of life we are in death, and that the quietest existences cannot escape tribulation. In her full-length novels disaster regularly threatens, and death overtakes;[7] in her short stories it is perhaps even more frequent; and even in *Cranford* accident and illness carry off Captain Brown and his elder daughter, banks fail, and old ladies like Miss Matty are left nearly destitute.

Few novelists make such use of the incidental details of life as Elizabeth Gaskell does. The world of *Wives and Daughters*, larger than Cranford, though less eventful than that of *North and South*, has its necessary share of

> 'natural sorrow, loss, or pain
> Which has been, and may be again'

all of which seem indeed, whatever may be their necessary services to plot and development, entirely natural, both probable and convincing, and before the event, uncertain. Mrs Hamley slips out of life gradually; Osborne, after a long period of doubt, dies suddenly; for neither of them does the author provide a death-scene, weaving their disappearance in with the events that continue on their course. She recognizes and uses also the smaller ailments and illnesses of life that, though they cause anxiety, do not lead to death. Lady Cumnor for example suffers throughout the story from a persistently increasing illness which intensifies her natural irritability, and results finally in an operation and slow convalescence. Elizabeth Gaskell does not

---

7 She was well aware of her propensity, once remarking that she thought 'a better title than *North and South* would have been "Death and Variations". There are five deaths, each beautifully suited to the character of the individual' (letter to Charles Dickens, 17 December 1854).

define the illness, for it is not necessary to do so, and it is more appropriate for the reader to share uncertainty and anxiety with the bulk of the characters. Such grave illness, and the intermittent minor ones – such as Molly's cold, which prevents her going to Cynthia's London wedding – not only make *Wives and Daughters* seem wrought from the stuff of life, but also intensify the feeling of unpredictable accident and chance in this most precisely-planned work.

Creating anxiety, a talent rare in the novel, for anxiety is neither an easily definable state, easy for a novelist to manipulate, nor one that readers expect to find, or to enjoy when they experience it, is one of Elizabeth Gaskell's great powers. She is equally good at rendering the consequences of anxiety in the sufferer. She attempted it before, on rather a grand scale, in *Mary Barton*, when Mary, after her long desperate efforts finding Jack Wilson, and giving evidence, sees Jem acquitted of murder, and collapses. Less sensational but infinitely more persuasive is her demonstration in *Wives and Daughters* that long strain and self control wear down both mind and body, and that moral fortitude cannot prevent physical consequences. Such consequences are a clue she provides to the mysterious Cynthia, who is both depressed and ill after encountering Mr Preston at the Charity Ball, and realizing again that she is still in his power. Although she declares to Mr Gibson,

'If there is one thing I dislike . . . it is the way doctors have of giving tablespoonfuls of nauseous mixtures as a certain remedy for sorrows and cares' (xxvii)

yet with physical recovery comes mental resilience. Later on, Molly suffers the long strain of day-to-day living with Mrs Gibson, of dealing with Cynthia's dilemma, of her long stay at Hamley supporting and comforting the Squire after Osborne's death, and looking after the unknown daughter-in-law and her child; after which the eventual relief brings wholly convincing exhaustion.

Altogether, although the events and emotions are generally far from happy ones – a quality *Wives and Daughters* shares with all of Elizabeth Gaskell's work except, perhaps, *Cranford* – the novel is not a dispiriting one, any more than are her others. Here, as is usual with her, she makes the reader keenly aware of the pleasures, comforts and compensations, small and unconsidered as some of them are, of everyday living. Among the chief of them are the sensuous responses to the natural scene – the seasons, weather, and physical

I*

activity – for which she has always had an unostentatiously Wordsworthian enthusiasm, and with which she endowed her characters.
She has frequently set her scenes outdoors, or with that domestic
mixture of in and out of doors which comes from open windows, or
changes from room to garden. Just as *Wives and Daughters* begins
with the child Molly's mixture of delight and pain in the grounds and
gardens of the Towers and its indoor splendour, so the action continues. The natural scenes and sensations of Hollingford and its
environs are modestly rural, like the Cheshire countryside on which
they are based, leaving the author no chance for grander scenes, like
the Welsh mountains in *Ruth*, nor the vast strangenesses of the sea
and the moors in *Sylvia's Lovers*. Nature in *Wives and Daughters*,
tamed and domesticated into flower and vegetable gardens, the land-
scaped parks of the great houses, and the fields and lanes of a farming
county, is not the less delightful, is even more skilfully worked into
the fabric of the whole, and always calls for participation of all the
senses: sound and smell and touch are as much a part of it as mere
looking. Many of the responses are Molly's, and are some of the many
things that endear to the reader a heroine with few outstanding
qualities, and no exciting history; the first day of her stay with the
Hamleys ends with cribbage:

> And so on, till the butler came in with a solemn look, placed a
> large prayer-book before his master, who huddled the cards
> away in a hurry, as if caught in an incongruous employment;
> and then the maids and men trooped in to prayers – the
> windows were still open, and the sounds of the solitary corn-
> crake, and of the owl hooting in the trees, mingled with the
> words spoken. Then to bed, and so ended the day.
>
> Molly looked out of her chamber-window – leaning on
> the sill, and snuffing up the night-odours of the honey-
> suckles. The soft velvet darkness hid all the things that were
> any distance from her; although she was as conscious of their
> presence as if she had seen them.
>
> 'I think I shall be happy here,' was in Molly's thoughts.
>
> (VI)

Such small, delightful descriptions as this never halt the action,
but advance it, as this one neatly makes the transition from family
prayers to Molly's bedroom, accounts for her feeling that she will be
happy – a prognostication which is true in the sense that Hamley will

always need her and offer her the real satisfactions of life, and is ironically at fault in that she will not only have to share in much of the Hamleys' future sorrow, but is also soon to be desperately miserable at her father's re-marriage. The delights are not only Molly's – they belong to all three chief narrative consciousnesses – nor are they all so idyllic. Roger Hamley, meeting Molly in her despair and misery

> had been out dredging in ponds and ditches, and had his wet sling-net, with its *imprisoned treasures of nastiness*, over his shoulder. (x, my italics)

and Mr Gibson also responds to what his frequent horseback journeys give him so much of:

> It was one of those still and lovely autumn days, when the red and yellow leaves are hanging-pegs to dewy brilliant gossamer-webs; when the hedges are full of trailing brambles, loaded with ripe blackberries; when the air is full of the farewell whistles and pipes of birds, clear and short – not the long full-throated warbles of spring; when the whirr of the partridge's wing is heard in the stubble-fields, as the sharp hoof-blow falls on the paved lanes; when here and there a leaf floats and flutters to the ground, although there is not a single breath of wind. The country surgeon felt the beauty of the seasons, perhaps more than most men. He saw more of it by day, by night, in storm and sunshine, or in soft cloudy weather. He never spoke about what he felt on the subject; indeed, he did not put his feelings into words; even to himself. But, if his mood ever approached the sentimental, it was on such days as this. (xxxiii)

By the time Elizabeth Gaskell gives this explanation, the reader has had many chances to recognize its truth, from little transitional observations between scene and scene:

> It was a brilliantly hot summer morning; men in their shirt-sleeves were in the field getting in the early harvest of oats. As Mr Gibson rode slowly along, he could see them over the tall hedge-rows, and even hear the soothing measured sound of the fall of the long swathes, as they were mown. The labourers seemed too hot to talk; the dog, guarding their coats and cans, lay panting loudly on the other side of the elm, under which

Mr Gibson stopped to survey the scene, and gain a little delay before the interview that he wished was well over. (x)

All such accounts precisely and unobtrusively chart the time and season, and so measure the pace from day to month to year that runs through the whole, giving a sense of time quite independent of the historical time of the period in which it is set, and working together with the timeless emotions of the human relationships, of which it is itself a part.

This sense of eternal as well as immediate values is reinforced by another of Elizabeth Gaskell's unobtrusive yet highly personal habits, which amounts to a feature of style. Plain and unadorned as her own writing is, it can absorb, in a surprising and delightfully unobtrusive way, innumerable echoes of others, which are never forced upon the reader, who is quite at liberty to miss them, since they are often unmarked and always unacknowledged, though very evidently conscious enough on her own part. The reverse of a literary or erudite writer, she is obviously a well-read and most responsive reader:

Fate is a cunning hussy, and builds up her plans as imperceptibly as a bird builds her nest; and with much the same kind *of unconsidered trifles.* (VII)

The house was so still, in its silence, it might have been the 'moated grange'. (VIII)

He was dainty in eating, and had anything but a Homeric appetite. However, Molly's hero was not to eat more than Ivanhoe, when he was Friar Tuck's guest. (XIV)

She woke up in the morning with a dull sense of something being wrong; the world was *out of joint*, and, if she were *born to set it right*, she did not know how to do it. (XXXVII)

She felt as if she could not understand it all; but as for that matter, what could she understand? Nothing. For a few minutes, her brain seemed in too great a whirl to comprehend anything, but that she was being carried on *in earth's diurnal course, with rocks, and stones, and trees,* with as little volition as if she were dead. (XXXIV)

These few of the very great number of such echoes, which the noticing reader will find, show how completely a part of her consciousness is her reading – Shakespeare, Tennyson, Scott, and Wordsworth, who are heard here, are joined by many others – and how unique is her unpretentious, telling way of using them. The power is one that has grown gradually with her from the beginning, coming into confident use in *Sylvia's Lovers*, where Biblical echoes prevail, and is plainly one of the skills that would have grown, had not death prevented it.

Although Elizabeth Gaskell's style in her narrative is always plain and unpretentious – so that it is easy to underestimate how accurate and communicative it is, and notice only that it has no noticeable features – she has always been good at representing natural speech. In *Wives and Daughters* she has a range of characters whose speech is not likely to have wide or striking variations of idiom or accent, and there is no use of dialect. She can therefore continue to depend, as she has always liked to do, on dialogue to carry on the business of the novel; many novelists make the varying speech mannerisms and idioms of the characters much of the pleasure of their art. As the nineteenth century continues, the technique becomes a steadily growing one, wherein the language of speakers becomes not only a source of entertainment, but the embodiment of ways of thought, just as much as is the content of their speech. Elizabeth Gaskell virtually ignores the frequent novelist's habit of giving characters *idées fixes*, or recurrent phrases or idioms such as are Dickens's forte, or such as George Eliot often uses, when, for instance, she bestows upon Mr Brooke in *Middlemarch* a rambling, interrupted manner, turning always to truism and reminiscence:

> 'Sir Humphrey Davy?' said Mr Brooke . . . 'Well, now Sir Humphry Davy: I dined with him years ago at Cartwright's, and Wordsworth was there too – the poet Wordsworth, you know. Now there was something singular. I was at Cambridge when Wordsworth was there, and I never met him – and I dined with him twenty years after at Cartwright's. There's an oddity in things, now. But Davy was there; he was a poet too. Or, as I may say, Wordsworth was poet one, and Davy was poet two. That was true in every sense, you know.' (*Middlemarch*, Book I, II)

> 'I shall never interfere with your wishes, my dear. People should have their own way in marriage, and that sort of thing – up to a certain point, you know. I have always said that, up to a certain point.' (ibid., IV)

'But you must have a scholar, and that sort of thing? Well, it
lies a little in our family. I had it myself – that love of knowledge, and going into everything – a little too much – it took
me too far; though that sort of thing doesn't often run in the
female line; or it runs underground like rivers in Greece, you
know. It comes out in the sons. Clever sons, clever mothers.
I went a good deal into that, at one time. However, my dear,
I have always said that people should do as they like in these
things up to a certain point.' (ibid., v)

Such uses of language are not only for comedy, they are a key to and
symptom of personality. George Eliot can also produce characteristic
speech whose elements are not extractable as catchphrases or recurrent idiom, as are Mr Brooke's 'up to a point', 'that sort of thing',
'you know', and 'I went into that a good deal'. Mrs Cadwallader,
also in *Middlemarch*, the astringent, strong-minded wife of the rector,
has a turn for epigram, always unexpected and varied: bargaining for
hens who eat their own eggs, she reacts with,

'O, the cannibals! Better sell them cheap at once. What will
you sell them a couple? One can't eat fowls of a bad character at
a high price.' (vi)

and produces this riposte on Mr Casaubon:

'He has not got red blood in his body', said Sir James. 'No,
somebody put a drop under a magnifying-glass and it was all
semi-colons and parentheses.' (viii)

The language of Elizabeth Gaskell's speakers is all of the latter
kind, where idiosyncrasy is not derived from catchphrases, or obviously repeated construction, but from personal modes of thought;
it is not a mere characteristic of speech, but a manifestation of inner
nature. Before her, it is noticeable in Charlotte Brontë, whose use
of speech is often unobtrusively precise. In *Jane Eyre*, for example,
whose narrator's own highly individual language seems to colour the
whole, it makes a modestly telling appearance in Mrs Fairfax, whose
faintly antique, even Austenian idiom reveals the ways of an earlier
generation:

'you know in winter time one feels dreary quite alone, in the
best quarters. I say alone – Leah is a nice girl to be sure, and
John and his wife are very decent people; but then you see they

are only servants, and one can't converse with them on terms of equality: one must keep them at due distance, for fear of losing one's authority. I'm sure last winter (it was a very severe one, if you recollect, and when it did not snow, it rained and blew), not a creature but the butcher and the postman came to the house, from November till February; and I really got quite melancholy with sitting night after night alone; I had Leah in to read to me sometimes; but I don't think the poor girl liked the task much: she felt it confining. In spring and summer one got on better: sunshine and long days make such a difference.' (*Jane Eyre*, XI)

The use of abstract nouns and impersonal constructions here, of introductory phrases like 'I'm sure', and of the adjectives 'decent', 'melancholy', 'confining', all suggest the usage of the turn of the eighteenth and nineteenth centuries.

Elizabeth Gaskell develops such use of speech from her earliest works; by the time she writes *Wives and Daughters* varied idiom flows so naturally as to be far beyond mere mannerism, and is always the manifestation of attitude, habit of mind, and process of thought. Cliché may suggest a simple mind, but need not be a call for disapproval. The Miss Brownings speak with the language of their age and class, using it in ways that define them – Miss Browning more incisively, Miss Phoebe with the soft vagueness of goodwill without perception that yet reaches rightness through innocence. It is the mode of *Cranford*, yet, though there is a resemblance between the Miss Brownings here and the Miss Jenkyns there, Miss Browning has none of Miss Jenkyns's Johnsonese Latinity, while Miss Phoebes has less of Miss Matty's gentle and dignified resolution. Miss Phoebe's account to Molly of Lady Harriet's visit gives the fine flavour of both sisters:

'... there was I in my black silk skull-cap, when Nancy put her head in, and whispered, "There's a lady downstairs – a real grand one, by her talk"; and in there came my Lady Harriet, so sweet and pretty in her ways, it was some time before I forgot I had never a cap on. Sister never wakened; or never roused up, so to say. She says she thought it was Nancy bringing in the tea, when she heard some one moving; for her ladyship, as soon as she saw the state of the case, came and knelt down on the rug by me, and begged my pardon so prettily for having followed

Nancy upstairs without waiting for permission; and was so taken
by my old lace, and wanted to know how I washed it, and where
you were, and when you'd be back, and when the happy couple
would be back; till sister wakened – she's always a little bit put
out, you know, when she first wakens from her afternoon nap –
and, without turning her head to see who it was, she said, quite
sharp – "Buzz, buzz, buzz! When will you learn that whisper-
ing is more fidgeting than talking out loud? I've not been able
to sleep at all, for the chatter you and Nancy have been keeping
up all this time." You know that was a little fancy of sister's,
for she'd been snoring away as naturally as could be. So I went
to her, and leant over her, and said in a low voice –

"Sister, it's her ladyship and me that has been conversing."

"Ladyship here, ladyship there! have you lost your wits,
Phoebe, that you talk such nonsense – and in your skull-cap,
too!"' (xv)

Cliché, in the form of the genteel idiom or the dead metaphor, serve
quite different ends in Mrs Gibson's language. She also, though
instantly identifiable from her speech, has yet no catchphrases,
though she has many repeating ideas and characteristic turns of
thought, and a weak head is revealed in startling false connections
and ragbag ramblings, whose words disclose but never define their
underlying purpose: as when she objects to calling upon Squire
Hamley, with Cynthia, after he has learned that his son and Cynthia
are engaged:

'I am sure I don't want him to come calling here . . . he was not
so very agreeable, the only time he did come. But I am that sort
of a character that I cannot put up with neglect of persons I love,
just because they are not smiled upon by fortune.' (xxxvi)

Finally persuaded, she can do what she always meant to do, as if it
were an uncongenial duty, making her own kind of profit from it as
the loosely-joined sentences reveal:

'Then I'll go!' said she, in the voice of a victim. 'And we'll
have a fly from the George, and get a livery-coat for Thomas,
which I've long been wanting; only dear Mr Gibson did not
like it, but on an occasion like this I'm sure he won't mind; and
Thomas shall go on the box, and –'

'But, mamma, I've my feelings too', said Cynthia.

'Nonsense, child! when all is so nicely arranged, too.'

(XXXVI)

The unexpectedness of Mrs Gibson's illogical mind, and the richly varied triteness of her expression, are what prevent this brilliantly humorous character from the tedium that would seem almost inescapable from a mind with so few ideas in it.

Mr Gibson's language, terse, and wry, expressing good sense in the least words, constantly reveals a pleasure in the twists of logic of its own thought, which the reader shares, even though the listener may not follow them. In this it contrasts with Squire Hamley's speech, which reveals a mind that works by emotional responses, that makes connections which have no logical sequence, but that always finds accurate language, and has a thematic relevance of which he is not consciously aware: after Mr Gibson learns of Cynthia's and Roger's engagement, he fulfils his promise to tell the Squire of any such happening:

'He's not the eldest son,' continued the Squire, talking as it were to himself. 'But it's not the match I should have planned for him . . . You say it's not an engagement yet? But I wonder what I'm doing! Hoping for my lad's disappointment in the folly he's set his heart on. – and just when he's been helping me. . . . Roger's "future wife"! he'll be wiser by the time he comes home. Two years among the black folks will have put more sense in him.'

'Possible, but not probable, I should say,' replied Mr Gibson. 'Black folk are not remarkable for their powers of reasoning, I believe; so that they haven't much chance of altering his opinion by argument, even if they understood each other's language; and certainly, if he shares my taste, their peculiarity of complexion will only make him appreciate white skins the more.' . . .

'What's the girl like in herself?'

'I don't know what you mean,' said Mr Gibson. But he did, only he was vexed, and did not choose to understand.

'Is she – well, is she like your Molly? – sweet-tempered and sensible – with her gloves always mended, and neat about the feet, and ready to do anything one asks her, just as if doing it was the very thing she liked best in the world?'

Mr Gibson's face relaxed now, and he could understand all the Squire's broken sentences and unexplained meanings.

'She's much prettier than Molly, to begin with, and has very winning ways. She's always well-dressed and smart-looking, and I know she hasn't much to spend on her clothes, and always does what she's asked to do, and is ready enough with her pretty, lively answers. I don't think I ever saw her out of temper, but then I'm not sure if she takes things keenly to heart, and a certain obtuseness of feeling goes a great way towards a character for good temper, I've noticed. Altogether I think Cynthia is one in a hundred.'

The Squire meditated a little. 'Your Molly is one in a thousand, to my mind. But then, you see, she comes of no family at all – and I don't suppose she'll have the chance of much money.' This he said as if he were thinking aloud, and without reference to Mr Gibson, but it nettled the latter, and he replied somewhat impatiently –

'Well, but, as there's no question of Molly in this business, I don't see the use of bringing her name in, and considering either her family or her fortune.'

'No, to be sure not,' said the Squire, rousing up. 'My wits had gone far afield, and I'll own I was only thinking what a pity it was she wouldn't do for Osborne.' (xxxv)

Tempting though it is to consider *Wives and Daughters* as Elizabeth Gaskell's crowning achievement, as her last best gift to English literature, and as a drawing together of all the powers she has developed in the twenty years of her writing life, and true as it is in many ways to say that this last novel does come from one at the height of her powers; yet *Wives and Daughters* is in no way a final or farewell performance, as Hardy's *Jude the Obscure* was a final novel of deliberate choice. Elizabeth Gaskell did not stop of her own choice; she died, leaving her last novel two chapters short. Her works show a greater variety of approach and subject than most writers have, and an outstanding flexibility in adopting and developing her own powers and techniques according to the nature of what she was doing. Like Jane Austen, she begins with excellence and proceeds to greatness. There is every reason to presume that, had she lived, she would have continued to write, not only as well as she has done, but with continually varying and increasing range.

Two quotations from novelists, George Eliot and Thomas Hardy, who both owe much to Elizabeth Gaskell's extension of the bounds of the novel, and whose own philosophies, thus put down, express those which she – whose writings are all in the practice, and never of the theory, of her art – herself acknowledges in all her writing, making a fitting conclusion. Hardy, writing in his notebook, is clarifying things for himself.

The real, if unavowed, purpose of fiction is to give pleasure by gratifying the love of the uncommon in human experience, mental or corporeal.

This is done all the more perfectly in proportion as the reader is illuded to believe the personages true and real like himself.

Solely to this latter end a work of fiction should be a precise transcript of ordinary life: but,

The uncommon would be absent and the interest lost, Hence;

The writer's problem is, how to strike a balance between the uncommon and the ordinary so as on the one hand to give interest, on the other to give reality.

In working out this problem, human nature must never be made abnormal, which is introducing incredibility. The uncommonness must be in the events, not the characters; and the writer's art lies in shaping that uncommonness while disguising its unlikelihood, if it be unlikely.[8]

All that is omitted from this estimate is Elizabeth Gaskell's sense of the social and moral purpose of fiction, which, since it also operates powerfully with Hardy, must be regarded as an unexpressed assumption.

George Eliot, reviewing *Modern Painters*, is doing as much as Hardy to clarify her own *desiderata*, in the process of assessing John Ruskin:

The truth of infinite value that he teaches us is realism – the doctrine that all truth and beauty are to be attained by a humble and faithful study of nature, and not by substituting vague forms, bred by imagination on the mists of feeling, in place of definite, substantial reality. The thorough acceptance of this doctrine would remould our life; and he who teaches its application

[8] Notebook entry, July 1881, in *The Life of Thomas Hardy* by Florence E. Hardy (London, 1962), Chapter XI, p. 150.

to any one department of human activity with such power as Mr Ruskin's is a prophet for his generation.[9]

Despite the dangerous vagueness of some of her terms, George Eliot is praising here the qualities that substantiate Elizabeth Gaskell's greatness. She has remoulded the novel, not simply by 'humble and faithful study of nature' in the novel, but by being so thoroughly master of the 'nature' she takes as her material, that it becomes a means, not an end. She has done much towards remoulding life as it can be used in art, and is a prophet for her own and the following generation in the English Novel.

[9] George Eliot, reviewing *Modern Painters, Westminster Review,* LXV (1856), pp. 343–4.

Bibliography

I have included, besides the works cited in the foregoing chapters, only those others which I have found particularly important, whether for their intrinsic value, or the profitable disagreement they provoke.

I Works by E. C. Gaskell

The Works of Mrs Gaskell, Smith, Elder & Co., 1906 (The Knutsford Edition), 8 vols.
The Life of Charlotte Brontë, Smith, Elder & Co., 1914 (Haworth Edition).
The Letters of Mrs Gaskell, ed. J. A. V. Chapple and Arthur Pollard, Manchester U.P., 1966.

II Works by Other Writers of Provincial Novels

BRONTË, ANNE
  Agnes Grey (1847)
  The Tenant of Wildfell Hall (1848)
BRONTË, CHARLOTTE
  Jane Eyre (1847)
  Shirley (1849)

All in The Shakespeare Head Brontë, ed. T. J. Wise and J. A. Symington, Oxford U.P., 1931–8.

ELIOT, GEORGE
Adam Bede (1859)
Mill on the Floss (1860)
Silas Marner (1861)　All published by
Felix Holt the Radical (1866)　Blackwood & Sons.
Middlemarch (1871)
The George Eliot Letters, ed. Gordon S. Haight, Yale U.P., 1954, 1956.

HARDY, THOMAS
Far from the Madding Crowd (1874)
The Return of the Native (1878)
The Trumpet-Major (1880)　All in the Wessex edition,
The Mayor of Casterbridge (1886)　Macmillan,
The Woodlanders (1887)　1912–31.
Tess of the D'Urbervilles (1891)
Jude the Obscure (1895)

TROLLOPE, ANTHONY
The Warden (1855)
Barchester Towers (1857)
Doctor Thorne (1858)　All in the World's
Framley Parsonage (1861)　Classics edition,
The Small House at Allington (1864)　Oxford U.P., 1918–32.
The Last Chronicle of Barset (1867)

III Other Works

BENNETT, JOAN, *George Eliot: Her Mind and Art* (Cambridge U.P., 1948).
BRIGGS, ASA, *Victorian People* (Odhams, 1954).
CARPENTER, S. C., *Church and People 1789–1889* (Seraph Books, 1959).
CECIL, LORD DAVID, *Early Victorian Novelists* (Constable, 1934).
CECIL, LORD DAVID, *Hardy the Novelist* (Cambridge U.P., 1942).
CHADWICK, MRS ELLIS H., *Mrs Gaskell: Haunts, Houses and Stories* (Isaac Pitman & Sons, 1913).
CLARK, G. KITSON, *The Making of Victorian England* (Methuen, 1962).

COLLINS, H. P., 'The naked sensibility: E. G.', *Essays in Criticism*, III (1953).

CROSS, J. W., *George Eliot's Life* (Blackwood, 1898).

DODSWORTH, MARTIN, 'Women without men at Cranford' *Essays in Criticism*, XIII (1963).

ELLIOT-BINNS, E. L., *Religion in the Victorian Era* (Lutterworth Press, 1946).

FFRENCH, Y., *Mrs G.* (Home & Van Thal, 1949).

G.B.S., 'Mrs Gaskell and her novels', *Cornhill Magazine*, 29 (February 1874).

GREEN, JOHN A., *A Bibliographical Guide to the Gaskell Collection in the Moss Side Library* (Manchester Reference Lib., 1911).

GREG, W. R., '*Mary Barton*', *Edinburgh Review*, CLXXX (April 1849).

GREG, WILLIAM R., 'The false morality of lady novelists' in *Literary and Social Judgements* (Trubner, 1869).

GUÉRARD, A. J., *Thomas Hardy: The Novels and Stories* (Harvard U.P., 1949).

HALDANE, ELIZABETH S., *Mrs Gaskell and Her Friends* (Hodder & Stoughton, 1930).

HALDANE, ELIZABETH S., *George Eliot and Her Times* (Hodder & Stoughton, 1927).

HANDLEY, GRAHAM, 'The chronology of *Sylvia's Lovers*', *Notes & Queries* (1965).

HARDY, BARBARA, *The Novels of George Eliot* (Athlone Press, 1959).

HARVEY, W. J., *Character and the Novel* (Chatto & Windus, 1965).

HERFORD, C. H., 'Mrs Gaskell', *Manchester Guardian* (29 September 1910).

HOPKINS, A. B., '*Mary Barton*: a Victorian best-seller', *The Trollopian* (1948).

HOPKINS, A. B., *Elizabeth Gaskell: Her Life and Work* (John Lehmann, 1952).

HOWITT, MARGARET, 'Stray notes about Mrs Gaskell', *Good Words* (September 1895).

JAMES, HENRY, Review of *Wives and Daughters* in *Notes & Reviews* (Harvard U.P., 1921).

JAMES, HENRY, *William Wetmore Story and his Friends* (Thames & Hudson, 1903).

LEHMANN, R., 'A neglected Victorian classic', *Penguin New Writing*, XXXII (1948).

'LYALL, EDNA' (E. E. Bayly), 'Mrs Gaskell', *Women Novelists of Queen Victoria's Reign* (1897).

PAYNE, GEORGE A., *Mrs Gaskell: A Brief Biography* (Sherratt & Hughes, 1929).

PAYNE, GEORGE A., *Mrs Gaskell and Knutsford* (Clarkson & Griffiths, 1900).

POLLARD, ARTHUR, 'The novels of Mrs G.', *Bulletin of the John Rylands Library*, XLIII (1961).

POLLARD, ARTHUR, *Mrs Gaskell: Novelist and Biographer* (Manchester U.P., 1965).

RITCHIE, LADY A. T., 'The author of *Cranford*', *Cornhill Magazine*, XCIV (1906).

RUBENIUS, AINA, 'The woman question in Mrs Gaskell's life and works', *Essays and Studies on English Language and Literature*, V (1950).

SHAEN, M. J., *Memorials of Two Sisters: Susanna and Catherine Winkworth* (Longmans, 1908).

SHORTER, C. K., *Charlotte Brontë and her Circle* (Hodder & Stoughton, 1914).

SUSSMAN, HERBERT L., *Victorians and the Machine* (Harvard U.P., 1968).

THOMSON, PATRICIA, *The Victorian Heroine* (Oxford U.P., 1956).

TILLOTSON, G. and K., *Mid-Victorian Studies* (Athlone Press, 1965).

TILLOTSON, K., *Novels of the Eighteen-Forties* (Oxford U.P., 1954).

WALLER, ROSS, 'Letters addressed to Mrs Gaskell by celebrated contemporaries', *Bulletin of the John Rylands Library*, XIX (January 1935).

WESTMINSTER REVIEW, Review of *Ruth* and *Villette* (January–April 1853).

WILLIAMS, RAYMOND, *Culture and Society 1780–1950* (Penguin, 1961).

WRIGHT, EDGAR, *Mrs Gaskell, the Basis for Reassessment* (Oxford U.P., 1965).

Index

The titles of novels have been abbreviated as follows:

MB *Mary Barton*
NS *North and South*
R *Ruth*
SL *Sylvia's Lovers*
WD *Wives and Daughters*

For individual characters in Elizabeth Gaskell's novels only the main discussions of important characters are entered.

Index